THE EMPIRE OF THE GREAT MOGOL

THE EMPIRE OF THE GREAT MOGOL

A Translation of De Laet's "Description of India and Fragment of Indian History"

Translated by

J.S. HOYLAND

and Annotated by

S.N. BANERJEE

MANOHAR
2026

Cover illustration: Abu'l Hasan. Celebrations at the accession of Jahangir. *Jahangirnama.* St. Petersburg Album. Mughal Court at Ajmer or Agra, ca. 1615-18, Institute of Oriental Studies, St. Petersburg.
Source: By Abu al-Hasan - Self-scanned, Public Domain, https://commons.wikimedia.org/w/index.php?curid=18791700.

Due to the academic and scholarly importance of this volume, we are reprinting/republishing it from the original source without any modifications or changes. Therefore, some misprints and errors may occur.

First published 1928
Reprinted 2026
First eBook edition 2025

ISBN 978-93-6080-562-3 (hardbound)
ISBN 978-93-6080-050-5 (eBook)

Published by
Ajay Kumar Jain *for*
Manohar Publishers & Distributors
4753/23 Ansari Road, Daryaganj
New Delhi 110 002

Printed and bound in India

PREFACE.

My own part in the production of this little book has been small—merely consisting in the somewhat laborious task of translating De Laet's crabbed Latin. The Introduction and notes have been written by my friend, Prof. S. N. Banerjee of Patiala.

Thanks are due to Dr. S. A. Khan of Allahabad University and to Mr. J. A. Chapman of the Imperial Library, Calcutta, for the loan of books: to Prof. J. N. Sarkar, the famous author of *Aurangzib*, for some suggestions regarding the annotation: and to Mr. S. Kumar (Superintendent, Imperial Library, Calcutta) for other help.

The annotator expresses his grateful thanks to Prof. S. H. Hodivala who has kindly gone through the book when in press and has made some suggestions and corrections which have been accepted.

JOHN S. HOYLAND.

Hislop College,

Nagpur.

INTRODUCTION.

Joannes De Laet, the Flemish geographer, philologist and naturalist, was born at Antwerp in 1593 and died at Leyden in 1649. His public life began at about 1625 when he 'occupied the position of the Director of the Company of the West Indies.' Later on he became one of the Directors of the Dutch East India Company. We do not know what part he played in the commercial extension of the Dutch nation in the East. But as a Director he was in touch with East Indian affairs. This enabled him to gain a knowledge of the East and especially of India, which knowledge he supplemented by a patient perusal of existing itineraries and geographies. The results of his studies he made available to the public by the publication in 1631 of the *De Imperio Magni Mogolis, sive India vera, Commentarius ex variis auctoribus congestus.*

De Laet was known in his own lifetime not as a Director of a commercial company but as a writer of accurate observation and wide interests. He was an intimate friend of Heinsius, Professor of Politics and Librarian in the University of Leyden and historiographer to Gustavus Adolphus of Sweden. In the British Museum Catalogue of Printed Books no less than 23 books are put down under the name of De Laet. It would be useless in this connection either to mention all the books or to discuss their merits. His first book was on the New World, and was published in 1625. He wrote both in Dutch and in Latin. The work here translated is in Latin.

We have it on the authority of Sir Roper Lethbridge that the *De Imperio Magni Mogolis* was regarded both by De Laet himself and by the public in his time as his most important and valuable work. It is a small duodecimo published by the famous Elzevirs of Leyden. It exists in two issues, both bearing the same date, 1631. The reprint has only a slight addition. The fact of two impressions in the same year attests to the warm reception accorded by the public. The book consists of two parts. The first part contains geographical, commercial and administrative details abstracted from various writings. The second part—known as Broecke's *Fragmentum*—gives a consecutive history of the reigns of Akbar and Jahangir.

After a fruitless attempt made in 1616, Pieter van den Broecke succeeded in 1620 in establishing a factory at Surat of which he became the President. He was the Director of what was then officially known as 'Western Quarters' comprising North and West India, Persia and Arabia. 'A gentleman of good breeding and very courteous,' he was also a shrewd man of business; and within the short space of seven years he secured in the regions under his charge the commercial preponderance of the Dutch, even rivalling the English, who had preceded the Dutch in the field. In the early part of 1621 a factory was established at Agra which offered a good market for the Dutch spice trade; and Francisco Pelsaert was placed at its head. Pelsaert wrote the *Remonstrantie* which has been translated into English by Mr. W. H. Moreland and Professor P. Geyl. In the *Introduction* the editors mention the fact that Pelsaert collected materials for a history of the Mughal Empire. These materials were incorporated by van den Broecke in the Fragment of Indian History which forms the second part of the present volume. The chronicle is said to have been sent to Holland in 1627 by the Director at Surat. The Dutch MS. of the Fragment was entrusted to De Laet, who translated it into Latin. Thus while the Fragment is associated with the name of van den Broecke, it appears to be primarily the work of Pelsaert, who is said to have mastered the language of the country and studied its history. While it is difficult to decide exactly van den Broecke's share in the work, there need be no doubt that De Laet's part was merely that of a translator and compiler, with the exception of a sprinkling of information concerning events that occurred after 1627. De Laet's interest in the affairs of the East, and the peculiar facilities which he enjoyed as a result of his position as Director and owing to his friendship with van den Broecke, enabled him to obtain quick and truthful information of happenings in India.

De Laet is pre-eminently a compiler; and his compilations are learned and laborious. No better illustration can be given than the first part of this book and above all, its first chapter. How assiduously he pieces together facts dug out of a host of writings and how closely reproduced they are! Ptolemy and Texeira, Roe and Pelsaert, Terry and Finch, Withington and Hawkins, Steele and Crowther, Benedict and Garcia are all largely drawn upon, making the *De Imperio Magni Mogolis* a monument of painstaking industry and a storehouse of varied information. The Empire and the Imperial administration, the court and its grandees, the towns and their splendour, the provinces and their administration, the country's trade and trade-routes, the articles of trade and the centres of production, the festivals and ceremonies of the court, the manners and pastimes of the rich, the pursuits of the common people and the economic condition of the country as a whole, are depicted with a realism of touch and a minuteness of detail which will make the

De Imperio Magni Mogolis enduringly useful. It is a complete Gazetteer of Jahangir's India. Although it is a compilation, it is a faithful and reliable compilation. Inaccuracies there are ; but that is a defect which it shares both with all contemporary foreign accounts and with all native chronicles. And these defects are more than offset by the large amount of acknowledged fact which it records.

The *Fragment of Indian History* forms an original source for the reigns of Akbar and Jahangir. It is one of the earliest and most informing, and as such deserves to be critically read for the period it covers. Vincent Smith is of opinion that it is based on some genuine Persian chronicle. This need not necessarily be so. In any case it would be difficult to specify the chronicle in question. The *Fragmentum* may be considered a digest of available books, hearsay reports and contemporary tradition.

Authorities :—

La Grande Encyclopedie, vol XXI.

P. P. Larousse. *Grand Dictionaire Universal*, vol. 10.

Bulletin de l'Academie royal de Belgique, pour 1852, tom XIX.

Calcutta Review, 1870.

J.R.A.S., 1915, 1923.

The Indian Antiquary, 1914, 1915.

Moreland's *Introduction* to Pelsaert's *Remonstrantie.*

Patiala,
May 23rd, 1927.

S. N. BANERJEE.

ABBREVIATIONS.

Ain	..	*Ain-i-Akbari* translated by Mr. Blochmann and Col. Jarrett.
A.R.	..	Archæological Survey Reports.
A.T.	..	A Handbook to Agra and the Taj, Sikandra, Fatehpur-Sikri and the neighbourhood, by E. B. Havell, Longmans, Green and Co., 1904.
Bernier	..	Travels in the Moghul Empire, second edition, by V. A. Smith, 1916.
B.G.	..	Bombay Gazetteer, first edition, by Sir J. Campbell.
B M.C.	..	Catalogue of Mughal coins in the British Museum, by S. Lane Poole.
C.R.	..	Calcutta Review, Vols LI (1870), LII (1871), LIV (1873).
E D.	..	Elliot and Dowson· Vols. 8, History of India as told by her own Historians.
E.F.I.	..	English Factories in India, edited by Sir W. Foster.
E.T.	..	Early Travels in India, 1583-1619, edited by Sir William Foster, Oxford University Press, 1921.
Erskine	..	History of Baber and Humayun.

Ferishta .. *Tarikhi-Ferishta* of Muhammad Bin Kasim, translated by John Briggs; Calcutta, 1909 Vols 4

Fryer .. A New Account of East India and Persia, being nine years' Travels, 1672-1681, by John Fryer, edited by W. Crooke, Vols. 3

H J. .. History of Jahangir, by Prof. Beni Prasad, Oxford University Press.

I A. .. The Indian Antiquary.

I G .. Imperial Gazetteer, Clarendon Press, 1908.

J.A.S.B. .. Journal of the Asiatic Society, Bengal.

J.P.H.S. . Journal of the Punjab Historical Society.

J.R.A.S. .. Journal of the Royal Society.

L M.C. .. Catalogue of coins in the Provincial Museum, Lucknow, by Prof. C. J. Brown.

L.R. .. Letters received by the East Indian Company from its servants in the East, edited by F. C. Danvers and Sir William Foster, 1901, Vols. 6.

Manucci . Storia do Mogor (1653-1608) by Niccolao Manucci, translated by W. Irvine, Vols. III, London, 1907

Monserrate .. The Commentary of Father Monserrate, edited by Prof. J. S. Hoyland and S. N. Banerjee

Pelsaert	..	The Remonstrantie, edited by Prof. P. Geyl and Mr. W. H. Moreland, under the title of Jahangir's India.
Rennell	..	Memoirs of a Map of Hindustan, or the Great Mogul Empire, by Major James Rennell, F.R.S., London, 1793.
Roe	..	The Embassy of Sir Thomas Roe to the Court of the Great Mogul (1615-19), edited by Sir William Foster (1899).
R.S.	..	*Riyazu-s-Salatin* by Ghulam Hussain Salim, edited by Maulvi Abdus Salam, published by the Asiatic Society, Bengal.
S.C.D.	..	The Seven Cities of Delhi by Gordon Risley Hearn, London, 1906.
Thevenot	..	The Travels of Monsieur de Thevenot, Part III, London, 1687.
T.J.	..	*Tuzuk-i-Jahangiri*, translated by Rogers and edited by H Beveridge, London, 1914
Whiteway	..	The Rise of the Portuguese Power in India, 1497-1550, by R. S. Whiteway, Constable, 1899.

CONTENTS

PAGE.

PART II

Note:—Words enclosed between square brackets have been inserted by the Translator or Commentator In some cases the spelling of names has been modernised in supplying titles to sections, etc.]

PART I.

GEOGRAPHY

AND

ADMINISTRATION

OF THE

MUGHAL EMPIRE

CHAPTER I.

TOPOGRAPHICAL DESCRIPTION OF INDIA OR OF THE EMPIRE OF THE GREAT MOGOL.

INTRODUCTION.

India, both on this side of and beyond the Ganges, was known even to the ancients, especially after the time of Alexander the Great, as is shown by the histories of his exploits composed by illustrious writers. Pliny, who studied very many of these histories which are now no longer extant, writes (Book VI, Chap 7) that the land inhabited by the Indian race begins from the mountains of Emodus and is bounded not only by that sea which lies towards the west, but also by the southern ocean, which he calls the Indian ocean (a name which we now apply to the former sea) He also says that the part of India which directly faces the east measures in all, including indentations, 1,875 miles, whilst in the south, according to Eratosthenes,[1] the coast measures 2,475 miles as far as the Indus, which is the western boundary of India.

[1] Eratosthenes (276-196 B C) was the learned President of the Library at Alexandria from 240 to 196 B C His observations on India are based on materials supplied by Patrokles, an officer in the service of Seleukos Nikator and Antiochus I. He speaks of the shape of India as rhomboidal, its four sides being composed of the Indus, the Himalayas and the shores of the Southern (Western) and Eastern Seas So far he was right But Eratosthenes imagined that the Indus flowed directly southwards, thus constituting the western side of the rhomboid and that the coastal orientation from the mouth of the Indus to Cape Comorin was south-south-easterly He further wrongly supposed that this coast measured 2,183 miles (De Laet says 2,475 miles) ; really it is 1,350 miles. The eastern coast from Cape Comorin to the mouth of the Ganges measured, according to Eratosthenes, 1,838 miles (De Laet writes 1,875 miles), whereas the actual distance again is 1,350 miles The distance from the Himalayas to the southernmost point of India is about 1,800 miles and not 2,750 miles as De Laet informs us.

However, he adds that a number of authors reckon the total length of India at forty days' and nights' voyage for a sailing vessel, whilst the breadth from north to south is 2,750 miles. I do not intend in this place either to refer to or to disprove these descriptions of the ancients, since the old names of districts, towns and races have in nearly all cases become obsolete, and the aspect of things is in our day far different from what it was in theirs. My intention is rather to describe the kingdom of the Great Mogol in its present-day condition, according to the observations made during recent years by men of various European races—Portuguese, English and Dutch.

BOUNDARIES OF THE EMPIRE.

Nowadays the Persians and Arabs call India Indostan. This country is bounded on the west by the river Indus, on the shore of which is the kingdom of Sind, whose inhabitants are called Abind [Sindhees ?]. The boundary may also be reckoned as the frontier of the kingdom of Macron (which is called by some Getche Maquerona). The inhabitants of this kingdom are Baluches, over whom in the year 1613 reigned Meleck Myrza [Malik Mirza] who formerly recognised the king of Persia as his sovereign, but afterwards threw off his yoke. This is that province which the ancients called Carmania. Its port is Guader, which is situated 25 degrees North of the Equator. Sinde is called by the Arabs and Persians the kingdom of Diul.[2] The river

[2] Debal was a celebrated seaport of Sind in the 17th century and is believed to have stood upon or near the site of modern Karachi. It was destroyed by the Mahomedans in 711 A D (E D I , p. 120). But another town bearing the same name was built to the east (J.R A S I., p. 29). To the Portuguese this came to be known as Diul-Sind to distinguish it from the resembling name of Diu in Kathiawar. The name Diul-Sind or Sindee was also applied to the Delta of the Indus (*cf* Kach-Makran). Diul has been identified with the famous port of Lari-Bandar by W. Foster (Roe.

which was called by the ancients the Indus is named by the Persians and Mogols the Pangab (that is, the five waters), because it carries to the sea the mingled waters of five rivers. One of these, according to Texeira, is the Behat, which rises near Kabul. The second is the Chanab which comes from Quexmir [Kashmir], a province which lies fifteen days' journey north of Lahore. The third is the Rabby (or Ravee) which passes by Lahore and is said to rise far to the north of that town. The other two rivers come from regions even more remote; they are the Via [Beas] and the Send[3] (or Sind). The last named gives its name to the others, which all flow into it. All the rivers join near Bakar, which lies about half way between Lahore and the Indian Ocean. I find that Dutch explorers declare that the Ravee, Behat and Sind rise in the mountains of Cassimer and join near Multan, a town 140 cos distant from Lahor. It is remarkable however that all the geographers who up to the present have drawn maps (of India) have made a great error in locating the mouth of this river Indus, for it is now sufficiently established that the mouth of that river is situated in latitude 24° 45′ N. Above the mouth is situated the town of Diul, which lies about 15 miles from the sea. I shall say more about the mouth of the Indus in the proper place.

---

p 122, see also J.A S B, Vol. 61, Part I, and Extra No.). Haig puts it at the ruin-covered site some 20 miles south-west of Thatta; De Laet makes it 15 miles from the sea (*vide infra*).

[3] The Sindhu or Indus (Sinthus of the *Periplus*) rises from the Kailash (the Hindu Olympus) to the north of the Manasarowar Lake at a height of 17,000 ft. Sindhu is also the Sanskrit term for ocean. probably to the early invaders coming through the north-western passes the river was as big as an ocean. I do not know what De Laet means exactly when he says that the 'Send' has given its name to the other rivers Sanskrit writers collectively called the rivers *Sapta Sindhavas* or seven Sindhus (or rivers): the Indus, the Jhelum, the Chenab, the Ravi, the Beas, the Sutlej and the Saraswati.

Provinces of the Empire.

The Empire of the great Mogol is of such an enormous size that some writers have declared that a caravan can scarcely cross it within the space of two years. The Englishman, Mr. Edward Therry, gives it the following boundaries.—In the east the kingdom of Maugh[4], in the west partly Persia, partly (towards the south) the ocean, in the north the Caucasus and Tartaria, in the south the kingdom of the Deccan and the Bay of Bengal He also declares that it is divided into 37 large provinces, which in former years were mostly separate kingdoms. The following are the names of the chief towns and the

---

[4] A name commonly applied to the natives of Arakan, particularly those bordering on Bengal or residing near the sea. As to the derivation of the word Maugh, more than one theory has been propounded *Hobson-Jobson* quoting Sir Arthur Phayre writes "There is good reason to conclude that the name is derived from Maga, the name of the ruling race for many centuries in Magadha (south Behar). The kings of Arakan were no doubt originally of this race, for though this is not distinctly expressed in the histories of Arakan, there are several legends of kings from Benares reigning in that country and one regarding a Brahman who marries a native princess and whose descendants reign for a long time I say this, although Buchanan appears to reject the theory" Some choose to derive the word from Magus or Magians, *i e*, Persian fire-worshippers The Maughs were Buddhists, and Muhammadan historians sometimes confounded Buddhists with fire-worshippers Whatever may be the etymology, the Maughs were a troublesome people who made capital out of their geographical position by carrying on filibustering raids into Bengal The annoyance they caused Jahangir is well reflected in his remarks in his *Memoirs* (T.J., Vol. I, 236) : "Briefly they are animals in the form of men They eat everything there is either on land or in the sea, and nothing is forbidden by their religion. In face they are like the Qara Qalmags, but their language is that of Tibet and quite unlike that of Turki. They are far from the Mussalman faith and separated from that of the Hindus."

rivers of these provinces, beginning from the western frontier :—

1. *Kandahar* (with capital of the same name) —This province lies towards the north-west, and marches with Persia, of which it was formerly a part, and indeed is so again at present, for the king of Persia Xa-Abas [Shah Abbas, 1586-1628] has recently recaptured it from the Mogols.

2 *Kabul*—This province is named from its chief town, and is the most distant portion of the Mogol Empire, marching with Tartaria in the north-west. In this province the river Nilab[5] rises, which flows southwards and joins the Indus I suspect that this Nilab is the same as the Behat which according to Peter Texeira (as has been noted above) rises near Kabul and is one of those five rivers which flow into the Indus It was called by Ptolemy either the Coas [Kabul river] or the Suastus [Swat river].

3 *Multan* (named from its capital of the same name).—This province is bounded on the west by Persia or Kandahar and on the south by Buckar. It lies on the banks of the Indus

5 The Nilab (*i e*, blue water) is the upper Indus and not the Behat or the Kabul river as De Laet and other European writers wrongly suppose Even in the 16th century a city named Nilab stood on the east bank of the Indus at a small distance below its conflux with the Kabul river It was an old city Ptolemy writes of a city of nearly the same name (Naulība) on the opposite bank of the Indus "The city of Attock in a manner," writes Rennell, "succeeded Nilab, their situations differing but little. It may be conceived from the apparent etymology that the city originally took its name from the river which was more generally known by the name of Nilab than Sinde It is certain that by strange want of accuracy, the name Nilab came to be applied also to an adjunct river, that is, to a part at least (between Attock and Peshawar) of the river Cabul" (Rennell, pp 95-96, Monserrate, pp. 121-122).

4. *Hajacan, or Hoagickan.*—This province[6] is bounded on the east by the River Indus and on the west by Lara, a province of Persia. It possesses no town of any note. It is called the kingdom of the Boloches (or Balaoches), about which race of people I will write elsewhere.

5. *Buckor* (*or Buckar*).—The capital of this province is called Buckor Suckor, it lies on the Indus. The province is divided into two by this river, to which also it owes its marvellous fertility It stretches to the north and east of Tatta. Its western boundary is the country of the fierce and warlike Baloaches.

6. *Tatta*[7] (so called from its capital) —This province lies on the banks of the Indus, which forms many beautiful and fertile islands in its course Lower down it unites into one stream near the city of Synde [Diul] which is famous for numbers and variety of its handicrafts.

7. *Soret* [Saurashtra].—The capital of this province (which is a small but rich one) is called Janagar [Junagarh]

---

6 Hajkan is mentioned by Abul Fazl as one of the Sarkars of **Multan** (*Ain* II 340) Rennell writes (p 178). "A large portion of Hajykan lies on the West of the Indus, opposite to Multan. It extends southward along the Indus until it meets the border of Sindy, and a small part of it was subject to Sindy The missionary itinerary (1662) mentions the Balloges (Bulloches) as the then possessors of Hajykan, which adjoined the kingdom of Persia and was inhabited by Baloches" The name is derived from Haji Khan whose overlordship the Balochees recognised and whose descendants ruled over the lower Derajat (E T, p. 292, *n*. 1 ; 314).

7 The town of Thatta is situated in 24° 45′ N. and 67° 58′ E. It is now in the Karachi district It was a Sarkar of the province of Sind. In Akbar's time and throughout the seventeenth century it was a busy entrepôt It decayed during the latter half of the eighteenth century.

It is bounded on the east and south-east by Guzurat and on the south by the ocean.

8. *Jeselmeere* (so called from its capital).—This province is bounded on the east by Soret, Buckor and Tatta.

9. *Attock* (so called from its capital)—This province is situated on the river Nilab, which comes from the north-west and flows into the Indus. The latter river divides this province from Haiacan.

10. *Pang-Ab*—This province, of which the capital is Lahor, is very large and fertile, being irrigated by those five rivers of which mention has already been made, and from which it derives its name Ptolemy alludes to the confluence of these five rivers,[8] *i.e*, the Coa or Suastus (these two rivers join a little above the boundary of this province), the Indus, the Bidaspes, the Rhuadis and the Zaradrus.

11. *Cassimere, Chismeer or Quexmir*.—The capital of this province is called Siranakar. The province lies upon both sides of the river Behat or Phat which winds in a meandering course with many islands, and finally falls into the Indus, or as others declare into the Ganges, though this latter appears to me less probable. The province is mountainous (it marches with Kabul) and rather cold, though less so than the kingdom of Thebet, which adjoins it on the east At a distance of 8 leucae[9] from the capital

---

[8] The rivers mentioned are the Kabul (Coa), the Swat (Suastus), the Indus, the Jhelum, the Ravi and the Sutlej The Sanskrit name of the Jhelum was Vitasta, the Greeks called it Hydaspes or Bydaspes, the Muhammadan historians called it Behat, locally in the Punjab Plains it is called Vehat, and in Kashmir Veth. Zaradrus is the Græcised form of the Sanskrit Satadru (Sutlej). Later on the Sutlej is referred to as Sietmegus (?)

[9] Leuca is a Gallic mile of 1,500 Roman paces. the ancient Roman pace was 58·1 English inches. In connection with

lies a large lake 5 leucae in circumference, in the middle of which is an island upon which a royal palace [10] has been built for the convenience of those hunting wild geese; these birds abound in the lake in vast numbers. Near to the river which flows through the middle of this lake towards the west, enormous trees are to be seen, whose leaves are somewhat similar to those of the chestnut, though their wood is different. When it is cut into planks, this wood presents the appearance of waves, and is very well suited for the making of boxes

12 *Bankish* [11]—The capital of this province is called Beishar or Bishur It lies to the south-east of Cassimere

13 *Jengapor or Jenupar*—This province [11a] is called after its capital, and lies on the bank of the river Kaul below Lahor and between that city and Agra

14. *Jenba or Jamba,* whose chief city is called by the same name [*Chamba*]—This province lies to the east of the Panjab, and is very mountainous

15. *Delly* (with capital city of the same name) lies between Jenba and Agra.—In this province rises the river

---

Haiderabad De Laet says that according to local measurement, each leuca was equal to 9 English miles The word seems to be rather loosely used The *lieue* of Bernier is 2½ miles, *i e*, one kos of northern India The *kos* of N India as calculated from the distance between kos-minars of Mughal times, is 2 miles 4 furlongs and 158 yards

10 On the Lanka island in the Wular lake may be seen the ruins of a Hindu temple and a mosque of the Sultan, Zain-ul-Abidin (1443-44) [See Bernier, p 416, *n* 2, and *Journals kept in Hyderabad, Kashmir, Sikkim and Nepal* by Sir Richard Temple, Vol II, pp 64, 120]

11 Prof Blochmann identifies it with Bangash in N W. Kohat, and Beishar with Bajaur Sir William Foster is inclined to identify it with Peshawar I accept the view of Blochmann. Really it is south-west, not south-east, of Kashmir.

11a Sir William Foster in annotating the corresponding passage of Terry, suggests Jaunpur, which is not probable Jammu, or Jaswal, the name of a Punjab Hill State (*Akbar-Nama* III. 51) is probable.

Jemini or Semena as others call it, which flows through Agra into the Ganges Delly is an ancient city and in former times was the capital of the old kings of India, of whom many monuments may still be seen there.

16 *Bando*[12] (with capital of the same name) lies to the west of Agra

17. *Maiovav or Malva*—This is a very fertile province, whose capital is Rantipore [Rantambhor], others give the name of its chief city as Ugen [Ujjain] which Thomas Roeus [Roe], the English Knight, calls the capital of Malva At a distance of one cos from this town flows the river Cepra, on whose bank is situated Calleada [Kaliyadaha], once the capital of the kings of Mando. This river is said to flow into the Gulf of Cambay

18 *Chitor* (with capital of the same name)—This is a large and very ancient kingdom, but its capital, whose walls are some 10 English miles in circumference, is in ruins, so that only the debris is left of more than a hundred most magnificent temples and of other buildings whose number is almost infinite The Mogol King Achabar captured this city from the servants of its Ranna and destroyed it But one prince fled into the fastnesses of the mountains and settled at the town of Odepore. In the year 1614 he was finally compelled to recognise the sovereignty of the Mogol. This kingdom is situated to the north-west of the province of Chandes [Khandesh] and to the north of Guzuratte.

19. *Guzuratte*—This most beautiful and opulent region is now, according to Texeira, called Cambay by the Portuguese after its chief port, which they frequently visit. Its capital is inland and is called Hamed-Eovat, that is the city of King Hamed [Ahmed, 1411-53] who founded it;

[12] Terry has it thus: "Bando confineth Agra on the west." In annotating it Sir William Foster identifies it with Banda, a district in U. P Probably Bandhu is meant (*Akbar-Nama* III, 1093; *vide infra p* 155).

it is now corruptly called Amadavar or Amadbat. This exceedingly rich region is watered by various rivers, Nardabah which flows past Baroah, the Tapte and others. It is penetrated by a huge gulf of the sea into which ancient geographers thought (wrongly) the Indus flowed.

20. *Candish.*—The capital of this province is called Burhampur and was once the capital of the kings of the Deccan. It was taken from them by the Mogol Emperor [Akbar]. It is a large and populous district through which flows the river Tabett or Tapte. This river flows into the Gulf of Cambay. Parthaspha,[13] a prince of mediocre importance and a tributary of the Great Mogol, rules over a district adjoining this province, which is the most southerly part of the Mogol dominions.

21. *Berar.*—The capital of this province is called Shahpore or Shahpur.[14] It is the southern province of the Empire and marches with Guzuratte and the mountainous districts of Ranna.

---

13 Pratap Sah was a Rathor chieftain of Baglana, the tract between Khandesh and the Surat coast His immediate predecessor Bharju (died in 1589) had imperfectly submitted to Akbar. Pratap acknowledged the suzerainty of Jahangir whom he visited at Mandu and left his son as hostage, the chieftainship was finally annexed by Aurangzeb In the *Ain-i-Akbari* we read that he commanded 3,000 cavalry and 10,000 infantry Baglana possessed seven forts, of which Mulher and Saler were the strongest. The chief's headquarters were at Jaitapur, near Mulher fort As the road from Surat to Burhanpur lay partly through his territory he claimed the right of levying toll at Daita, from which however Roe got exemption. A safe-conduct for transport of royal treasures through his territory was obtained in 1622. In De Laet the name of the Raja appears under various guises as Parthaspha, Pectoshavus. *Vide infra*. (*Ain*. II. 251; Roe II. 87 *n*. 460 *n*., Sarkar's *Aurangzib*, Vol. I. 50-53).

14 After the annexation of Berar to the Mughal Empire in 1596 Prince Murad, the viceroy, fixed his head-quarters at Shahpur. It grew apace into a fine city (*Ain* II. 229) It is in the Akola district of Berar see *Fragment*, Section XVII).

22. *Narvar.*—The capital of this province is Gehud. It is watered by a very beautiful stream which flows into the Ganges.

23. *Guvaliar or Gualoor.*—This province is called after its capital, which possesses an exceedingly strong fortress in which noble prisoners are confined. In the same place the king has numerous treasuries, which contain a great quantity of silver and gold, both coined and uncoined.

24. *Agra*—This province is named after its capital, which is not a very old place Some appear to call it Parrop[15] and Purbeth It is a very large city and is situated in the very heart of the Empire. Agra and Lahore, which are now by far the most important cities of the Empire, are 400 English miles apart The intervening regions are level The cities are connected by a royal highway[16], which is adorned with a double line of trees like a pleasant promenade

25 *Sambal or Sambel*—This province, which is called after its capital city, is divided from Narvar by the river Jemini which runs into the Ganges below the city of Halebasee. The province lies to the north-west of this river junction and seems to be called by some the Do'ab, that is the district between the two rivers.

26. *Bakar*—This province,[16a] whose chief city is called Bikaneer, is situated on the west bank of the Ganges.

---

15 There seems to be some mistake here Purrob (East) was generally applied to the country round about Allahabad. Purbeth may stand for mountain

16 Babur planned and his successors completed the road. Terry describes "the walke of four hundred miles shaded by great trees on both sides" and adds that "this is looked upon by the travellers who have found the comfort of that cool shade as one of the rarest and most beneficial works in the whole world." Coryat says much the same

16a I am indebted to Prof. S H Hodivala for pointing out that Bakar is identical with Bhagore of Tod. Beeka wrested Bhagore from the Bhattis and founded Bikanir in 1489.

27. *Nagrakut or Nakarkut* [Nagarkot or Kangra].—This is a mountainous province and is the northernmost of the Empire. Its capital bears the same name as the province and contains a most magnificent shrine whose floor and ceiling are covered with plates of gold. In this shrine there is an idol called Matta,[17] to worship which many thousands of Indians gather every year, they offer to it small pieces of their own tongues which they cut off for the purpose In this same province lies Callamaka [Jwala-mukhi], which is also a celebrated place of pilgrimage, for every day flames are seen to break forth from amongst some high rocks where there is a spring of cold water The barbarous and superstitious crowd prostrates itself before these flames and worships them.

28. *Siba* [18]—The capital of this province is Hardwair, the place where the Ganges is believed to issue from a rock which the superstitious common people imagine to resemble a cow's head [Gau-mukhi] The Indian peoples venerate the cow above all other animals Every day they bathe their bodies in the waves of the river at this place The province is mountainous and lies to the south of Nakarkut.

29. *Kakares.*[19]—The chief towns in this province are Dankala and Purhola. It is a very extensive region, and mountainous, being divided from Tartary by the

---

[17] The famous temple of Mata Devi or Bajreshwari Debi at Bhawan, a suburb of Kangra Abul Fazl and Finch also mention the cutting off of tongues (E T, 180, *Ain* II 313; T.J. Vol. II, 224, Terry, p 82)

[18] Siba was once an independent principality, now a part of the Kangra district

[19] The country of the Gakkhars was in the north-west of the Punjab. Here the Gakkhars and not the Khokhars are referred to Dangali was made the capital by the chieftain Rajar Khan (1152-1186 A.D) After the destruction of Dangali by Sher Shah,

ranges of the Caucasus. It is the northernmost part of the Empire, lying to the north of Cassimere.

30 *Gor* [Gaur or Bengal].—This province, which is called after its capital city, is also a mountainous one. The river Persely [20] rises in it and flows into the Ganges.

31. *Pitan or Peitan* [21]—This province, whose capital bears the same name, is watered by the river Kanda, which joins the Ganges at the border of the province. It is a mountainous district and lies to the east of Jamba.

32. *Kanduana.*[22]—The capital of this province is Kerahkatenck The province is separated from Peitan [Patna] by the river Persely. It forms with Gor, the northern district of the Empire.

33. *Patna*—(so called from its capital).—This is a very fertile province watered by four rivers, of which the Ganges and the Persely form the western and eastern boundaries of the province, respectively. The other two rivers are the Jemini and the Kandah.

the Gakkhar chief, Sultan Adam made Pharwala his headquarters. It had a strong fort (J A S.B , Vol XL, Part I, 1871, p 88).

20 Persely is a mistake for Sersely which again is a mistake for Sersety or Saraswati, " which after the Jamuna is the principal (legendary) tributary of the Ganges Terry, so also De Laet, follows the legend and makes the Saraswati flow into the Ganges near Allahabad " (J A S B , 1873, p 244) I am not certain that Gor is Bengal, because the latter is separately mentioned (No. 37) See below Note 22 It may refer to Koch (Kuch Behar)

21 Paithan or Pathankot De Laet evidently means the whole hill tract of the Sirmur range as far as the Alaknanda The river Kanda is possibly the Markanda which, however, does not flow into the Ganges

22 Gondwana and the capital Garh-Katanga (Jubbulpur). Terry, from whom De Laet copies, says that " this and Gor are the north-east bounds of this Monarchy," and Blochmann, commenting on it, writes " If Gor is the north-east boundary of the Empire, it is Gaur of Silhat or the Garo Hills " (J.A.S.B., 1873, p. 243).

34. *Jesual.*[23]—The capital of this province is Rajapore or Ragapor. It lies to the east of Patna and marches with Bengal on the south-east.

35. *Mevat* [Mewat].—The capital of this province is called Narnol. It is a mountainous region lying to the east of the Ganges.

36. *Udessaor, Udeza* [Orissa].—The capital of this province is called Jokanat or Jekanat [Jagannath]. It is the most remote province of the Empire towards the east and adjoins the kingdom of Maug, whose inhabitants are very fierce and extremely barbarous.

37. *Bengala.*—This is a very large and fertile region bounded on the south by the Bay of Bengal, into which the Ganges discharges itself through four huge mouths The chief cities of the province are Ragmehell [Rajmahal] and Dekaka [Dacca]. The nearest land to the south-west is Choromandel. The province has many ports, both small and great, which are frequently visited by the Portuguese. It contains many districts such as Philipatan [24] and Sataghan [25] The chief of these districts are Purop [26] and Patan which were once governed by a line of very powerful kings [Kararani dynasty].

---

[23] Foster suggests Jaswan in Hoshiarpur District He identifies Rajapore with Rajpura, 15 miles from Patiala. Van den Broucke puts Jesual east of Morang in the Himalayan tract In Blaev's map it is marked out as a place for elephants, from which Blochmann concludes that Rajapore refers to Raipur in C. P. I find it difficult to identify the place.

[24] Probably Pipli is meant. It is near Balasore (Orissa). The Portuguese settled there in 1599 and for many years it was a centre of their power.

[25] Satgaon, now a ruined town in the Hugly district, Bengal. It was once the mercantile capital of Bengal Its decay dates from the silting up of the river Saraswati during the first half of the sixteenth century (R.S , p. 29 , Rennell, p 57).

[26] I am unable exactly to identify the district of Purop. The word or its variant was applied to Allahabad and Oudh; and some.

Another writer [Sir Thomas Roe] who declares that he obtained the names of the provinces from a list in the Royal library gives the same total number and practically the same names, except that he does not mention Jeselmeere, but substitutes for it, in order to bring the total number up to 37, the province of Roch[27] on the border of Bengal, which has no town of any note.

Peter Texeira, in his account of the kingdom of Persia, enumerates several provinces of India, but not nearly so many as I have just mentioned He speaks of the province of Utrad [Otrar] on the Jaxartes with a capital of the same name, but does not say where it is situated. He also writes that the kingdom of Cachc [Cutch] produces most excellent horses. These are called Cachy after that kingdom which seem to be situated to the north of Cambay.

Size of the Empire.

The total length of the Empire from north-west to south-east is at least a thousand cos, each of which is equal to two or two and a half English miles. Two cos are equal to one Dutch mile. From north to south it measures 1,400 English miles The southernmost part is only 20° from the Equator, but the northern frontier is about 43° north. Its breadth from north to south-west is 1,500 miles.

The Fathers of the Society of Jesus declare that this Empire extends northwards from the coast of Cambay for 400 leucae and east to west (*i.e.*, from Bengal to the Indus) the distance is 600 leucae.

---

times it included Behar even. It generally meant the East country (*i.e.*, *Purab*, East). Pelsaert (and De Laet elsewhere) speaks of Bengal as Bengalen Purop Finch speaks of Patna as being a great city in Purop (E.T. p 147)

27 Rukh is the term for Arakan Some say that it stands for Koch or Kuch Behar. I think the former explanation is better.

So much is common knowledge about the size of this Empire. Let us now address ourselves to a description of the provinces one by one, beginning with those which lie on the sea coast.

GUJARAT.

Guzuratte, or as it is nowadays called by the Portuguese Cambay, is a maritime province of India, part of which juts out into the Indian Ocean like a peninsula, and has a large gulf on each side of it The southern of these two gulfs is 80 miles across at its entrance and narrows gradually It is about 40 miles deep and runs north-eastward This province is bounded on the west by the Indian Ocean and on the north by a great gulf (beyond which lie the provinces of Soret, Jeselmeere and Bando). On the east it is bounded by Chitor and Chandis, and on the south by the kingdom of the Decan The province used to be much larger, stretching indeed from the Indian Ocean to Gualer, an 8 days' journey from Amadabat; and to the south it used to extend as far as Daman The following are the names of its chief towns, which lie on the sea coast or on the two gulfs, Suratta, Brochia, Cambaia, Mangorol, Patan Diu, Kerimar, Nagsari Menhovva, Dongessar, Dlasghan, Mangerol, Pore, Onnapar, and Goga.[28]

The annual revenue of this province from taxation and tribute is said by the Dutch to amount to 150 tons of gold.

---

28 I am unable to identify the last eight places except Gogha which was a port, situated in 12° 41 N and 72° 17 E. Its natives were reckoned the best sailors or lascars in India. Its decay dated from the rise of Surat The English considered it unsuitable for their fleet in 1618 (*Ain* II 247, E F.I., 1618-22, pp. 29-30). Prof. Hodivala thus identifies them: Prabhas Patan (Patan Diu), Kodinar, Nageshri, Mahuva, Dungar, Tatāja, Mangrol, Por or Porbandar and Una.

SURAT.

The port which is to-day most frequented by the English and Dutch is Suratte, which lies 20° 40′ north of the equator on the bank of the river Tapte (which is called by others the Tynde) This river comes down from Barampore, and flows into the Indian Ocean 20 English miles below the town. Ships of a moderate size can ascend the river as far as the town Suratte is a place of medium size with a large number of fine houses belonging to merchants. Near by is a large fort surrounded with a wall of sandstone and defended by a number of warlike engines, some of which are of exceptional size The fort has only one gate which opens upon a most beautiful plain called by the people the Medon [Maidan]. On this side the town is open, but on all other sides it is fenced by a dry ditch and an earthen rampart with three gates, of which one opens upon the road to Variauvv [Variao], a small village, where travellers to Cambay cross the river [Tapti]. The second gate is in the direction of Brampore; and the third in that of Uonsaray or Nassaray [Nausari], which town is 10 cos distant from Suratte or (according to the Dutch) 6 Dutch miles At Nonsaray a large number of cotton fabrics are woven, from that place to the town of Gondoree [Gandevi] is 10 cos, and a little further lies Belsaca[29], close to the boundary of Daman. On the other side of the fortress of Suratte is Telonium,* where the port duties are paid. There is a market here. Close to the town is to be seen a tank [Gopi talao] excavated in the living rock. It has more than a hundred corners; each

[29] Bulsar is 40 miles south of Surat The place was well-known in contemporary history for having caused friction between Akbar and the Portuguese (Monserrate, pp. 166-67). At places, as here, De Laet draws materials from Finch In Finch the letter *c* is to be taken for *r*. So Belsaca is Belsara, Beca is Bera, Necanpore is Neranpore, Pectosphavus is Pertosphavus.

* It is not the name of a place, but some word meaning "Custom-house."

of its sides is 28 fathoms long and the steps which lead down to it are also of stone. It is a work of admirable execution, from the point of view both of size and elegance of workmanship. About 3 English miles above the mouth of the river Tapte lies an island which is totally submerged during the rainy season; on the northern side of this island is a landing stage where large vessels discharge and embark their cargo This place is said to be 21° 10′ north of the equator From this island up to Suratte the river is navigable to ships of a burden of 50 dolia.* As you go up the river you see the fortress which has just been mentioned on your right, and on the left bank a little below the city is the pleasant town of Raneli [Rander]. The inhabitants of this place are called Naites,[30] and speak a different dialect from that of Suratte For the most part they are sailors The streets of Raneli are narrow and the houses lofty, being ascended by several flights of steps Balsara or Belsaca is 14 Dutch miles south of Suratte

CAMBAY.

The port of Cambay, which is greatly frequented by the Portuguese is situated at the end of the Gulf, which looks towards the south. It is 18 or 20 Dutch miles north of Brochia or Baroche The road thither is dangerous, being beset by robbers, for the inhabitants of this province are exceedingly wicked, and extort tribute from travellers even against the direct command of the Emperor.

* Is it the Russian weight ? One Dolia=0·684 Grs Lethbridge translates it as ton which is probable Finch also writes tun

30 Shortly after the beginning of the thirteenth century (*c.* 1225 A.D) a colony of Arab merchants and sailors is said to have settled at Rander They attacked the Jains who at that time ruled at Rander, drove them out of the city and converted the temples into mosques. Under the name of Nayates they traded to distant countries and became famous for their wealth and hospitality. They are spoken of as a race of more courage and policy than the Banias (B G , II., p. 299)

I find from the English that Cambay is 38 cos from Amadabat, the road, which is sandy, passing through forests, and being beset by robbers. Cambay lies 1½ or 2 miles from the sea, close to an inlet, which near the city is 4 or 5 miles wide and narrows gradually above. On the opposite bank of this inlet lies the village of Sarode. The inlet can be crossed by a ford when the tide is out, but not without danger or in the absence of an experienced guide. The crossing by boat, when the tide is in, is also dangerous on account of the violence of the currents, which are said hereabouts sometimes to form seven whirlpools

The city of Cambay is twice as big as Suratte and is surrounded by a triple wall of brick. Its houses are lofty and magnificent, its streets straight and well paved, each one of them being closed by a separate gate at night. In the middle of the town are three very extensive market places The inhabitants are for the most part Baneanes. There are large numbers of monkeys in the town, which do a great deal of damage and often wound passengers in the streets with tiles which they fling from the roof of the houses. The port is so crowded that not infrequently 200 vessels may be seen here at one and the same time

[*Ahmedabad*].—The capital of this province is Hamed Euvat or as it is commonly called, Amadabat or Amadavar. This city is almost as large as London, having a circumference of 6 Dutch miles. It is 23° and a few minutes north of the equator and 18 Dutch miles from Cambay. It is situated on a plain near the bank of a small river, and is surrounded by a strong wall with many gates and turrets. It has a large and excellently fortified citadel. The houses of the townsmen are equal in magnificence to any in Asia or Africa. The streets are broad and well paved. The city is a great trading centre; every ten or twenty days 200 carts leave for Cambay laden with every description of merchandise. Many of the inhabitants are merchants (mostly rich Baneanes) or master craftsmen, so that a force of six thousand horsemen can without difficulty be maintained here. The gates of this city are strictly guarded, and no one can come in or go out without the governor's permission. These precautions are taken owing to the proximity of a stronghold belonging to the brigand-chief Badur,[31] who lives fifty cos to the east of the city. His fort is so strongly defended both by nature and by art that the great Mogol has been unable to dislodge him from it. Indeed within the past few years this freebooter (accompanied by one hundred thousand horsemen, whom he has attracted to himself by the hope of liberty and spoil) has suddenly attacked and miserably plundered Cambay. In the mountains also, between Amadanar and the town of Trape [Traj], there lives a certain Rahja, who can put seventeen thousand horse and foot into the field. His followers are called Colles or Quillees,[32] and live in solitary places, which render them immune from attack on

---

31 Bahadur, son of Muzaffar Shah III, the last king of Gujarat. In 1606 he, "proclaiming liberty and laws of good fellowship," sacked and held Cambay for fourteen days (William Finch, 1608-12, in Kerr's *Voyages*, Vol VIII, p 275, 302) Hawkins (1608-13) speaks of him as "one of the three arch-enemies which with all his (Jahangir's) forces cannot be called in" (E T, 100). Bahadur died in 1615

32 The Kolis were a predatory tribe spreading mainly over the country between Cambay and Ahmedabad, and the well-wooded nature of the country afforded them the desired shelter. During the Mughal period they were great disturbers of the peace in Western India, and the rough-and-ready way of controlling them may be gathered from the two following quotations from two different types of writers Nizam-ud-din, in his *Tabakat-i-Akbari* (E.D., V 447), writes: "I attacked and laid waste nearly 50 villages of the Kolis and Grassias, and I built forts in seven different places to keep them in check . . . Having put Chait Rawat to death, I removed Karmi Koli, Krishna Koli and Lakha Rajput who were the principal Grassias of these parts and left

the part of the Mogol Empire. Further to the east lives another Rahja who can gather ten thousand cavalry. He dwells in an impregnable fortress situated on a deserted plain, and though he is a vassal of Gydney Caun,[33] frequently refuses to pay him tribute.

In the district around Amadabat indigo is produced, though of a quality far inferior to that of Biana. The people call it Cickel [32a] The town and district are ruled by a governor, a judge called the Cahi [Kazi] and a Cutwall [Kotwal].

Not far from this town begin the mountains of Maroa (Mewar) which cover an immense space, extending for 150 cos along the road which leads to Agra, and for about 200 along that to Ougen. For the most part these mountains are quite impassable. On their top stands an impregnable fortress called Gur-Chitto [Garh-Chitore], the stronghold of a powerful Rana or Rahja, whom neither the old kings of Potan nor up to the present the Mogols have been able to subdue. The Indians, who were formerly all heathens, have from ancient times venerated this Rana in a similar manner to that in which Roman Catholics venerate the Pope of Rome. His dominions are everywhere protected by trackless mountains, and wherever an entrance might be forced exceedingly strong fortifications have been erected. This

garrisons in their places" Nicholas Withington writes "And the 19th day we came to Bollodo, a fort kept by Newlooke Abram (a brave soldier) for the Mogull, whoe was that day retorned from battle, bringing home with him 169 heads of the coolies, a thievish caste of montteners (mountaineers) that live by robbing and spoyling poor passengers on the heigh waye" (E T., p. 209). Probably these heads were utilized in erecting *Chor minars!*

[32a] Prof. J. N Sarkar points out that the name is derived from Chikli, a well-known place near Surat. I think the name is some sort of corruption from Sarkhej.

[33] Ghaznin or Ghazin Khan of Jalor (*Ain.* I. 493; E D., V. 440, T. J. 353). Elsewhere De Laet says that his forefathers were heathens (Hindus). At least his father bore a Muhammadan name, Malik Khanji Afghan

ruler had in a very brief time gathered twelve thousand horsemen. He is lord of many large and beautiful cities. At the distance of one leuca from the city of Amadabat may be seen a fine tomb. It is that of a certain Cahi, the tutor of a king of Guzuratte, who superintended the building of the whole tomb, and is himself (together with three others) buried in another shrine near by. The tomb [34] is entirely built of beautifully polished marble, the surrounding platform being also of marble. It contains three halls, in one of which are 440 marble columns, 30 palms high, with epistyles and bases in the Corinthian style, truly a royal piece of work, and one well worth seeing. On one side is a tomb constructed with marvellous skill, over which very fine view may be obtained from a number of elegant windows

Sarques or Sirhesa[35] is a large village three cos (*i.e.*, 1½ Dutch miles) distant from Amadabat Here the tombs of the old kings of Guzuratte may be seen in a very beautiful temple, to visit which numerous Indians come from all directions. About a cos distant from this place is a magnificent palace with a lovely garden around it, constructed

[34] The reference here is probably to the group of buildings "sacred to the memory of Shah Alam, the son of Kutb-ul-Alam of Batva, who, till his death in 1475, as the guide of Sultan Mahmud Begara's youth and afterwards as one of the most revered of Musulman religious teachers, held a high place in Ahmedabad" (B G., Vol IV, on Ahmedabad, p 286) From the description of the buildings it appears that the reference cannot be to the Mosque of Miya Khan Chishti, whose family claimed the office of the city judge or Kazi (Cahi)

[35] Sarkhej is about 5 miles from Ahmedabad. It contains the tombs of Mahmud Begara (1459-1511) and his son Muzaffar II (1511-25) and Rajbai, Muzaffar's queen Sarkhej was one of Mahmud Begara's favourite resorts The Sarkhej buildings are almost purely Hindu in style, with only the faintest Musalman feeling. The place was famous for its indigo, the Dutch established a factory there in 1620 (B G, Vol IV, II, p 291-292)

by a leading Mogol chieftain, Chou-Chin-Nauw[36] who defeated the last king of Guzuratte at this place in a fierce battle, and brought his kingdom under the control of the great Mogol Much indigo is produced at this village of Sarques, and is called after the name[37] of the place. It is inferior only to that of Biana, and great mountains of it are exported to Europe. Before we leave this capital of Amadabat it will be worth while to add the following details, which I have obtained from Dutch sources. The city is the headquarters of 35 large rural areas, which contain 2,995 villages The revenue from these villages is brought together first to the rural headquarters, and is thence sent to Amadabat The total annual revenue comes to more than 6 millions of gold pieces In the year 1626 the governor of Amadabat was Chan-Syan [Khan Jahan Lodhi], the most powerful of all the vassals of the Mogols. Together with his sons, of whom he had a large number, he was in charge of a contingent of 15,000 horse (although under ordinary circumstances he does not provide for more than 5,000 or 6,000), and he used this circumstance as a means of misappropriating for his own purpose this vast revenue The public funds are chiefly collected from the agriculturalists, for there are no duties on goods carried into or out of the city

---

36 Mirza Abdur Rahim, Khan Khanan, defeated Muzaffar III, king of Gujarat, in January 1584 at Sarkhej and converted the battlefield into a garden, called Fateh Bagh (the garden of victory), for long one of the chief sights of Ahmedabad As viceroy (1583-1590) Khan Khanan laboured for the prosperity of Ahmedabad and Sarkhej (B G, Vol IV, on Ahmedabad, p 252)

37 Finch calls it Cickell, known to European merchants as "Flat" because the product was prepared in the form of cakes; whereas that from Biana was known as 'round' because it was rolled up in balls Between 1620-30 the price of 'round' fluctuated between 5*s* and 6*s* and that of 'flat' was 4*s*. per lb in the London market.

[*Broach*].—The place second in importance to the capital is Baroche or Brochia, which is 21° 55′ north of the equator, and lies 23 cos or 12 Dutch miles north of Suratte, and 15 Dutch miles east of Cambay. It is situated on the bank of a most beautiful river, which comes down from afar in the mountains and enters the sea six (or according to others eight) Dutch miles below the city. About four miles below the town, near to the village of Hansot, which lies on the south bank, the river divides into two branches, which surround an island in some places half a leuca broad and in others only a quarter. This island is cut up by various water-courses The river finally flows into the sea by two mouths whose outer margins are two and a half miles apart. The city of Baroche is built on a lofty hill, and is surrounded by a wall. Hence it is a very strong place both by nature and by art. At the foot of the hill is situated a suburb almost as large as the city itself, inhabited by artisans and sailors. The annual revenue obtained from this place is 200,000 mamudei (each of which is equal to ten Dutch stuferi). The land around the city is extremely fertile and bear abundantly every kind of crop. Three other cities were formerly under Baroche as revenue-headquarters, but now have their own governors. These are Medapore (70 miles inland), Brodera [Baroda] three days' journey distant, and Jounbansser [Jambuser] 8 miles away. The road from Suratte to Brochia passes through the villages of Periaw [Variao] and Cosumbay [Kosamba]. Four miles from Brochia is a place where magnificent gems are dug from the ground, called Achates [Agates]. The neighbouring district is pleasant and populous. It abounds in palm-trees of the forest variety, from which (as also from another tree, called the Tarru) the people obtain a certain liquor which they call Tarrien [*Tari*, toddy] and Suren [*Sura*, liquor]. In a certain town between Brochia and Amadavat is buried a Mussalman saint, named Polle Nedonii.[38] To visit his tomb pilgrims gather from all the provinces of India, in desire for wealth, children, or other benefits. One may see these pilgrims on their way, some of them laden with ponderous chains, others wearing a muzzle on their faces, which is only removed for the purposes of taking food, others burdened in other ways; but they falsely declare, and superstitiously believe, that as soon as they have devoutly offered their adoration to the saint, their chains burst asunder, and the muzzles break open, of their own accord.

Janbayssar, or Jounbasser, or Gianniser [Jambusar] is a large village, nine or ten Dutch miles distant from Brochia, on the road which leads thence to Cambay. Here also indigo is produced, but of inferior quality.

[*Baroda*].—Radiapore [Rajapur ?] or rather Brodera (this is the common form of the name, the city being situated only about a mile and a half from an older place named Brodera, and having gradually attracted the inhabitants of the latter to itself) is 42 cos distant from Amadavat, and 30 (*i e*, 15 Dutch miles) south of Brochia: it is the same distance east of Cambay, and 14 Dutch miles from Jaunbausar. It is a very beautiful inland town, situated on a sandy plain, near the bank of a small river called the Wassah.[39] It is surrounded on all sides by a wall with

38 Pir Ali Medinai (?) Sir Roper Lethbridge thus writes: "A pious Mahomedan will immediately recognise in this name a corruption of Boulee Mudum, the name of one of the most celebrated saints of Islam He is elsewhere called Pir Muhiudi He came from Medina (hence the name) at an early period and settled near Ahmedabad" (C R., 1870, Vol LI, p. 353 *n*) It is no wild conjecture to suggest that the reference might be to the Pirana monastery of Giramtha, some 9 miles south of Ahmedabad The founder was Imamshah who was supposed to have miraculous powers (B G., Vol IV, 287-90).

39 The Mahi. Nicholas Withington in his Travel calls it Wasseth which is a corruption of Vāsad, the place where the high road crossed the river (E.T., 205).

many towers. The inhabitants are for the most part Baneanes. There are 210 villages in the surrounding district, none of which is more than 20 or 25 Dutch miles from the city. Much the most important of these is Lindikera, which lies 16 cos east of Brodera, at this place a great quantity of lac is collected every year, being brought from the mountains which stand 15 or 16 cos from the village.

Niriaud is a large town 14 cos distant from Brodera, and 10 from Amadavat here also a large amount of indigo is collected Gandeve (this is perhaps the same place as the Gandoree briefly mentioned above) lies nine Dutch miles distant from Suratte, to the south it is three miles from the sea, and is on the bank of a small river. it is a small town, or rather, a large village, whose inhabitants are mostly weavers In the same province is also situated the fortress of Jeloure [Jalor] This is built on the top of a mountain, which is ascended by a broad road three cos in length, paved with stone at the end of the first cos is a gate, which is guarded by soldiers above this the road is fenced on each side by a wall as far as the end of the second cos, where there is a double gateway the fortress itself has three gates, of which the first is protected by sheets of iron, and the third by sharp iron spikes · within the gates, on the right hand side, is a most beautiful mosque, and on the left the governor's palace, which is built on the extreme top of the mountain. In the same place may be seen a Pagoda built by the forefathers of Gydne-Caun [Ghaznin Khan] who were heathens, though he himself embraced Mahumetism and usurped the throne of his elder brother from whom he seized this fortress and handed it over to the great Mogol. About half a cos within the fort is a square tank hewn out of the rock, this tank is said to be 50 cubits deep: its water is exceedingly clear and good. A little further on is a plain shaded by very beautiful trees: and on the top of a pyramidical hill is the tomb of king

Hassuard[40], who was respected in these parts during his lifetime for his warlike courage and after his death for his supposed saintliness The circumference of this fortress is about eight cos. It is reckoned to stand on the boundary of the kingdom of Guzuratte.

[*Diu*] —On the coast of this kingdom, or rather on a projecting portion of the peninsula which looks towards the south, is situated the town of Diu, where the Portuguese have a port Texeira states that the name of this town is pronounced Dive both by Indians and by others (the latter part of the name being slurred over) This word signifies in the common speech an island (thus Ange-dive means 'Five islands,' Nale-dive 'Four island' or as the Portuguese pronounce it 'Maldiva,' and so on).

The town is called 'the island' *par excellence*, or (for the sake of differentiating it from others) Dive-Now-Laka,* *i e*, 'the island of nine millions' (thus I translate the word Cuentos which the Portuguese use in their reckonings). For the people narrate that once long ago the daughter of the ruler of this island asked her father for a gift, whereupon he granted her the revenue for one day, which came to nine Lekas of the coins of that kingdom The Portuguese first built the fort in the year 1535 A D, with the permission of Badurius[41] who was then the governor of Cambay. Afterwards they acquired possession also of the old town, which they still hold together with the fort A little to

---

40 Prof Hodivala points out that it is a corruption of Husain Khangsawar, a soldier and a saint who lies buried at Taragarh in Ajmer. Finch from whom De Laet copied, confounded Ajmer with Jalor (*See Akbar Nama* III 305, Badāoni II 143)

* Not infrequently has De Laet confounded lakh with million.

41 Sultan Bahadur Shah (1526-36), king of Gujarat, concluded on Oct 5th, 1535, a treaty with the Portuguese governor, Nuno da Cunha, granting the site for a fortress at Diu "The King of Portugal was to have no claim to any of the customs and receipts; but the curious and noteworthy clause of the peace is that in which both agree to prevent religious proselytizing." (Whiteway, pp 224-42. Bahadur's relations with the Portuguese will be found in the pages following)

the north of east from Diu lies Madafeldabar, [Muzaffarabad, now called Ja'afarabad] by the side of a sandbar-encumbered inlet of the sea. About ten miles to the north of that place is Mohar, [Mahuva], where may be seen the ruins of a large town, though now there are very few inhabitants.

THE PROVINCE OF KHANDESH.

[*Khandesh*].—The next province to the east of the province of Guzuratte or Cambay is that of Chandies, which the Portuguese also call Sanda. The route from Guzratte is as follows.—from Suratte to the village of Combariauw [Kumbharia] three cos: thence to the large village of Mutta [Mota] seven cos: thence to the town of Caroden [Karod], which lies on the south bank of the river on which Surate stands, eight cos. This town has a fort with a garrison of 200 Pathan cavalry. Thence to the large village of Curca which lies to the north of the river, twelve cos. On the way lies Beca [Viara], a fort with a tank and grove of trees From Curca to Nacanpore [Narainpur] is ten cos: this is a large town, whose ruler is named Pectosphavus [Pratap Sah]. To the right of the town appear unbroken mountain ranges, the same which I have mentioned as beginning near Amadabat and containing the numerous strongholds of Badur [Bahadur], who is strong enough to defy all the forces of the king of the Mogols. These mountains, whose general direction is towards Barampore, contain large numbers of wild elephants. It is eight cos from Nacanpore to Dayta (Dhaita). On the way is a river full of rocks and rather hard to cross. Dayta is a very large city, with a citadel almost surrounded by the river. The neighbouring country is very fertile. Dutch writers state that Dayta is 120 cos east of Brodera. From Dayta to Badur [Bhadwar] is ten cos. Badur is a filthy place, and a nest of robbers. Here a kind of wine is manufactured from the fruit of the Meva [Mahua]. It is unwholesome unless boiled. This is the last town owing allegiance to Pectospavus [Pratap Sah], a small Hindu Raja or chieftain who dwells amongst the trackless mountains which occupy a great stretch of country east of Curca. This chieftain holds two fine towns, Salere and Mulere,[42] where the coins called Mamudies are minted. Each of these towns has a strong citadel approached by a very narrow pathway, on each side of which 80 small forts have been conetructed to defend the way. Amongst the mountains are fertile fields and pastures. Achabar, the king of the Indians, spent seven whole years in besieging these strongholds, and eventually made a treaty with the Rahja by which he was permitted to retain Nacampore, Dayta and Badur on condition that he abstained from molesting travellers on the plains. As a result the Rahja is nowadays on friendly terms with the Great Mogol and sends him gifts every year: one of his sons is held as a hostage at Barampore The Rahja is said to possess 4,000 magnificent horses and 100 elephants

From Badur to the city of Nonderbar [Nondurbar] is eight cos Near the latter place many ancient monuments may be seen It possesses a fort and a very fine tank. From Nonderbat to Lingul [Nimgul] is ten cos: the road is very muddy. Lingul has a small fort. the inhabitants have a bad name for brigandage. From Lingul to Sindkerry is ten cos This is a large but unpleasant place. Moreover it stands on the bank of a river whose water is salty and unwholesome From Sindkerry to Taulnere

42 Both Salher and Mulher are in the Nausari district The latter fort contained a mint where the coins of Pratap Sah were struck The *mahmudis* were the coins of the independent Muslim kings of Gujarat After its conquest by Akbar, the coinage of rupaiyas was introduced at the royal mints of Ahmedabad and sometime after of Surat The coining of Mahmudis was continued by Pratap Sah at the fort of Mulher till 1637; his Mahmudis were struck in Akbar's name. Five mahmudis made two rupees. See Note on Chapter VI.

[Thalner] is ten cos: the road is infested with robbers. Taulnere is a fine city with a fort and a river which cannot be forded in the rainy season. From Taulnere to Chupra, another large town, is 15 cos · thence to the village of Rawd [Aravad] six cos thence to Beawle [Byaval], a large city with a fort, ten thence to Ravere, a large town, 17: thence to Barampore 10. from Barampore to the lovely city of Badurpore [Bahadurpur], 2 cos

[*Burhanpur*] —Barampore or Bramport, which (as mentioned above) is the capital of this province, is a very large city, but is an ill-built place and, on account of its low lying position and intemperate climate, is notoriously unhealthy On the north it has a large and well-fortified citadel situated on the bank of the river which flows down to Surate In the river stands a rock bearing the figure of an elephant,[43] so well executed that it frequently deceives elephants which come down to drink the water of the river. The common people worship this figure, as they do other remarkable works of nature Two leucae from the city lies the park [Lal Bagh] of the great noble Chan Channae [Khan i-Khanan]; the road thither is shaded by trees on either side, in the park are most beautiful promenades and a square tank surrounded by a wall and shaded by trees English writers state that the city is 28° north of the equator; some of them say that Brampore lies 233 miles due east of Suratte and that the whole of the intervening region is barren Dutch writers say that the distance is 80 Dutch miles.

[*Asirgarh*] —The road from Brampore to Agra, the present capital of the Great Mogol, is at first steep and

---

43 Thevenot throws more light on the matter. "The elephant (which that statue represents) died in that place before Cha Gehan . . . who would needs erect a monument to the beast because he loved it, and the Gentiles besmear it with colours as they do their Pagods." (Part III, p. 72)

rough, leading through lofty mountain ranges, the same which start near Amadabat. Not far from the road stands a very strong fort, called Hassere.[44] It is situated on the top of a lofty mountain, and is of great size, for it is said to be able to accommodate 40,000 or 50,000 horsemen. Inside there are large tanks and pastures Under the last king of Gujaratte it is said to have been equipped with 600 warlike engines Achabar, the Emperor of the Mogols, compelled it to surrender after a long siege. They say that innumerable worms live in the water of the tanks, so that those who drink the water swell up and burst asunder. This it was that brought about the surrender of the fort to Achabar The English say that the fort lies 16 cos from Brampore, but the Dutch say 15 only.

From Brampore to the large village of Barre [Borgaon] is 12 cos, the road (as has been mentioned) being difficult: to the small village of Camla, 11 cos to Magergom [Mogargaon], a large village, 4 to Kergom (Khirgaon a big town), 10. All this way the road is difficult, steep and full of obstacles To the small village of Berkul [Balkhar] is 13 cos: thence to the town of Taxapore [Tarapur] 8. On the way the river Narvor [Narbada] is crossed. This is believed to flow down to Biochia.

[*Mandu*].—Taxapore is a moderate sized town, with a beautiful citadel. It stands on the bank of the river; when this is crossed with camels one must keep a little to the left, where there are rapids. The bed of the river is about an English mile in width. From Taxapore to Mandoa the distance is 3 cos, the pathway is narrow and ascends a steep

[44] Asirgarh was one of the strongest forts in India in the sixteenth century. It commanded the route from Hindustan to the Deccan It capitulated to Akbar in the beginning of 1601. Vincent Smith ascribes the surrender to treachery (*Akbar the Great Mogul*, pp. 272-300). [I.A., 1918, pp. 180-83, *Fragment*. Sect. XIX.]

and rocky mountain (the mountains here widen out between north and south). At the steepest pitch of the mountain is the gateway of the ancient city of Mandoa [45] above which stands a citadel containing a palace. The walls of the city surround the whole mountain and are many miles in circumference. On the left of the entrance, perched on a pyramidical mountain, stands a very strong fort, and in other situations there are 10 or 12 more such forts. Some two cos within the gateway just mentioned are to be seen the remains of the old city, which, with the exception of a few tombs and temples, is entirely in ruins. The old city was 4 cos broad from north to south, and 10 or 12 from east to west Scattered about the city are 16 tanks. The present city of Mandoa is very beautiful, but is far smaller than the old city. It has many fine buildings cut out of the living rock, and lofty gateways of a

[45] Nearly all European travellers have been struck by the architectural relics of Mandu and have given a glowing description of them Mandu or Mandapadurga was one of the last strongholds of the Paramar dynasty of Malwa

From 1405 to 1526 A D , two provincial independent dynasties, the Ghoris and the Khaljis, ruled over Malwa, with their capital at Mandu, then known as Shadiabad The mosque referred to in the text is the Jami Masjid commenced by Sultan Hushang (1406-34) and completed by Mahmud Khalji (*c.* 1440 A D). Ferishta relates that after his return to Mandu from a victorious campaign against the Rana of Chitor, Sultan Mahmud Khalji, in 1443 A D , built a school and a tower seven storeys high, opposite the mosque of Sultan Hushang At a later date in the absence of a suitable central site, the College building and the Tower were utilized as a splendid frame, existing ready to hand, in which to set the mausoleum containing the tombs of the four kings mentioned by De Laet The four kings are Sultan Mahmud himself (1435-75), his father Malik Mughis and his successors, Ghiyasuddin (1475-1500) and Nasiruddin (1500-1510)". The mausoleum of the Khaljis is mentioned by Abul Fazl as one of the sights of Mandu. It is a mass of ruins now (A.R., 1903-4, pp. 30-45).

type which I have never seen elsewhere. As one enters from the south, one sees on the left a fine mosque, and near to it a magnificent palace where are the splendid tombs of four kings. Beside this palace rises a tower 170 steps high, with balconies, windows, fine columns and arches. On the northern side of the city there is a strong gateway at the top of a steep descent, and beyond this are six more gateways, all well defended and with strong flanking-walls. To the right and left, though the mountain is hard to ascend and seems sufficiently defended by nature, the wall is continued with strong bastions, so that the place is quite impregnable. They say that Hamawne [Humayun], the Mogol emperor, captured this place from Shec Sha-Selim [46] (whose forefathers 400 years before had captured it from the Indians) partly by force and partly by guile. This Sha-Selim was a very powerful king of Delhi, and had inflicted upon Hamawne so heavy a defeat that he was compelled to fly into Persia, whence he returned with Persia reinforcements and in his turn defeated Selym, who however took refuge in the mountains and hiding now here, now there, avoided conquest during the whole reign of Hamawne and a good part of that of Achabar. Outside the walls of the city on this side there used to be large suburbs of which now only the ruins are to be seen. Dutch writers declare that Mandoa lies 50 Dutch miles east of Brochia.

THE PROVINCE OF MALWA.

To the north of Chandis is the province of Malwa, whose soil is very fertile and produces a great quantity of opium. The road to Agra, which so far we have been following, proceeds as follows:—From Mendoa to Lunehaira.

---

[46] The account given here of Humayun's reconquest of his Indian possessions is confused and wrong. The facts are too well known to need repetition.

(Lunera), a small saray or public inn, is 4 cos along a very rough road: to Dupalpore, a small town, 4 cos, the road being more smooth: to Oughi [Ujjain], a beautiful city, 12: to the village of Conoseia, 11 · to Sunnenarry [Sunera], a small town, 8. the road is difficult and infested by brigands, for the mountains which lie to the left hand are the home of savages who are constantly attacking travellers · they are said to be called Graciae [47] To the village of Pimpelgom [Pipliagaon] is 10 cos on the way a little aside from the royal highway lies the great town of Sarangpore with a fortified citadel to the south of it To the village of Cukra [Kakarwar], which produces great quantities of every kind of corn and of the wine made from the Meira [Mahua], is 7 cos · to the large village of Delout 12 about half of this stage is difficult owing to mountains and crags, and is beset by robbers, the rest is easy. To the small village of Burrouw [Barrai] 7 cos here there is plenty of corn but little meat to be had, meat is indeed hard to obtain on all this route To the small town of Suchesera 7 cos; to Syrange [Sironj], one of the chief cities of this province, 9: this is a large town surrounded by pleasant gardens, in which a great quantity of Betle [Pan] is grown. From Syrange to Cuchenary [Kachner], a Saray, 8 cos. to Sadura [Shahdaura] 5. to Collebag [Kalabagh] 7 to Qualere [Kulharas] 12 · this is a pleasant town surrounded by tamarind and mango trees thence to Cypry [Sipri] 7 this stage is difficult and notorious for robbers Cypry is a walled city, its houses are fine, and are roofed with hewn stone. To Norwar 12 cos this stage is lonely and infested with brig-

[47] Grassias The word *gras* (meaning mouthful in Sanskrit) was applied to land given for subsistence to cadets of chieftain's families Afterwards in practice the term came to signify the blackmail paid by a village to purchase the forbearance and protection of a neighbouring brigand Thence the word *grassia* came to mean a professional robber. It was a generic term which included the species Koli (*q v.*)

ands : Norwar is situated at the foot of some mountains, at the top of these is a fort, up to which one may ascend by means of a narrow pathway paved with stone: the ascent is difficult and is defended by three gates with an appropriate guard. No stranger may enter the fort without a permit from the king. The town of Norwar is large and spacious The whole hill is said to have once been surrounded by a wall with bastions and many engines of war: for it was the boundary of the kingdom of Mandoa ; but now the walls are ruinous

The Province of Gwalior.

To the east of Malva is the province of Gualiar. The following is the account of the route through it:—From Narwar to Palachau [Paraich] 7 cos. to Antri, a large town, 12 to Gualere, 6 This city, which is capital of the province and gives it its name, is very beautiful and is defended by a fortress On the eastern side of the city at the top of a steep and precipitous mountain lie the ruins of a building in which many great men are said to have been buried. To the west of the city is a rocky hill which is everywhere precipitous and is girt by a strong wall whose circumference is some 6 cos or more. At the entrance to the pathway which leads up from the city to this fortress is a guard-house, defended by very lofty walls, where members of the garrison keep watch: above this the ascent is made by a narrow pathway, paved with stone and protected by a wall to right and left. the way is barred by three gateways one above the other, each of which is strongly guarded in front of the fourth and last gateway stands the figure of an elephant skilfully carved in stone: this gateway is magnificently built of green and blue marble, at its top are several tall turrets, which are gilded. Here dwells the governor of the place, and in the same spot noble captives are imprisoned. The king is said to have three prisons of this kind: one here; a second at Rantipore [Rantambhor], 40 cos from Gualere, whither are sent nobles who have been condemned to death; these are generally imprisoned there for two months, after which the governor of the fortress brings them forth, makes them stand on the top of the wall, gives them a drink of milk [48], and then flings them down on to the rocks below. The third prison is in the fortress of Rotas, in the province of Bengal, whither are sent those condemned to life-long incarceration: it is very rarely that they escape thence. The range of mountains, near to which Gualere stands, has a very fertile soil, on it are situated three or four tanks and many fine buildings. To the north-west of the city is an enormous field, enclosed on all sides by a wall, in which are most beautiful gardens and pleasure grounds. This fortified city was once the frontier post between the kingdom of Delhy and that of Mandoa From Gualere to Mendaker [Mundiakhera] is nine cos, and thence to Doulpore [Dholpur] ten.

THE PROVINCE OF AGRA.

One passes from the province of Gualere (or Gualiar) into that of Agra across the river Cambere [Chambal] which I believe to form the boundary between the two provinces. According to the English this river is as large as the Thames. Beyond the river the road is narrow and difficult, passing between mountains for two cos, as far as Doulpore, a Hindu town, near to which is a very strong and spacious fort, everywhere surrounded by a deep ditch, within which is a four-fold wall. This fort, access to which is very difficult, is about three-fourths of a mile in

48 This portion is taken from Finch who has it thus: "giving them a dishe of milke, which having drunke, he is cast down thence on the rockes." It was a decoction of the milky juice of the poppy (E.T., 145).

diameter. Hence to Jaju is nine cos, and it is as many more to Agra.

Agra is 28° 30′ (or as some say 45′) north of the equator. It is said to have been a mere village before the times of King Achabar, but is now a spacious and very populous city, whose streets (most of which are narrow, except that in which the market is held) are always crowded with people. It lies in a semicircular position on the bank of the river Jemini or Semaena Many beautiful palaces of nobles overlook this stream, and the view of the riverside which is six or more cos in length is very beautiful indeed. Near the river also is the royal citadel, which is the greatest and most magnificent in the whole East, for it is almost four English miles in circumference, and is everywhere surrounded by a wall built of squared stone. Within this wall is a double rampart of earth, and within this are the palace of the king and the audience chamber, with other buildings of incredible magnificence. The city itself has neither wall nor earthen rampart, but only a deep ditch The suburbs are very extensive. King Achabar is said to have made this city his capital first in 1566 and to have constructed several gateways [49] for its defence and adornment, which are named Madhar Derwasa, Tziartzou Derwasa, Nim Derwasa, Pouto Derwasa, and Noery Derwasa. The city is much longer than it is broad; for all the inhabitants have desired to be near the river, and hence have built their houses along its banks. The following is the list of the palaces of the nobles,[50] begin-

[49] All about Agra given here is taken from Pelsaert. Mr. Moreland (*Jahangir's India*, p 1) ascertains that four of these five names survive in modern street nomenclature The fifth is Pouto, which is probably Puttu The gateways then were Madari, Chabarsu, Nim, Puttu and Nuri

[50] Most of the nobles herein mentioned can be identified. Some of them were dead at the time when De Laet wrote. The list is taken from Pelsaert (*Jahangir's India*, p. 2). Bador Chan

ning from the north :—First that of Bador Khan who was once governor of Hasseic: next that of Rodzia Bofios, father of Ray Rottongh, who used to be governor of Barampore and was in charge of 5,000 cavalry : then that of Ebrahim Chan, leader of 3,000 cavalry then that of Rostam Kandahary, leader of 5,000 · then that of Radja Kissendas, leader of 3,000 . then that of Ethegat Chan, younger brother of Assof Khan, leader of 5,000 · then that of Chazady Chanoms, sister of the king and formerly wife of Madoftar Khan then that of Goulziar Begem, mother of the king . then that of Codha Momet Thahar, leader of 2,000: then that of Codha Benziu, leader of 1,000: then that of Ozier Chan, leader of 5,000 then that of Tzoach-Poeraz (a large building in which live the concubines of the late king Achabar) then that of Ethebar Chan the eunuch who, when he lived, was governor of Agra · then that of Bager Chan, leader of 3,000 then that of Mirza Abouzayth, leader of 1,500 . then that of Assof Chan, leader of 8,000 (by far the most magnificent of all these palaces) : then that of Ethamaedoulet, leader of 5,000 then that of Prince Sultan Khrom who during the lifetime of his father was

---

was Miran Bahadur Shah, once ruler of Khandesh (Hassere is Asirgarh) Radzia Bofios is Raja Bhoj, father of Rao Rattan of Bundi who defended Burhanpur against the rebellious prince Shah Jahan in the nineteenth year of Jahangir's reign Raja Bhoj served under Man Singh against the Afghans of Orissa and under Abul Fazl in the Deccan He incurred the displeasure of Jahangir by refusing to marry his grand-daughter to the Emperor and committed suicide in 1607 He was a Chauhan (*Ain*. I 458 , C.R , LII, 1871, p 68 *n*) Ibrahim Khan was one of the brothers of Nur Jahan (H J , 105-6, 190, 376-9) Mirza Rustam of Kandahar (grandson of Shah Ismail of Persia) was commander-in-chief, in Jahangir's reign, of the Kandahar expedition. Raja Kishen Das (Tunwar) was accountant of the stables under Akbar and Jahangir Itiqad Khan was another brother of Nur Jahan (H.J., 190, 326, 352) Shazadi Khanam was a daughter of Akbar, born in Nov. 1569 of a concubine. She was the wife of Muzaffar

leader of 20,000: then that of Chan Sian, leader of 5,000: then that of Codha Abdulhassan, leader of 5,000: then that of Rochia Sultan Begem, unmarried sister of the king: then comes the royal fortress, whose walls are 25 cubits high and are made of red stone.

[*Agra Fort*]—The fortress, which stands on rising ground, is a wonderful place, and is most beautiful to look at from all view points, especially from the river bank; for on that side are galleries with golden windows, from

---

Husain Mirza Goulzier Begem is either Gulzar or Gul-izar Begam. Nowhere else is the personal name of Jahangir's mother recorded, her official title was Maryam-uz-Zamani There was one Gulizar (Kamran's daughter) whose niece was married to Jahangir Codha Mamet Thahar is probably Khwaja Mahmud Tahir Khwaja Bansi was steward of Prince Khurram Wazier Khan Hakim Alimuddin of Chiniot (Punjab) was made commander of 5,000 on Shah Jahan's accession, and died in the fourteenth year of his reign, as Subadar of Agra Prof J N Sarkar points out that Tzoach-Poeraz is Sohagpura (see his *Mughal Administration* Second Ed P 194, No 59) Itibar Khan was governor of Agra (H J, 361) Bakir Khan Najm-i-Sani, a grandee of Jahangir's and Shah Jahan's court, was married to Khadija Begam, daughter of Nur Jahan's sister, and died in the tenth year of Shah Jahan's reign as governor of Allahabad (C R, LII, p 69 *n*) Mirza Abu Sayid, grandson of Itimad-ud-dowlah, died in the beginning of Aurangzeb's reign Asaf Khan was elder brother of Nur Jahàn. His name was Abul Hasan, he received the title of Asaf Khan in 1614, and was father of the celebrated Taj Mahal (Arjumand Banu Begam). A man of very high abilities, he played a very important role in subsequent history, especially in the complicated party strife leading ultimately to the accession of his son-in-law Shah Jahan (H.J, 189-90) Ghias Beg, Itimad-ud-dowlah, was father of Nur Jahan and of the three brothers mentioned above, died in 1621-22 His mausoleum on the left bank of the river is well known (H J, 132, 142, 325) Sultan Chrom is Sultan Khurram or Shah Jahan The last three names are those of Khan Jahan Lodi (H. J, p 265 *ff*). Khwaja Abul Hasan (frequent references to him will be found in the *Fragment*) and Ruqayya Sultan Begam. I do not find anywhere that Jahangir had a sister named Ruqayya Sultan. One of that name was Hindal's daughter and Akbar's wife.

which the king is wont to look on at elephant fights. Behind these galleries lies the audience chamber, which is called the Gussai-can.[51] This is a magnificent building, square in shape, and constructed of alabaster covered with gold plates. Beneath are situated the women's apartments (called the Mahal) belonging to Nourzian Begem, the favourite wife of the last emperor Ziangier [Jahangir]. The rest of the fort is occupied by various buildings, the most important of which are women's apartments, such as that of Mariam Makany, [52] the wife of Achabar and mother of Ziangier: there are also the three palaces in which the king's concubines are accommodated, of which one is called Lethevar (*i.e.*, Sunday), the second Mongel (*i.e.*, Tuesday), and the third Zenisser (*i.e.*, Saturday): for on these days the king is wont to visit the said palaces. There is also a fifth palace for women, in which live foreign concubines of the king. This is called the Bengaly Mahal. On leaving the fort one comes to the greater market, where horses, camels, oxen and every kind of merchandise are sold. Further on are the palaces[53] of Mirza Abdulla, the son of Khan Azem, leader of 3,000 horse: of Aga Nours,

---

51 Ghusl-Khana, *i.e.*, a bath-room. The name however was applied to the semi-private apartment in a Mughal palace. Manucci says: "it is a privileged and ordered place" (Vol. II, p. 463). Ordinarily only the principal officers were summoned there. The name originated in the practice of Sher Shah who, while drying his long locks of hair after a bath, called his ministers there to discuss State affairs. *Vide* p. 94.

52 It should be Mariam-uz-Zamani. Marium Makani was Akbar's mother. Pelsaert commits the same error.

53 Mirza Abdullah and Mirza Khurram were the sons of Mirza Aziz Kokah (Khan Azam). So Mirza Khrom of De Laet was not the son of Khan Alam. Abdullah received the title of Sarfaraz Khan under Jahangir (*Ain*. I. 328, 492). Khurram was the governor of Junagarh under Akbar, received the title of Kamil Khan under Jahangir and accompanied Shah Jahan to the Deccan. Pelsaert says that Aga Nur was the provost of Jahangir's army.

leader of 3,000: of Zehenna Khan, leader of 2,000: of Mirza Khrom, son of Khan Alems, leader of 2,000: of Mahabot Khan, leader of 8,000 · of Khan Alem, leader of 5,000: of Rodja Bartzing, leader of 3,000 · of Radja Mantzing, leader of 2,000

[*Sikandra*].—On the opposite bank of the river lies the finely built city of Secundra which is inhabited mainly by Baneanes. Hither are brought all kinds of merchandise from Purob, Bengala, Purbet and Bouten [54]; these pay dues to the queen before they are taken across the river. This city also is almost 2 cos in length, and contains some magnificent palaces, such as that of Sultan Perwesi [Prince Parvez] There are also lovely pleasure-grounds, chief amongst which is that of Etham Doulat, the recently deceased father of Assof Khan and of Queen Nourzian, in whose memory a most magnificent tomb is being built at a cost [55] estimated at more than 10 million rupees.

[*Fatehpur*]—In the same province is situated Fettipore, [56] 12 cos from Agra It was once a splendid city which Achbar surrounded with, a wall, and where he had

---

Zehenna Khan may be Zain Khan Kokah Radja Bartzing is Raja Bir Singh who rose to be commander of 4,000 personel and 2,200 horse Radja Mantzing is Raja Madho Singh.

54 Bhutan is meant The text refers to goods brought from the countries in the East—Allahabad, Behar, Bengal and Bhutan. Purbet may be connected with Bouten to mean the mountainous country of Bhutan

55 Pelsaert says that 'the tomb has already cost 3,50,000 rupees and will cost 10,00,000 more' Pelsaert is more reliable.

56 The original name of the village was Sikri. It came to have the joint name of Fatehpur-Sikri after Akbar's successful Gujarat campaign De Laet's explanation that it was named Fatehpur after the birth of Salim is wrong (Monserrate, p. 30, n. 64). Equally wrong is the meaning given to the word Sikri (Sykary). Finch has confused it with the word *Shikar* (hunting). European

his capital before removing it to Agra. The ramparts are still left, but the city is almost deserted. Its houses have collapsed, and the ground has been utilised for fields and gardens, so that when one stands in the middle of the city one might seem to be in the country. The town is three English miles broad from gate to gate, but it is very dangerous to walk through it at night. There used also to be large suburbs, but these are now entirely in ruins. Within the north gate is a very large market

writers usually thus utilized their smattering of the native tongue, *e.g.*, Terry derives the name Delhi from *dil*, heart, centre of the empire. The Muhammadan saint referred to in the text is Shaikh Salim Chishti (1479-1572) Akbar, desirous of a son, visited the hermitage of the saint, who blessed him with the fulfilment of his desire, and the son Salim, named after the saint, was born, and his birthplace was made the capital In the words of Jahangir, in the course of 14 or 15 years the hills and desert of the village of Sikri which abounded in beasts of prey were converted into a magnificent city, comprising numerous gardens, elegant edifices and pavilions It remained the capital from 1570 to 1585, that is to say, for 15 years, and not for 50 years as De Laet says. Why was it abandoned? The place did not possess any natural advantages, Akbar obtained what he had wanted, and the Shaikh had long been dead Moreover political considerations necessitated Akbar's presence on the frontier, and hence the royal residence was shifted to Lahore for the next 13 years. Havell mentions a fable that the abandonment was due to the distractions caused to the saint by the din and bustle of a great city

The city was nearly seven miles in circumference, protected on three sides by a strong wall and on the north-western by a large artificial lake which supplied water to the inhabitants The city wall was pierced by nine gates, of which four were principal Finch mentions 'four faire gates', so too Father Monserrate The principal four gates were. (1) Agra Gate to the north-east, (2) Ajmer Gate to the west, (3) Delhi Gate to the north (Circus Gate of Father Monserrate) and (4) Gwalior Gate (Dholpur gate of Father Monserrate). A visitor usually enters by the Agra Gate on the north-east, De Laet refers to it as the north gate: The place mentioned in the text is the Mahal-i-Khas. Further beyond

place, a mile long, paved with stone and surrounded with buildings. At the end of this a palace is to be seen, adorned with much magnificent building, and beyond this the most glorious mosque in the whole East. One ascends to this mosque up 25 or 30 steps, through a very lofty and beautiful gateway, which can be seen from a great distance. Within this is a large courtyard paved with the living rock, and surrounded by colonnades with lofty columns and large domes. Near the gate a splendid tomb is to be seen, in which a certain Mahometan saint is buried who belonged to the sect called Kalenders He is said to have built this mosque at his own expense Beneath the city lies a tank, which is the sole source of drinking water, for the other springs and streams are brackish and unwholesome This scarcity of water is said to have compelled the king to abandon the city, which thus had a very short lifetime (only about 50 years) between its foundation and its virtual extinction. The place was formerly called Sykary, *i.e*, a net, but on his return from an expedition abroad, and after the birth of the son who afterwards became emperor, Achbar wished it to be called Fetipore, *i e*, the wish fulfilled Outside the walls towards the north-west lies a swamp two or three cos long, abounding in fish and

---

the Daftar Khana and Jodh Bai's palace is the Jami Masjid. The lofty and beautiful gate of the masjid is the Buland Darwaza. The Great Mosque is one of the most magnificent of Akbar's buildings It was built in honour of the saint Shaikh Salim Chishti An inscription over the main archway of the Mosque gives the date of its completion as 1571 A D But the Buland Darwaza or Lofty Gate (176 ft in height) was not built till 1575-6 A D It was, according to Smith, intended to serve as a memorial of the conquest of Gujarat in 1573 Within the quadrangle of the Great Mosque, opposite to the Buland Darwaza, is the mausoleum of Shaikh Salim Chishti It was built some years later. For other details about Fatehpur see Monserrate, pp 30-32; A.T, pp 107-31; and E. W. Smith's · *The Moghul Architecture of Fatehpur Sikri*, for the life of Shaikh Chishti, see H.J, p. 3-11.

birds. This marsh is almost entirely covered by a kind of grass which produces the fruit called Hermodactylus. Another kind of grass produces the Camolochacheri [*kanwal kakri*]. Both these kinds of fruit are productive of cold. The Hermodactylus is protected by a three-cornered shell of texture resembling wood, armed with sharp thorns at each corner; when still green the fruit is soft and of a not unpleasant taste, but doubtless chill-producing; the common people call it the Singara [water-chestnut], it grows also here and there in the tanks around Agra. The Camolochacheri is shaped like a small ladle, and contains inside six or eight kernels, which are joined together by a white membrane.

In this same province is Bayana or Byana, which is famous for its excellent woad. The route thither from Agra is as follows: to Menhapore [Mundiapura] (a great junction of roads), 7 cos near this a county mansion may be seen (or Moholl as they call it) belonging to the mother of the queen · it is surrounded by a fine garden which is excellently cultivated Thence to Cannova is 11 cos. Along this road (*i e*, that leading from Agra to Asmere, a distance of 130 cos) it is worthy of note that each cos is marked out by a stone column, and that at every eight cos a woman's apartment has been constructed, which can accommodate 16 ladies with their servants · these were erected by king Achabar, who having no sons walked on foot from Agra to Assmere where is the tomb of the Mahumetan Saint Hogee Modee [57] who is regarded with the greatest veneration.

Cannova is a small country town, around which the best indigo (or *nîl*) is collected; its excellence is due to the heavy soil and brackish water, the effect of which is that

---

[57] Khwaja Muinuddin died at Ajmer in 1239 A.D. Jahangir alls him "the fountain-head of most of the saints of India."

the indigo is much more easily broken up than that grown in places where the water is sweet. The Dutch writers state that Cannova is ten cos from Byana, and has under it the following villages:—Mahal and Phoubas (each 2 cos distant from Cannova), Tzourtsonda (1½ cos), Dabet (2), Mahalpore and Garassa (1), Dannachan (2), Bockolyt (1), Barawat (1½), Zrazewolia (1½), Phettapore (5). From Connova to Ouche is 3 cos: to Candere (a filthy village) 6: 2 cos from here stands one of those palaces which I have mentioned as having been constructed by the king every 8 cos. It is a square building. Within the outer gate is a hall called the Hall of the king's Darsany,[58] leading off which are some other small rooms: within the second gateway are the women's apartments, also square in shape: along each side are four bedrooms for the king's concubines, and of these there are 16 in all · in the middle of each side and at each corner are spacious halls called Devoncan,[59] hung with rich tapestries, in the middle of the whole palace is the king's bedroom.

Byana[60] was once a large and beautiful town, but is now in decay. It has only two sarayas and a long street or bazar (*i e.*, market) with a few cottages. The finer houses have either already collapsed or threaten to do so very soon. There are but few inhabitants. Yet from this town the best indigo exported from India to Europe takes

58 It is so named probably because the kings used to sit there to allow the people to have *darshan* (sight).

59 Diwan-Khana was the hall of semi-public audience, as contrasted with the Ghusl-khana

60 Biana indigo was the best; next that of Sarkhej (*q v.*) It has already been mentioned that Biana indigo was known as 'round.' In the Aleppo market the indigo of northern India, mainly from Biana, was known as Lahori, from the fact that caravans were made up in Lahore and thence carried overland to Aleppo. Pelsaert's Section 3 may be read with profit.

its name; but this (I find from Dutch writers) is gathered from a tract of land 20 or 30 cos in length, in which there are 5 chief centres, each having several villages placed under it for revenue purposes. One of these centres is Cannova, which I have already mentioned, the second is Byana, which is the headquarters of the following villages:—

Ibrahamie Dabat [Ibrahimabad], one cos from Byana, Serco (4 cos), Ochien [6 cos], Patchiona [Pachuana], 5 cos, Birampoer (4 cos), Mehepore [Malikpur], 4 cos, Tzonova [Sanawa], 4 cos, Pinijora (6 cos), Nau Nova (6 cos), etc. The third centre is Bassouwer (10 cos east of Byana). The fourth is Hindaun (10 cos from Byana). The fifth is Tora (10 cos from Byana).

There are other indigo-producing centres in this province, *e.g.*, Koil [Aligarh] and Gorza [Khurja] 30 cos from Agra across the river Semena, but the indigo obtained there is not reckoned nearly as good as that of Byana, and has not hitherto been exported to Europe.

Three or four cos north-west of Byana are the ruins of a splendid palace and of other buildings. Similar ruins may be seen on the summit of a crag near Scanderbad [Sikandarabad] about the same distance south of Byana. The pathway leading up to these ruins is steep and narrow and is paved with stone; it can only be climbed on foot; immediately within the narrow gateway to the right, on the very edge of the cliff, there is a most beautiful tomb, with several monuments inside it which are still undamaged. Above this one ascends by a paved roadway to the royal palace, which is now in ruins, and is inhabited only by a few shepherds called Goagers [Gujars]. At the foot of the mountain towards Scanderbad is a lovely valley, enclosed by a wall, in which are many gardens.

The town of Scanderbad was once the capital of a most powerful Pathan King.[61] Its walls are 8 cos in length, and are even built along the edge of cliffs which would themselves prevent attack. It is now only the abode of shepherds; for king Achabar drove the tyrant Scha Selim from this stronghold and entirely destroyed the town, just as he did also with Mandoa.

The Province of Delhi.

The route from Agra to Lahore passes through the famous kingdom of Dely or Delhi. From the capital to Rawnocta [Rankata] is 12 cos. to the Saray of Bady [Bad-i Sarai] 10 to Achabarpore, 12 This was once a large town, but is now only frequented by pilgrims on account of many Mahumetan saints whose tombs are here. To Houdle [Hodal] is 13 cos to Pulwool [Palwal] 12: to Ferreedabad [Faridabad] 12: to Delly 10 On the way the vast ruins of the ancient city of Delly[62] are seen on the left. The Indians say that it once had 9 fortresses and 52 gates, but to-day it is only an abode of shepherds. Not far from these ruins a branch of the river Jemini or Gemena is crossed by a stone bridge[63] from which a broad avenue,

[61] Sultan Sikander Ghazi (1489-1517), the second king of the Lodhi dynasty, is referred to The remark about Akbar and Salim Shah does not tally with known facts of history.

[62] Carr Stephens states (*Archæology of Delhi*, p 91) that according to tradition the city of Tughlakabad had 52 gates. Hence the reference here is to the ruins of Tughlakabad built (5 miles to the east of old Delhi round the Kutb) by Ghiyasuddin Tughluq Shah (1321-25) De Laet's remark that 'today it is only an abode of shepherds' reminds one of the curse of the saint, Nizamuddin Aulya who, hindered by the Sultan in the construction of his own dwelling pronounced the curse "May it (Tughlakabad) remain deserted or may it be a habitation of Gujars."

[63] The Bara Palah bridge leading to Humayun's tomb where are buried many members of the House of Timur It is called the Dormitory of the House of Timur.

thickly shaded by tall trees, leads to the tomb of Hamaunis, the grandfather of Selim, who became emperor in 1609 [1605]: a little further on is a royal palace, now partially ruined.

[*Delhi*].—The present city of Delly is also of great size, being two cos in length; it is surrounded by a strong wall, which is however ruinous in parts, many of the houses within the walls are also in ruins; both inside and outside the walls there are many finely built tombs of the Pathan kings, numbering about 20 in all. It used to be regarded a religious duty that the kings of India should be crowned in this city. Two cos from the city lies the hunting-palace of the Pathan kings. It is said to have been built by the powerful monarch Sultan Berusa [Feroz Shah]. In that place, amongst other ancient monuments, a very lofty obelisk[64] is to be seen, which is said by some to bear an inscription in Greek and to have been built by Alexander

64 While annotating Father Monserrate's Commentary, I contented myself with merely stating the reference to the Asoka Lāt. Father Monserrate's remark did not call for a detailed note. Finch (E.T., 156) Coryat (E.T., 248), Roe (103) and Terry (81) have mentioned the column. De Laet copied it from Finch, Terry heard from Tom Coryat, Roe probably had it also on Coryat's authority. Of all these writers, it is Tom Coryat who is most explicit on this point and hence most erroneous. "I have been in a citie in this countrie called Detee (Delhi) where Alexander the Great joyned battell with Poros, King of India, and conquered him; and in token of his victorie erected a brass pillar, which remaineth there to this day." This is a fine specimen of the "crudities hastily gobled up by Tom Coryat in five months travels." The pen of Coryat has transferred the Karri Plain to Delhi and metamorphosed stone into brass. The pillar was erected (*c.* 243-42 B.C.) by Asoka (B.C. 273-32) to instruct his people in the Dhamma, and not by the Greek invader to commemorate his victory over Porus at the Karri Plain, and the script used in the inscription is Brahmi, not Greek. There are (in addition to the one of wrought iron in the courtyard of the Kutb Minar) two such pillars, one in the Kothila of Feroz Shah and

the Great. Similar obelisks are said to be found in various parts of India. One such, 100 cubits long, was lately discovered buried in the earth near Fettipore; but whilst it was being with great difficulty conveyed to Agra, it was carelessly broken on the way.

THE PROVINCE OF THE PUNJAB.

The following is the route from Delly to Lahore, the capital of the province of the Panjab :—From Delly to Nalero [Narela], 14 cos : to Gonowre [Ganaur], 14 : to Pannepat, 14 : to Karnal, 14 : all this part of the way is exceptionally dangerous from robbers : to Tanassar [Thaneswar], a fortified place, 14 : near this town is a most beautiful tank surrounded by temples, or Pagodas as the Indians call them; in these temples idols are to be seen, which the Indians most superstitiously worship. Not far away are wells of Salammoniac. Thence to Shabad (or 10 cos : to Amballa, 12 : to Holloway [Aluwa-Shahabad Saray], 14 : to Siryna, 7 : this city[65] has a beautiful tank,

---

the other in the grounds of the hunting-lodge of the same Sultan Reference here is to the latter It originally stood at Mirath (Meerut) and was removed in 1356 by the orders of Sultan Feroz to grace his hunting park. "This pillar was much injured by a gunpowder explosion, broken into five pieces and rather roughly put together" (S C D, p. 28) It was re-erected by the present Government in 1867. The other pillar in the Kothila of Feroz Tughlaq (it originally stood at Topra in the Ambala district) was removed by the same Sultan in the same year. The process of removal is very interesting and is described in E D., III., 350; Carr Stephens, p 131. It is regrettable that the column at Fatehpur was carelessly broken on the way while being conveyed.

65 Sihrind. The reference below is probably to the garden of Hafiz Rakhnah, the delight of all beholders. He was a grandee of Humayun's court (*Ain.* II, 281). Both the mosque and the park are mentioned by Monserrate (pp. 101-2) and Manrique (J.P.H.S., I., 87-88).

in the middle of which is a temple approached by a stone bridge of 15 arches : a cos distant from this tank is a royal park approached by a canal and a paved road, 50 feet broad, between a fine avenue of trees. This park is square shaped, each of its sides being more than a cos long. It is surrounded by a brick wall. Within are all kinds of fruit trees, plants and flowers. Some writers say that 50,000 rupees are yearly spent on this park. In the middle, where broad pathways bordered with tall cypress trees meet in the form of a cross, a royal palace is to be seen, beautifully built, and surrounded by a fine colonnade. It contains 8 women's apartments ; upstairs are 8 more bed chambers, and at the top is a fine dining hall.

From Syrina to Dorapay [Doraha] is 15 cos : to Pulloce Saray [Phillaur-ki-Sarai] 13 : to Nikodar 12 : to Sultanpore 11 : to Fettipore[66] 7. Selim, the last emperor of India, is said to have built this Saray in memory of a successful battle which was here fought by his army against his own eldest son, Sultan Cusheroo, who was put to flight. The circumstances were, they say, as follows :—Selim had grievously offended his father Achabar, and fearing to meet him withdrew to Purropia [Purab, East,] and occupied the strong fortress of Halebassa [Allahabad]. Thereupon Achabar named his grandson Cusheroo heir of the Empire. But on the death of Achabar and before Cusheroo could consolidate his power Selim by the help of his friends attacked the fort of Agra, possessed himself of his father's treasure, pursued his son towards Lahor, routed him at this place, soon afterwards captured him, threw him into prison, and was supposed (but, as afterwards appeared, falsely) to have put out his eyes. From Fettipore to

66 Fathpur (town of victory). Bhairowal, on the Beas, was named Fathpur (Fatehpur) in memory of the victory gained by the royal forces over Khusrau (April, 1606). Full details of Khusrau's career and revolt will be found in the *Fragment*.

Hogemoheede [Tarn Taran ?] is 10 cos : to Concanna Saray [Khan-Khanan Sarai], 12 : to Lahor, 7.

[*Lahore*].—Lahore is by far the largest city in the East, for the circumference of its ditch (recently built by order of the king) and wall (built under Selim) is 24 cos In the time of the Patan kings it was a mere village, Multan being then a much more important place ; but it was enlarged by Hamaun. The city suburbs are six cos long. The royal citadel is surrounded by a very strong brick wall. There are 12 gates,[67] 9 of which lead into the suburbs, whilst 3 open upon the river. The streets of the city are fine, and are paved with stone. The inhabitants are chiefly Banianes and artisans. The buildings are well-built and lofty ; they are constructed of brick ; many of those belonging to Hindus are approached by flights of six or seven steps, steep and difficult to climb, for the sake of safety and of privacy from passers-by. The citadel is situated on the bank of the beautiful river Ravee, which lower down joins the Indus and is navigable for boats of 60 dolia burden and more. Many of these boats ply between Lahor and the trading centre of Tatta in Sinde after the rainy season is over The voyage takes about 40 days. Multhan, Seetpore, Buchur, Rauree [Rohri] are passed

[67] Dr Vogel thinks that the gates here referred to, are of the whole fortified city, and not of the citadel (J P.H.S., I, 39). Manucci mentions the names of the gates (Vol II, p 185). Dr. Vogel writes: "The palace of Lahore (described by Finch, De Laet and Herbert) consisted evidently of the large quadrangle of the *Diwan-i-Am* constructed by Akbar, and the smaller square adjoining it to the north which is now usually designated as the Quadrangle of Jahangir. These are no doubt the two courts pointing out the two ways—one to the king's Durbar and the other to the Diwan Khana. Dr. Vogel's *Historical Notes on the Lahore Fort* (J.P.H.S., Vol. I, pp. 38-55) and Maulvie Nur Baksh's article on *The Lahore Fort* (A.R., 1902-3) are of value for the palace described here as well as for the later additions of Shah Jahan

on the way. The river Ravee comes from the east, out of the mountains of Kassimer (or so some say), and flows past the northern side of the city. The royal palace lies on its bank, within the citadel; the approach to the citadel from the city lies through a great gateway and thence through a second small gate into a square courtyard where the royal guards are on duty; within this, through another gateway, to the left, is an inner courtyard, in which the king's Durbar is to be seen. around this are a large number of guard-posts for the nobles who are on guard; within this is a third courtyard, in the middle of which the king's Devoncan may be seen, with several bed-chambers in which the king is wont to rest from 8 to 11 in the evening. On the wall of this building is a picture of the king, sitting with crossed legs under a splendid canopy; on his right are his sons[68] Sultan Porvesius, Caroonius and Timoret. next to them are his brothers Sha Morat [Shah Murad] and Dan Sha [Danyal Shah]. next to them Emyrza Sheriff,[69] the eldest brother of Can Asom (they say he was so rich and luxurious that he would never allow the garments which his concubines, of whom he kept more than 100, had once worn to be touched by anyone else but had them buried in the ground till they rotted away; he also kept 500 torchbearers, who are called Massalgees [Mashalchis] and when he returned from Agra to his palace, a distance of at least a cos, every single one of these torch-

---

[68] Parvez and Khurrum were the sons of Jahangir; Tahmuras was his nephew, being a son of Danyal We are told by European writers that the sons of Danyal (at least 2 out of 3) were made Christians. Hawkins says that 'Jahangir wanted to make them hateful to the Moors' (E T, 116). Roe and Terry say that they renounced their new faith when the Jesuits refused to provide Portuguese wives to them. Tahmuras was put to death by order of Shah Jahan in January 1628.

[69] Sharif Khan. The description about Can Asom applies to Mirza Aziz (Khan Azam). But Sharif was the uncle of Aziz.

bearers had to be in his right place, so that the whole way was lined with them) : next[70] to him is Emyrza Rosthan, once king of Candahar, then Cancanna, Cuttuph Caun, Rohia Monisengo, Caun Asom, Asoph Caun, Scheck Fereed, Kalishcoun and Rahja Juggonath (upon whose death they say that seven of his friends, including his sister and his brother's son, of their own free will mounted his funeral pyre). To the left[71] of the king is Rahja Bousingh who is driving away flies with a fly-flap, Rahja Ramdas, who bears the king's sword, Cleriff Can, Mocrib Boucan, Rahja Bossu, Rahja Rausing, Moje Kesso and Lalla Bersing. In the same colonnade in which is this excellent picture of the king, on the right hand wall above the door, may be seen a statue of our Saviour and the Virgin mother In this palace are very many halls and women's apartments, which it would be tedious to describe But mention must be made of one colonnade on the wall of which are portraits of the ancestors of king Selim, *i e*, his father Achabar, his grandfather Hamaune and his great-grandfather Babar, who first invaded India with 30 nobles dressed in the disguise of Kalendars,[72] as I shall recount elsewhere The

[70] The nobles mentioned are Mirza Rustam, Khan-i-Khanan (Abdur Rahim), Qutbuddin Khan, Raja Man Singh, Khan Azam (Mirza Aziz), Asaf Khan, Shaikh Farid, Qulij Khan, and Raja Jagannath (son of Raja Behari Mal)

[71] The nobles are easily identified They are respectively Raja Bhao Singh (son and successor of Raja Man), Raja Ram Das Kachhwaha (son of Raja Raj Singh), Shariff Khan (*Amir-ul-Umara*, T.J , I, 14-15), Mukarrab Khan (H J , 105-7, 405-407, 421), Raja Basu of Pathankot (see *Fragment*, Section XXII), Raja Rai Singh of Bikanir, Raja Keshoo Das Maru and Lala Bir Singh.

[72] Sir Edward Maclagan, in annotating the corresponding statement of Finch, writes: "I have not found the incident mentioned in the ordinary histories but the story of Babur going as a Yogi to Delhi in 1507 (?) is given in Valentyn, pp 188-9" (J P H.S , I, 127, *n.* 4). De Laet has it in Chapter IX. It may be guessed that the unfounded story once gained wide currency.

river is crossed to the west of the citadel, and from thence a road leads towards Kabul. The whole region beyond the river is most pleasant. Some writers[73] give a slightly different route from Delly to Lahor, as follows:—Delly to Bunyra, 10 cos: to Cullower, 12: to Pampetta (a small but beautiful town), 12: to Carnal, 12: to Tanissor, 14: to Sahbad, 10. to Gangur or Mogal Saray, 15: to Sina (an ancient city, noted for cotton weaving), 14. to Duratia, 15. to Pullower, 11. Before reaching this place the great river Sietmegus [Sutlej], which flows westwards into the Indus, must be crossed in boats. From Pullower to the small town of Nicoudar, 11: to Saltanpore, an ancient town standing on the southern bank of a river: to Chuirmal, 11, before reaching which place the river Van must be crossed: it is a very wide stream which flows westwards and finally falls into the Indus. Thence Canacanna Saray is 17 cos: and Lahor 7 more.

The whole country between Agra and Lahor is well cultivated and is the most fertile part of India, bearing

Manucci (Vol I, p 111) in his strange list of Pathan kings, puts the name of the 25th king as Sultan Babar Calandar (the Poor Lion). Ferishta states that after the occupation of Delhi, Babur distributed with prodigal generosity all the public treasures not only to the men of his camp but sent a part of them also to Kabul to be divided among his subjects Ferishta (Vol II, 49) then goes on "Such generosity bordering on prodigality procured for Babur the name of Kulundar (begging friar) whose practice it is to keep nothing for to-morrow" Probably this is the substratum of truth in the legend mentioned by the European writers.

73 Sir Edward Maclagan suggests that the stages from Delhi herein given are Narela, Ghanaur, Panipat, Karnal, Theneswar, Shahabad, the Ghaggar river, Sihrind, Dauraha, Philaur (crossing the river Sutlej, erroneously called here Sietmegus), Nakodar, Sultanpur, then crossing the river Bain or the Khalna and the Beas to Chirmal and thence to Khan Khanan Sarai. This route is taken from the journal of the Journey of Richard Steele and William Crowther, 1615.

all kinds of crops abundantly. Much sugar is produced. The road is bordered by trees on either side which bear fruit something like the mulberry. Every 5 or 6 cos is a saray, built by the king or some noble, where travellers may obtain sleeping and stable accommodation. Once a traveller has occupied the rooms allotted to him, nobody else may turn him out.

THE PROVINCE OF KABUL.

The road from Lahor to Kabul is infested by Pathan brigands, and although the king has established 23 guard-stations of troops at regular intervals, none the less travellers are frequently robbed by these brigands, who in the year 1611 actually attacked and looted the city of Kabul itself. The stages of the journey are as follows:—

From Lahor to Googes Saray [Kacha Sarai] 10 cos: the river Ravee must be crossed to Emenbad [Aminabad], a fine town, 8: to Chumaguckor [Chima Gakhar], a large city, 12: to Guzarat, a notable trading centre, 14: on the way, 7 cos from Guzarat, the great river Chantrow [Chenab] must be crossed. From Guzarat to Khowaspore, 12: to Loutre-Rotas* (a place with a strong fortress on the top of a mountain) 15: this was once the frontier post of the Pathan kingdom. To Hattea 15: to Puchow [Pakka] 4: to Raulepende [Rawalpindi] 14· to Collapanne [Kalapani] 15: to Hassan Abdal 4 this is a fine town on the bank of a small river, near to which lie some beautiful tanks containing countless fish, upon whose snouts Achabar† is said to have fixed gold rings; the water is so clear and pure that one can everywhere see the bottom From Hassan Abdal to Attock (a city on the Indus with

---

* Prof. Hodivala points out that Loutre is a mistake for *Khurd* which means little. The place was called Rohtas-i-Khurd to distinguish it from the other Rohtas in Behar.

† Jahangir fastened pearls! (T.J., I, p. 99)

a very strong fort) 15: to Pishore [Peshawar] 36: to Alleck Mosque [Ali Masjid] 10: this part of the way is rendered dangerous by enemies of the king, who can bring together ten to twelve thousand horsemen. To Ducka [Dakka] 12: to Beshoule [Basawal] 6: to Abareech [Bariku] 6: to Alebog [Ali Boghan] 11, (this place stands on the Cow [Kabul], a large river flowing from Kabul): to Gelalabad, 14: to Loure Charebog, 4: 73a to Budde Charbog, 6. to Nomle, 8· to Gondoma [Gandamak]: to Surcrood Saray [Surkhab Sarai] 4· here a small river is crossed whose water is reddish and is said to be beneficial to stomach complaints. to Zagdeie [Jagdalak] 8· to Abereeck [Ab-i-Barik] 8: to Dowabad [Doaba] 8: across a mountain region to Buttocanche [Butkhak] 8. to Kamree [Bikrami] 3: to Kabul, 3

Kabul—Kabul is a very large city. It has two citadels and many Sarays. It used to be the capital of the ancestors of the present king of India About 20 cos beyond the city lies Chore-Cullow [Charikar], a very fine town, and 20 cos further is the large town of Gorebond [Ghorband] on the frontier of the province of Usheck [Uzbeg] whose capital is Samarcand. The kingdom of Kabul (says Texeira) was once subject to Persia: the journey thence to Lahor used to take three months, owing to the great detours which had to be made to avoid robber-infested districts: now that many guard-posts have been erected at regular intervals along the royal highway, the journey takes 20 or 25 days. From this province a kind of mirabolam derives its name, being called the Kebuli in the manufactories. The Arabs and Persians call this fruit the Alilah which name the Indians have corrupted into Arare [Har-ra]. They say that caravans take

---

73a The three places may be Charbag-Khurd, Charbag-Kalan Nimla-bag (Sarkar's *The India of Aurangzib*, p. ciii) Budde of De Laet may be Bada = large.

two or three months to travel from Kabul to Cascar, which is a very large kingdom subject to the Tartars: its chief trading centre is called Yar-Chaun [Yarkhand], whence great quantities of silk, musk, rhubarb and other merchandise are exported: these are brought to this province from China: the journey from Kascar to the frontier of China is said to take only three months My statement about the length of time which used to be taken on the journey from Lahor to Kabul is confirmed by the itinerary of the Portuguese Jesuit Benedict à Goes (given in Trigentius). He set out from Lahor on January 6, 1603, reached Athoc (or Attock) in a month, thence Gidele in 20 days, and Kabul in 20 more from Kabul he went on to Ciarcor, and thence to Parva, the last town of the Mogol Empire.

The Province of Kashmir

From the city of Lahor there is also the following route to the great province of Kassimere. As far as Guzarat the route is the same as that to Kabul · thence one turns north to Bimbar, 16 cos: to Joagek Hotely [Jogi-ki-hatli] 14: to Cinquesque-Hotely [Changas Hatli] 10: to Peckly,[74] 10 · to Conowa,[75] 12: to the Hastehaunck-gate[76] over the mountains (at the top of which is a beautiful plain) 8: thence to the capital, Kassimere or Syrinakar, through a

---

[74] Sir Aurel Stein suggests that geographically it ought to be Suj Sarai or very near it But he suggests that it may be the hilly district of Pakhli But Pakhli is considerably away from the Pir Panjal route and in fact a branch route runs from Chingas Sarai *via* Pakhli to Kashmir Either Finch (from whom De Laet copies) or his informant confused the two routes (J P H S., Vol VI, p 147)

[75] Sir Aurel Stein suggests that the location of Conowa may be at or near Pushiana and that it may be connected in some way with Kambuva, which Kalhan, the author of *Rajtarangini*, mentions as the designation of an ancient watch-station on the route across the Pir Panjal Pass.

[76] The ridge of Hastivanj overlooking the Pir Panjal from the south. The term 'gate' (*ghat*) has since ancient times been specifically applied in Kashmir to the passes which lead to the valley across the enclosing mountain ranges.

most lovely district, 7. This city stands on the river Bohat; it is surrounded by a very fertile plain about 50 cos long and 50 broad: the women of this region are said to be white. Kassimere has a cold climate, and suffers from frost and deep snow in winter. Kascar is near by, but such impassable mountains lie between that there is no route possible to caravans between the two countries; it is but rarely and with great difficulty that the mountains can be crossed on foot. Amongst these mountains lives a chieftain called Tibbon.[77] He has no great wealth, but a few years ago sent his daughter to Selim, the king of India, in order to contract a marriage alliance with him. The same region marches with the two kingdoms of Thebet, whose chief export is saffron.

THE ROUTE FROM KABUL TO KASHGAR.

The above-mentioned Itinerary of Benedict à Goes gives an account of the route from the kingdom of Kabul to Cascar, which is worth quoting here. He set out from Parva, the frontier town of Kabul, and after a most difficult journey of 5 days through lofty and precipitous mountains came down into the region of Aingara and 15 days later reached Calcia, whose inhabitants are said to resemble the Dutch. Thence, after a 10 days' journey, he came to Gialalabattia, where the Bramenes took tribute from him in the name of king Bruarates. Thence he travelled 15 days to Talhan, thence to Cheman, which belongs to Abdulahan, king of Samarhan[a], Burgavia, Bacharat and other provinces: thence he had a difficult journey of 8 days to Badascian and Ciarcunar: thence Serpanill was 10 days, and Sarcil (a region full of villages) 20. Two days further on is the snow-covered Ciecialith range. After

---

[77] In 1590 Salim married a daughter of Ali Rai, the chief of Skardo (Baltistan or Little Tibet) brought by the Mughal ambassador, Haji Mirza Beg Kabuli (*Ain*. I., 310).

a. Samarkand, Balkh and Bukhara

crossing this, and losing many of his fellow travellers from the cold, he came to Taughetar in the kingdom of Cascar. Fifteen days further on is Joconich and then Hiarchon (or Yarchaun), the capital of the kingdom of Cascar. He left Hiarchon with a caravan in the middle of November, 1604, and had a difficult 35 days' journey through mountains and deserts (called the desert of Caracathay) to Ortograch Gazo, Cascia, Dellae, Saregabedal Ugan and Cucian : thence 15 days more brought him to Cialin, which was ruled by a bastard son of the king of Cascar. Thence in 20 days he came to Pucian, then to the strongly fortified town of Turphon : then to Aramuth : then to Camul, the frontier post of the kingdom of Cialis : a journey of 9 days more brought him to the wall which protects China from the north.

The Regions Lying East and South of Lahor.

Up the stream of the Ravee, and on its banks as one goes northward, is the country ruled by the Rajha Bossow,[78] whose capital is called Temmery and is 50 cos from Lahor. He is a powerful chieftain, though subject to the Mogol Emperor, with whom he is a great favourite. Many valuable herbs are found in his territory, being collected amongst the mountains. Near by is the country of another Rahja, called Tulloch Chan. His capital is Negarcut, 80 cos from Lahor and as many from Siryna. The town contains a famous temple or Pagoda, called Je or Durga [Bajreswari Debi] about which marvellous tales are told. On account of the inaccessible mountains amongst which he lives this prince sometimes becomes insolent and shows scant respect to the Mogols.

---

78 Raja Basu. Frequent references to him will be found in the *Fragment* Temmery stands for Dhameri, the old name of Nurpur, near Pathankot in Kangra. Basu died in the fifteenth year of the reign of Jahangir.

East of Negarcut lives Decomperga,[79] a very important prince, whose capital is Colsery, 150 cos from Agra. His state is so thickly populated that in a very brief time he can collect an army of 50,000, chiefly infantry, for he has but few cavalry.

East of this again, between the rivers Jemina and Ganges, lies the state ruled by Rahja Mansa,[80] who is so rich that he eats his food from dishes of solid gold. His capital is Serenagar. His territory which is very fertile is shut in by snow-covered mountains, called the Dow Lager [Dhaulagiri] though the distance north of the equator is not more than 40° Serenagar is 200 cos from Agra and 50 from Syrina.

On the other side of the Ganges lives a very powerful prince called Rahja Rodorow [Rudra Chand of Kumaon], who rules a very large mountain region which is said to march with China. The capital is called Camoio. He can collect vast forces of infantry, but can make no use of cavalry on account of the roughness of the mountains · elephants are impossible on account of the cold. He has however a kind of horse called Gunts which seem to have been specially made by nature to climb inaccessible mountains.

South of this, across the Ganges, is the territory of the powerful Rahja Mugg which produces great numbers of horses and elephants. He is also said to possess a very rich diamond mine. East of this amongst the branches of the Ganges lives a Pathan chieftain,[81] belonging to the

---

79 Sir William Foster suggests Dharm Parkash of Sirmur, though the Raja had been dead for over 40 years Dr Vogel suggests Ude Chand Parkash, Raja of Sirmur Kalsi was the ancient capital of the State

80 Raja Man Sah of Garhwal. Srinagar was the capital of the Garhwal Rajas.

81 The reference probably is to Miyan Isa Khan Lohani or to Usman, ruler of Bhati. Both had died at the time when De Laet wrote. Raja Mugg may refer to the Zemindar of Khokhara (T J. I, 315) where diamonds could be had.

stock of the kings of Delly. The Mogol has never been able to conquer him on account of the devious branches of the Ganges and the many islands amongst which he lives. His territory adjoins the province of Purropia, into which he makes frequent incursions, so that the Mogol king is compelled to go to the expense of keeping up a large army to hold him in check.

The Mogols hold all the region down to the mouths of the Ganges, with the exception of one fortress[82] which is held by Portuguese exiles. Across the Ganges lies the very powerful kingdom of Arracon which is bounded on the east by Siam, Ova and Jangoma.[83] Between Tanossarin and Arracan lies the kingdom of Pagu, now mostly deserted; to the south of this lie Queda,[84] Malacca, etc. On the shore of the sea the Mogol king has two chief ports, Ougolee,[85] which the Portuguese have occupied, and Pipilee (or Petepolis), which lies 15° 36′ from the equator.

---

[82] Sondwip, off Chittagong, was a nest of Portuguese pirates

[83] Portuguese name for Kiang-mai or Zimme, in the north-western part of Siam.

[84] Quedda was a port (also a small kingdom) on the west coast of the Malay Peninsula, it was tributary to Siam

[85] Hugly. Satgoan (*q v*) declined and Hugly rose to importance The latter had supplanted the former by the time the *Ain-i-Akbari* was completed, say by 1598 · for Abul Fazl mentions the two ports of Satgaon and Hugly situated at a distance of half a kos from each other By that time the Portuguese had already a permanent settlement there The Rev Father H. Hosten argues that the name Hugly is derived from O Goli or Golu, *i.e.*, the store house (erected by the Portuguese). The two settlements of Chittagong and Satgoan were respectively called Porto Grande (Great Port) and Porto Piqueno (Small Port). When the latter declined in importance Hugly came to be known as the Porto Piqueno. Many facts have been brought to light by the Rev. Father Henry Hosten, S.J., in his instructive article · *A week at the Bandel Convent, Hugli*, in *Bengal, Past and Present*, Vol. X, 1915, pp. 36-120, see also *Bengal District Gazetteer : Hooghly* Chap. ·

Southwards, beyond the province of Orissa, is the province of Golconda, which Selim tried to subdue in 1609. Its chief port is Mosulipoton, 15° 57′ N.; but the capital is Braganadar [86] or Golconda, a city founded only recently. Further south on the coast is the kingdom of Bisnagar [Vijayanagar] in which the Portuguese hold the towns of San Thoma [St. Thome] and Negapatan. I shall describe these more fully below.

THE PROVINCE OF PURROPIA.

[*Allahabad*].—The route from Agra to Halabasse, the chief fortress in Purropia, is as follows :—

From Agra across the river Jemina to Amedipore, [Itimadpur] 7 cos (here much indigo is grown. it is called Cole and is of inferior quality, being either used in India or exported to Samarcand and Casgar : it is never sent to Europe) · thence to Itay [Etawah] 12 (this was once the capital of one of the Pathan kings, but the town is now in ruins there is a fort here on the top of a hill precipitous on all sides : it is

---

III, *History of Portuguese in Bengal* by J J A Campos, pp 63-65. Mr W. H. Moreland, in *India at the death of Akbar* (Appendix C), argues that Porto meant Estuary, not seaport, in reference to Bengal in the sixteenth century so Porto Grande referred to the Meghna estuary.

[86] Bhagnagar. The following quotation will explain: "In the year 998 A H (1589-90 A D) the king (Muhammad Quli Qutb Shah, 1580-1611 A D) determined to remove the seat of his government on account of the confined situation of Golconda, which from many causes, particularly the want of water, became extremely unhealthy: he accordingly fixed on a spot situated at the distance of five kos from his former capital (Golconda) on the river Moosy where he laid the foundation of a new city which was called Bhagnuggur ("The fortunate city") after his avourable mistress Bhagmutty; but after her death he ordered it to be called Hyderabad (after his son) although for many years it retained its original name." (Ferishta, II, 451-52; Thevenot, III, 94).

surrounded by a double wall, on the gateway of which a human face is carved which the Indians superstitiously worship, pouring over it quantities of oil) · thence to Choppergat, 12 cos (here there is a magnificent Saray which seems more like a fortress than a resting-place for travellers) : to Menepore, 12 cos: thence along the Ganges to Halabasse, 22. This city, which used to be called Praya, is situated on the bank of the Ganges; various Pathan kings tried in vain to build a citadel here; but the Mogol king Achabar at last succeeded in laying solid foundations and (so they say) employed more than 20,000 workmen on it for many years. Nevertheless the citadel is not yet completed; it stands in the angle where the Jemina river flows into the Ganges, and is surrounded by a triple wall: the outer wall, which is the highest of the three, is built of squared stone of a reddish colour In the courtyard within a column or obelisk [Asoka Pillar] may be seen, 50 feet high above the ground and believed to go much deeper below. It is clearly the work of some great prince, the Indians believe of Alexander Here also is a most magnificent palace of the king, beneath which in a subterranean cavern are some temples, monuments (as the Indians vainly believe) of Baba Adam and Mamma Havah [Eve] and their early descendants For they believe that the first man either was created here or at least lived here for a long time, and they regard themselves as belonging to his religion. Pilgrims come to visit these monuments from all the provinces of India, and before approaching them bathe in the Ganges and shave off their hair and beard: by so doing they believe themselves to be cleansed from all their sins. In October and November, when the snows have melted, the river may be descended in boats from here towards Bengal, but the voyage is somewhat dangerous. Four cos below the city, on the right and left banks of the Ganges, are two very strong fortresses, Harrayle [Arail] and Hussoe [Jhusi], founded by the Pathans. In this same province is situated the deserted city of Potana [Patna ?] in whose citadel the royal treasures are guarded. The Pathan kings derived their name[87] from this city, or perhaps rather gave their own name to it; they emerged from the mountains between Candahar and Kabul, invaded India, defeated Rasa Pethory [Prithviraj], the king of Delly, and for a long time were the rulers of India, till the Mogols drove them out in their turn.

THE ROUTE FROM AGRA TO JOUNPORE.

One hundred and thirty cos east of Agra is Cannove [Kanouj], a large unwalled city at the foot of a mountain, on whose top is a well-fortified citadel. The Ganges used to wash the foot of this mountain, but has now made a new course for itself 4 cos distant, though the old channel (which is of no great size) is still called the Ganges. From Cannove to Lacanouw is 30 cos. this is a great trading centre: thence to Oudee (an ancient city, once the seat of Pathan kings, but now almost deserted), 50 cos. Not far from this city may be seen the ruins of the fort and palace of Ramchand, whom the Indians regard as God Most High: they say that he took on him human flesh that he might see the great *tamasha* of the world. Amongst these ruins live certain Bramenes who carefully note down the name of all such pilgrims as duly perform their ceremonial ablutions in the neighbouring river. They say that this custom has been kept up for many centuries. About two miles from these rivers is a cave

87 I have no opinion to give regarding the philological gymnastics involved in the derivation of Pathan from Patna; Tughlaq is said to be similarly derived from Kutlugh. The word Pathan is a corruption of *pukhtanah*, dwellers in hills (from *pukht*, hill).

with a narrow mouth but so spacious within and with so many ramifications that it is difficult to find one's way out again. They believe that the ashes of the god are hidden heie. Pilgrims come to this place from all parts of India, and after worshipping the idol take away with them some grains of charred rice as proof of their visit. This rice they believe to have been kept here for many centuries. From Oudee to Achabarpore is 30 cos (about 30 cos from this place, but away from the route, is Bonarce, a famous emporium for the products of Bengal). From Acharbarpore to Jounpore is 30 cos. This town stands on the bank of a river which is crossed by a fine bridge : on this bridge many houses have been built. There is a citadel of the old Pathan kings and some good buildings. The city is said to be about 8 or 10 cos in circumference. From Jounpore one may return to Agra by another route through Halebasse, which is 110 cos distant: the road lies for 30 cos through a lovely and unbroken forest.

The Route from Agra to Ahmedabad.

There is a route from Agra to Amadavar in the province of Guzuratte through Fettipore, Scanderbad, Hindoine [Hindaun], Chenigo [Chandangaon], Mogol Seray, Nonnigong (this place lies at the foot of some mountains which are ruled by two Rahjas of moderate importance : beyond, the mountains of Marva, mentioned above, extend southward over a great extent of country). The road then leads through Gamgram, Charroit (capital of the ancestors of Rahja Maniseng), Landany, [Ladana], Mousalde [Mozabad] and Bramderande [Bandar Sindri] to Asmeere, an impregnable fortress situated on the top of a precipitous mountain, the path up which is difficult, and is three cos long.

Ajmere.—The town of Asmeere is of moderate size, situated at the foot of the mountain and surrounded with a stone wall and a broad moat. Its houses are yellow in colour; outside the walls many antiquities may be seen The town is specially famous for the tomb of Hoghe-Mondee [Khwaja Muinuddin], a saint held in the greatest veneration by the Mogols: the tomb is approached through three very large courtyards, of which the first occupies about an acre of land, and is paved with black and white marble: in this courtyard are many tombs of Mahumetan saints: to the left lies a beautiful tank enclosed on all sides by a wall. The second courtyard is paved in the same way, but the pavement is of much finer workmanship. in the middle hangs a lamp-stand with many lamps. The third courtyard is entered through a bronze gate of exquisite workmanship, and is far more beautiful than the others, especially at the opening of the tomb itself, whose door is studded with pearl-bearing shells; the pavement around the tomb is entirely of marble, and the tomb itself is adorned with gold and pearl-bearing shells, the epitaph being inscribed in Persian. Not far away is the saint's cell, whence he was wont to utter responses and oracles as if from the tripod (of Delphi); to the east of the tomb are three more courtyards with tombs, whilst to the north and west are fine houses in which the priests live No one is allowed to enter the precincts except with bare feet. Thomas Roe, the ambassador of the king of Great Britain to the Mogol, says that not far from Asmeere, in a beautiful and very fertile plain, lies the town of Godah, [Kota] which is well-fortified and finely built, but already ruinous. It was once the capital of a Rashboot prince whom Achabar Sha conquered. It contains many monuments skilfully cut from the living rock and a large number of tombs surrounded by strong walls. Roe also observes that Asmeere is situated 25° 30′ north of the equator, 200 English miles or ten days' journey south of Agra and 450 miles north of Barampore.

From Asmeere the road leads to Cairo (Garao); to Mearta [Mirtha], (which possesses a very strong castle, beautiful tanks and three idol-temples endowed with very rich offerings): to Pipera [Pipar], Jongesgong [Jogikagaon], Severange, Candempe [Khandap], Jeloure, Mudra, Bilmoll [Bhinmal], once a very large city about 24 cos in circumference, now ruined, though the line of the walls can still be plainly made out. finally to Amadavar.

Another Route from Agra to Asmeere.

From Agra to Fettipore, 12 cos. to Bramobad, 12: to Hendowne, 12. to Mogol Seray, 14 to Lalscotte, 12: to Chadfoole, 13· to Pipela, 7 to Mosobad, 13: to Badersondre (a small village), 10. to Mondil, 12: to Asmeere, 2.

The Route from Ahmedabad to Loure-bander, the Famous Port of Tutta.

The following is the route from Amadavat to Tutta, or Tatta, the emporium of Sind: to Cassumparo: to Callitalowny (a fine fortress) to Calwalla (a pleasant village), 7 cos (this place was given by King Achabar to certain women and their descendants on condition that they taught their children the art of dancing): to Carrya (a strong fortress with a large garrison), 8 to Deccanaura [Dekawara]: to Bolloda, 10 (this is a fort held by the Mogols, the governor being Newlock Abram Cabras,[88] who rules over a people notorious for brigandage called Colies). to the fort of Sariandgo, 13 cos. to Radimpore (a great town with a citadel): thence through an arid and waterless desert for 60 cos to the village of Nagar Parkar; in this desert live many wild asses, stags, foxes and other wild beasts.

---

88 This route is taken from Nicholas Withington, 1612-16. The name of the governor was probably Nurulla Ibrahim Kabuli.

Thence as far as Inne [Juma], which is only half a day's journey from Tutta, the country is inhabited by savages who recognise no ruler, but plunder travellers at their will or take blackmail from them in exchange for a safe-conduct. If the king sends his armed forces against them they burn their huts, which are only made of straw, and withdraw to rugged mountains. From Parkar to Burdiano is 24 cos (the water in the intervening region is scanty, brackish and unwholesome): thence to Nuraquimiron, a small town, the road lies through a similar desert, the distance being 57 cos: thence to Gundaiuw, 10 cos: to Sarruna (a large town, with a fort, and inhabited by Rashpots), 10: finally to Tutta, 14.

[*Thatta*].—Tutta is by far the largest trading centre in India; its chief part is Loure-bander,[89] which is 3 days' journey distant from the town and possesses a commodious harbour just outside the mouth of the Indus. Insects are here far less of a pest than in the other Indian ports, especially Surate. The journey hence to the capital Lahor takes two months, but the reverse journey only one. Merchandise can also be brought on camels from the other capital, Agra, as far as Buckar on the Indus, whence the port is 15 or 16 days distant. This route is much shorter than that from Agra to Surate, but robbers render it very dangerous. The English have discovered that the mouth of that most noble river, the Indus, is 24° 38′ north of the equator: Duil (this must not be confused with Dive) is 15 miles distant. Here lives the governor of this province of Sind, in a well-fortified citadel.

[89] Lahori Bandar was a much frequented seaport of Thatta. Abul Fazl states that in the *sarkar* of Thatta no less than 40,000 boats of all kinds could be found (*Ain* II, p. 338). The port was under an officer called Mir Bandar. For the vigilant port arrangements see *Tarikh-i-Tahiri* (E.D. I, p. 277).

The Route from Lahor to Kandahar.

The following is the route[90] from the metropolis of Lahor to Kandahar: to Chack Sunder, a small town, 11 cos: to Non-Saray, 15: to Muttetay, 8: to Quemal Chan, 19: to Herpack, 16: to Alicasavan, 12: to Trumban, 12: to Sedoushall, 14: to Callixeckebande, 15: to Multhan, 12: this is a large and ancient city situated about 3 cos from the bank of the Indus: the river must be crossed: to Petto-alle, a small village, 20 cos. Here another river must be crossed, and a little further on a third smaller one, called the Lacca. The route thence lies through steep mountains and deserts infested with robbers, to Chatza [Katzia], a small fort with a mud wall, where the Mogol keeps a garrison to control robbers, though the soldiers are indeed themselves not very different from robbers. Nothing can be obtained on the way except (in a few places) a little grass for the beasts of burden. The inhabitants of these mountains are called Agwanes, and are notorious for brigandage. From Chatza to Duckee (a town inhabited by these same savages, where the Mogol has a citadel and cantonments,) is 72 cos: on this part of the way the savages sell all kinds of supplies to travellers at fairly cheap prices. To Secota (three closely-adjoining villages, situated in the shape of a

---

[90] The stages of this route are Chak Sunder, Naushera, Mopalkee Kamal Khan, Harapa, Chak Ali Shah, Tulamba, Siddhu Sarai, Khatti-churkiabadi and Multan. This is copied from the Journal of the Journey of Steele and Crowther (J P H.S., Vol. I 132, *n*. 3, see also Sarkar's *The India of Aurangzib*, p. cvii) Petoali (also mentioned by Manrique) and the Lacca river have not been identified. The route from Multan to Kandahar noticed by European travellers is the same But Manrique is more vivid and clear. The places on the route herein given are: Katzai, Duki, Secot (a parghana of three villages), then *via* the durras or defiles (Durues of De Laet) of the Khoja Amran mountains to Pesinga (Peshingaon ?), thence to Kandahar (J.P.H.S. I, 165).

triangle at the foot of the mountains), 14 cos: thence to a mountain-pass, called locally Durues, which can be held by a very few men against a great army, is about 24 cos. To Pesinga, a fort not unlike Duckee, 23 cos. From this place to Kandahar is 60 cos, through desolate mountains where scarcely any supplies can be obtained. The mountainous parts of this kingdom of Kandahar are inhabited by fierce tribes called Agwanes[91] and Petanes: their physique is strong and their colour is a little lighter than that of the Indians, but they are notorious for brigandage and atrocities, and though, through their fear of the Mogols and their zest for trading (for they are well off for cattle and agricultural produce), they are said to have begun to treat travellers a little better during recent years, yet not infrequently they seize small or ill-prepared bodies of strangers, drag them away into the recesses of the mountains, and enslave them: they even mutilate their captives to prevent their escaping.

Kandahar—Kandahar is an ancient city, said once to have been inhabited by Baneanes: the governor of the province now lives here, with a Mogol garrison of 12,000 or 15,000 cavalry, who are maintained in this place because the frontier of Persia is close at hand to the north The city is protected on the west by a steep, rugged mountain, and on the south and east by a strong wall · the suburbs are larger than the city itself owing to the crowds of merchants who resort hither and need accommodation. Grain is very abundant, but very dear owing to the crowds of strangers, and also because the

---

91 The word Afghan (having the same meaning as Pathan, *vide supra*) is a corruption of the Armenian word, Aghwan, a term originally applied to the Albanians settled in W. Afghanistan. Strictly speaking, Afghans are the dwellers in the Kandahar country and Pathans are those of the Suleiman range and its offshoots.

whole region between this city and Hispaan, the capital of Persia, is so barren that in many places not even grass can be obtained, whilst water is very scarce, brackish and unwholesome. From Kandahar to the village of Seriabe is 10 cos: to Deribag, a small village, 12; to Cushecuna, the frontier post between the dominions of the Mogols and of Persia, 8.

THE KINGDOM OF BENGAL.

The kingdom of Bengal has only recently been conquered by the Mogols and brought under their control: it is very large, being said to extend for 120 leucae along the sea-coast, whilst its breadth inland is but little less. The river Chabaris[92] (also called the Guenga and judged by many of the ancients to be the same as the Ganges) flows through the province from the north-west (according to English observers) and receives very many tributaries on both sides, but especially from the north. The province produces quantities of rice, wheat, sugar, ginger, pepper, cotton and silk: the climate is fairly healthy. The chief town is called Gouro[93] and the second Bengala[94]: both cities are finely built and rich. From the latter is named (or

---

[92] The Camberis or Chabris is the Chambal (Sans *Charmanvati*). Some travellers, descending the Ganges from the Chambal, would naturally call the river by the same name throughout (C.R., 1871, p. 96 *n*)

[93] *Gaur* It was the ancient capital of Bengal but is now in ruins, situated in 24° 54′ N and 88° 8′ E on a deserted channel of the Ganges It is in the Malda district (I G., Vol. XII, 186-191).

[94] The Italian traveller, Ludovico di Varthema (1503-8), writes · "We took the route towards the city of Banghalla which is distant from Tarnassari (Tenassrim) seven hundred miles, at which we arrived in eleven days by sea The city was one of the best that I had hitherto seen and has a very great realm." Varthema sailed up the Padma, his city of Banghalla is either Chittagong or Sonargaon. De Laet refers to the latter city. It was a large city and the provincial capital of the eastern division

perhaps from the province itself) the gulf which used to be called the Gangetic Gulf, but is now commonly known as the Gulf of Bengal. Another town is Chatigan. Tanda[95] also is a famous centre of trade: it lies about a mile from the bank of the Ganges. Banaras is a very large town, also on the bank of the Ganges. Patanow is a fine place, with broad street, though the houses are poor, being built of sods: it used to be the capital of a very large and splendid kingdom, now ruled by the Mogols. Orixa also belongs to the same province, and was an independent

---

of Bengal before Dacca was built. It is situated on one of the branches of the Brahmaputra, about 13 miles from Dacca, and was famous for the manufacture of fine cotton cloth But according to Rennell, there was a city of the name of Bengalla situated near the eastern mouth of the Ganges but the site of it has since been washed away. "Bangalla appears to have been in existence during the early part of the last century (17th century)" *Bengal District Gazetteer*: Hooghly, Chap. III, pp. 43-45; Rennell, p. 57. The best opinion now-a-days considers that by it a European traveller invariably refers to the chief port at the time of his visit. Thus the term has been applied to a variety of places: Sonargaon, Satgaon, Chittagong, and even such places as Hugly and Chandernagar (J.A.S.B, 1875, p. 182, *Ibid.*, 1913, pp 444-5). There never was a city called Bengala De Laet copying from other accounts fell into the misconception of taking it for a town of the time De Laet's account has some resemblance to that of Peter Heylin's *Cosmographie*

95 *Tanda or Tanra.* Sulaiman Kararani in 1564 transferred the capital from Gaur to Tanda. It is supposed to have been a *char* of the Ganges to the south-west of Gaur, though the name is still borne by a piece of land near Lakhipur on the Rajmahal Road. The place retained its importance till the time of Raja Man Singh. The *char* on which the town was situated has been entirely swept away by the river. It was sometimes called Khawaspur Tanda from the original name of the district in which it was situated (Rennell, p. 56; *Bengal Dist. Gazetteer* · *Malda* 4, 21-22, 99) Ralph Fitch speaks of the place as the centre of a great "traffique in cotton and cotton cloth" (E.T., 24). It disappeared into the river about 1826.

kingdom till subdued by the Pathans and later by the Mogols. The natives of this province are of subtle but depraved character; the men are notorious for thefts and robbery, the women for immodesty and vice. By religion they are Mahumetans.

THE KINGDOM OF GOLCONDA.

Musilipatnam,[96] the chief port of the kingdom of Golconda, lies on the Gangetic Gulf, 16° 30′ north of the equator. It is a small but crowded town, unwalled, with poor buildings, and badly situated, for all its wells are brackish: it was once a fishermen's hamlet but has become a port for the convenience of merchants. The climate is healthy: the year is divided into three seasons: the first of which comprises March, April, May and June, and is called summer; in these months the heat is almost intolerable, the wind itself, which blows from the west, being exceedingly hot. In July, August, September and October it rains almost continuously, and sometimes with such violence as to wash away the houses: it is to these rains however and to consequent floods that the land owes its fertility. In the remaining four months the heat is bearable. The soil is so fertile that in many places two crops of rice are obtained, and in some places three: wheat also is grown, and other kinds of grain unknown to Europeans. This kingdom is named after Golconda, its chief city, and the residence of its prince; this place is called by the Mahumetans

---

96 *Masulipatam.* It was then a great shipping centre on the Coromandel Coast. For an account of the trade of Metchlepatam see Christopher Hotton, 1676-1677. The name of the port-town is generally considered to be a variant of the vernacular term Machhli-patnam, *i.e.*, Fish-town Colonel Yule however is of opinion that the coast was called Maesolia by Ptolemy (Masalia of the *Periplus*) and the important town on it came to have the name of Masulipatam. The Dutch established a factory there about 1615, the English in 1622 and the French in 1669.

and Persians Hidrabad: it lies 28 leucae distant from Musulipatna according to the local measurement, by which each leuca is equal to 9 English miles: the journey takes 10 days. The city of Golconda is second to none in the East as regards its climate and the fertility of its surrounding district. The king has a palace here of very great size (its circumference is 9 English miles), it is everywhere surrounded with a wall: the buildings are of stone and the most important of them are gilded The elegance and wealth of the prince are very great, for he rivals the Mogol Emperor in the number of his elephants and the amount of his riches, and excels him in the size of his realm. The prince is a Mahumetan by religion, and a Persian by descent: he belongs also to the Persian sect. His family name, handed down from his ancestors, is Gotub Sha. He does not acknowledge the suzerainty of the Mogol, but merely pays him respect by sending him friendly presents each year His annual revenue is said to be 20 lacks, or millions of pagodas, a pagoda[97] being equal in weight and value to a French crown. He is the sole lord of all lands, and assigns them to his feudatories in return for large payments of tribute. There are 66 fortified castles along the frontiers and in the interior of his dominions; each of these castles has its governor (or Nayk as he is called) and garrison: they are mostly built on high craggy hills, up which there is generally only one narrow pathway; no one is admitted to them without an order from the prince. Such craggy hills are called Conda. One of the fortresses, which is called Condapoly [Kondapilli], near

---

[97] The word Pagod or Pagoda has three meanings: (1) an idol temple, (2) an idol, (3) a kind of coin, usually gold, current in Southern India. The coin was of two types—new Pagoda worth 3 rupees and old Pagoda, 100 of which went to 125 new. The coin was also called *hun* (Moreland's *From Akbar to Aurangzeb*, p 332, Appendix D.)

a city of the same name, is of huge extent and embraces in its circumference six castles built one above the other: each has its own tanks and groves (both of forest trees and of fruit trees) and its rice fields: the garrison of each is 12,000. Between this fortress and the next, which is called Condavera [Kondavir] and is 25 English miles distant, are guard-towers, placed at regular intervals, from which the guards signal news to each other in the briefest possible time by means of torches.

In this kingdom very rich diamond mines were discovered a few years ago quite by accident at the foot of a great mountain, not far from the river Christena, where the land is very rough and barren · they lie about 108 English miles from the fort of Musolipatnam. The king was in the habit of letting out these mines at an annual hire of 300,000 pagodas, on condition that all the diamonds found weighing more than 10 carats should be brought to his treasury In the year 1622 however the miners were forbidden by the king to dig any further, in order (it is said by some) to prevent the price of diamonds falling too low in consequence of the large numbers that were being found, others declare that the mines were closed because the Mogol Emperor had demanded through an ambassador that three measures of the most precious diamonds should be sent as tribute to himself; it seems more probable however that the greed of the miners has now exhausted the mines · for William Metholdy [98], the Englishman, says that he visited these mines and discovered

[98] William Methwold was sent to Surat as a factor in 1616. From Surat he was despatched to Tiku and Bantam, whence he went back to Musulipatam in 1618, in 1633 was appointed President at Surat at £500 per annum in succession to Thomas Rastell. As President he concluded the Anglo-Portuguese Convention in 1635 with the Viceroy at Goa He returned home in 1639, was made Deputy Director, which post he held from 1643 till his death in 1653 (E.F.I., 1618-21, p 1 n; L.R., Vol. V, 1617, p. 124 n.)

from those who knew what was going on, that more than 30,000 workmen were there employed on that work of avarice and greed : some dug up the soil, others carried it out in baskets, others baled out the water by a slow and laborious method, raising it from hand to hand in certain vessels (for these barbarians are almost ignorant of machinery). The miners drive shafts straight downwards into the bowels of the earth to a depth of 12 or 15 fathoms, and pour the earth excavated, which is of reddish colour with veins of yellowish or whitish chalk, over a flat space prepared for the purpose, to a depth of 4 or 5 thumbs; when this soil has been thoroughly dried by the sun, they pulverise it with stones, pick out and throw away the flints mixed in with it, and pass the remainder through a sieve ; as they do this, sometimes few, sometimes many gems are found, and sometimes none at all, in which case the time and labour are wasted. Other kinds of precious stones are also dug up in this region, but of less value. The other products of this kingdom are iron and steel. It has no gold, silver or copper mines. It also exports Bezoar stones,[99] every kind of cotton fabric, especially finely dyed and printed fabrics (in which art these people

[99] Texeira (p. 230), Manucci and Lockyer (*Account of India*, 1711, p 268) and others mention these stones. Manucci writes: "In Gulkandah is a district called Bezoar (Baizwada?) near the country of Chanda In that part goats are very numerous and in them grow the bezoar stones. It is from this place that the stones take their name It is found that these stones grow in the smaller intestines of the goat" Manucci also mentions bezoar stones extracted from the body of monkeys in Borneo (Vol III, pp. 191-92) The word is derived from *pad-zahr*, poison stone or an antidote to poison. Biron has a chapter on this stone in his book *Curiosities of Nature and Art* Fryer writes "Bezoar is tried sundry ways: As the rubbing chalk upon a paper, then rubbing the stone hard upon the chalk, if it leave an olive colour, it is good. Also touch any with a red hot iron, which you suspect because the colour is lighter than ordinarily they use to be, and

excel the other Indians, using for the purpose a plant called Chay [Indian madder] which gives a rich-coloured and very fast red dye), indigo, etc. Ships of a considerable size are also built (sometimes as large as 600 or more dolia) of excellent timber, but not as handy or as well suited for fighting as are European ships: in these ships they sail for purposes of trade to Moha [100] on the Red Sea in the month of January, returning in September or October. They also make voyages in September to Achinum, Areccan, Pegu and Tanassarin, returning in April.

The Route from Agra to Chatigan, the Port of Bengal.

From Agra the river Jemena is descended to Prague (as Rudolph Fitch, the Englishman, calls it: I have called it Halabasse above and have noted that it was once called Praye). This is the place where the Jemena loses itself in the Ganges: from Prague [Prayag] the Ganges (which here begins to be a very broad stream) is descended as far as Bannaras, a large town, whose inhabitants are heathens and hardened idolaters: from Bannaras one proceeds to Patenaw (there are many towns in between these two, and many tributaries flow into the Ganges). Patenaw is a large town, oblong in shape: in the neighbourhood there are said to be many gold mines: the houses are of moderate size, mostly built of mud and thatched: but the streets are quite wide. From Patenaw one proceeds to Tanda in the province of Gour in the kingdom of Bengal:

if they fry like resin or wax, they are naught. Sometimes they are tried by putting into clear water, and if there arise upon them small white bubbles, they are good; if none, they are doubtful." (Fryer II, p. 141).

100 Mokha, 13° 20′ N. and 48° 20′ E., was the busy port of the Red Sea. The *Periplus* writes of the port of Muza as being crowded with Arab ship-masters and sailors and heaped with bales of merchandise, trading with Barygaza (Broach). It was a slave mart also.

Tanda is one leuca distant from the bank of the Ganges, for the river here often overflows its banks and floods the neighbouring fields · finally one reaches Chatigan, a fine town 23° north of the equator and one leuca distant from Ugeli (or Porto Piqueno as it is called by the Portuguese). Not far distant from this port is another called Angeli [101] in the province of Orixa, whose capital (also called Orixa) is six days' journey distant from Chatigan.

The Province of Multan.

The province of Multan is very large, and remarkably fertile: it is well situated for purposes of trade on account of the three rivers which pass through it and which join not far from the capital. The city of Multan or Moltan is 120 cos distant from the royal city of Lahor it is on the trade route from Persia through Kandahar to the provinces of India. The three rivers mentioned above are the Ravee, the Bahat (or Behat) and the Sind or Indus , their current is swift. The chief products of the province are sugar (great quantities of which are conveyed in boats down the Indus to Tatta and in the opposite direction to Lahor): also nut-gall, opium, sulphur, linen and cotton goods (in great quantities) Many camels are also reared here , and the skill of the inhabitants in building arches is famous.

101 Hijjili An old village in the Midnapur District at the mouth of the Rasulpur river The original site has long since been washed away. It was the centre of an extensive salt manufacture Cargoes were also landed there for transport up the Hugly. For Satgaon, *vide ante, n.* 85.

CHAPTER II.

AN ACCOUNT OF THE CLIMATE AND SOIL.

[THIS chapter contains an account of the seasons, the prevailing winds, Indian grains, cattle, horses, camels, wild beasts, trees (especially the toddy palm), flowers, rivers—the water of the Ganges is considered the most pleasant and wholesome, hence the Emperor has this water brought to him in bottles wherever he goes and drinks it alone—, tanks, wines, fishes, indigo (and the methods of treating it), spices, assafœtida, opium (and the *post* made from it), salt-making, sugar, etc.]

CHAPTER III.*

THE CHARACTER, CUSTOMS, INSTITUTIONS AND SUPERSTITIONS OF THE INHABITANTS.

The inhabitants and natives of Indostan were formerly heathen and profane idolaters (or, to call them by the common name, 'Hindoi'): but after the conquest of Temirlane they became mixed[1] with Mahumetans. Many Persians and Tartars also live here, also Abyssinians and Armenians, and members of almost all the races of Asia and also of Europe. There are amongst them even some Jews, who are generally held in contempt. The inhabitants are of stature equal to that of Europeans, and are generally erect and well-built; for few or none are found who are bent or hunch-backed. Their complexion is brown or olive-tinted: their hair black but not curly. They dislike a white complexion, saying this is the colour of lepers, of whom there are many among them. Most Mahumetans, except the priests whom they call Moloes [Mullahs], shave off the beard, but leave a moustache: they shave the whole head except a tuft[2] around the crown, which they leave in order that Mahumet may pull them up to heaven by it. All of them bathe frequently, and anoint themselves with precious ointment or oil.

Dress, etc.—The clothes, both of men and women, are made of cotton cloth on almost the same pattern, *i.e.*, a tight tunic, with a belt round the waist, coming down to the knees, under this they wear breeches which come down

---

* The materials of this chapter are mostly taken from Pelsaert and Terry. De Laet gives a bowdlerized version of Pelsaert's Section 12, The Manner of Life.

1 Bernier says: 'The country contains hundreds of Gentiles to one Moghul or even to one Mahometan' (p. 209).

2 Evidently he is speaking of the Hindus, especially Brahmans.

to the ankles: their feet are bare except for open sandals, which can be easily taken off when they enter a house: for their floors, according to their condition in life, are carpeted either with valuable rugs, which are made in India no less skilfully than in Persia, or with some cheaper covering, upon which they sit cross-legged, like tailors, when they are talking or eating. On their heads they wear a fine cotton wrapping, called a sash [turban-cloth], either white or coloured: when paying respects to their superiors they never take this covering off, but bow low, touch the ground with the right hand and then place it on the top of the head to indicate that those to whom they thus pay their respects may even tread on their heads. In greeting an equal they grasp the beard and in turn utter their good wishes in well-chosen phrases, such as *Greeb-a-Nemoas* [*Gharib-nawaz*] which means I pray that you may be upheld by the intercession of the poor.

The Mahumetan women do not come out into public unless they are poor or immodest; they veil their heads and draw the hair forward in a knot from the back; those who are rich adorn themselves with many jewels: some pierce one of the nostrils in order to be able to wear a gold nose-ring ornamented with gems when they so desire. They suffer much less than other mortals in child-birth: for not infrequently they bear a child at the end of a day's journey and on the next day ride forward carrying the infant in their arms.

The houses of the inhabitants are generally low and flat-roofed: they have many windows to admit the air: these are unglazed. The more important edifices are built of brick or hewn stone: both in town and country the houses are surrounded by many trees, so that when one sees a city from a distance it seems more like a series of groves than a city. There are no inns in which board is supplied to travellers: but in the larger cities and towns there are buildings called Sarays, not inhabited, but in which travellers can obtain accommodation, though it is necessary to supply one's own beds, furniture and cooks, as also the tents which one uses in places where there is no Saray The poorer people, both men and women, ride on horses, donkeys, mules and camels, or sometimes in carts, which hold only two or three and are drawn by oxen: these are only closed in when women are riding in them, in which case they are entirely enclosed· the oxen are looked after as carefully as horses, and are so well trained to their work that they can do 20 miles a day. The richer people, and the nobles, ride on elephants, or in Pallancas, as they are called, which resemble the litters used by the ancients and are carried by porters.

Hunting, etc.—Indians are extremely fond of hunting and hawking: their hunting dogs are similar to ours, but smaller: they also tame leopards for hunting purposes; these follow the quarry with great bounds. They show great cunning in catching water-birds; for they take the skin of a bird of the same kind to those they wish to catch and stuff it so skilfully that it seems a real bird: they then immerse themselves in the water up to the neck, cover their heads with the sham bird, and thus make their way into the flock of wild birds, which they catch by seizing their feet from below the water.

There are also clever archers who skilfully fashion small bows out of buffaloes' horns, and arrows out of light reeds which they carefully dry for the purpose: with these they can kill birds even on the wing. At home they are very fond of the game of chess. They also use playing-cards, but these are very different from ours. They enjoy looking on at boxing-matches and at conjuring-shows given by snake-charmers, who carry their snakes about with them, and even allow them to bite them. They greatly enjoy the tricks of apes and monkeys which abound in innumerable quantities in India; they are white in colour and exceedingly agile; they hide in birds' nests in a very extraordinary way. In each of the larger cities and towns markets are held twice daily, once a little before sunrise and again a little before sunset; almost everything is sold by weight. During the heat of the day the people sit at home: the richer sort have servants who fan them with large leather fly-flaps and thus cool the air: they also have medical attendants who massage their arms and other members—a very common practice in the east, designed to stimulate the circulation of the blood. Praise must be given to the faithfulness of the Mahumetans and heathen servants who look after foreign travellers so well that they can journey in perfect safety in all directions: they accompany their master on foot and equipped with arms: their wages are quite low, for they only receive some five shillings a month, in addition to their food. The Indians are also extremely devoted to their parents, preferring to die of famine themselves rather than that their parents should suffer hunger. Some, amongst both Mahumetans and heathens, are of remarkable courage and audacity, notably the Baloches or Boloches, who inhabit the province of Haiaca [Hajikhan] on the borders of Persia, and the Patans in the province of the same name in the kingdom of Bengal. Amongst the various sects of heathen there is only one nation, the Rasboots, infamous for brigandage. these Rasboots plunder travellers without distinction and cruelly put them to death: they are however very brave soldiers. The other inhabitants of these regions are cowardly, and love quarrelling rather than fighting. So that the king is in the habit of saying that one Portuguese is better than three Indians, and one Englishman or Dutchman[3] better than two Portuguese.

[3] Terry writes: "One Portugal will beat three of them, and one Englishman three Portugals." This statement, in passing through a Dutchman's hands, has got an additional word inserted!

Shipping.—The ships which make the annual voyage from Surate to Moha on the Red Sea are of huge size, but are carelessly built, and, though they carry many guns, cannot defend themselves properly. Each of them sometimes carries as many as 1,700 men, who sail not only for purposes of trade but in order to proceed to Medina and worship at the tomb of Mahumet. Those who have once performed this pilgrimage are afterwards called Haggei, *i.e.*, Saint. The ship generally sails in the month of March and returns about the end of September in the following year: the voyage could indeed be accomplished in as short a time as two months, but in the rainy season such fierce hurricanes occur in the Indian ocean that navigation is attended with the greatest danger. The ships bring back from Moha hardly anything but gold and silver.[3a] Metals are also imported from other regions, and it is a capital crime to re-export them. All gold and silver, whether minted or unminted, is melted and refined and coins are then struck which bear an inscription in Persian characters recording the name and greatness of the king: for the gold and silver used for the coinage are unalloyed.

Language.—The language of the common people is peculiar to themselves It is quite easy to pronounce, and is written from left to right, in the same way as our languages. The language of the educated classes is Persian or Arabic, but these classes are not numerous, owing to the lack of books and manuscripts, of which they have few: yet their character and industry seems to show that if they could obtain education they would excel in every branch of learning. They have several of the smaller

3a Partly owing to her geographical position and partly owing to her being the supplier of luxuries to the civilized world, India was, in the words of Bernier, an abyss of gold and silver. Even as early as the first century A.D. Pliny lamented the drain of gold into India

works of Aristotle (whom they call Aplis[4]) in Arabic : they are well acquainted also with the teaching of Avicenna[5] who was born at Samarcand under Temirlane.

Diseases.—The common diseases of India are dysenteries, fevers (the best cure for which they hold to be fasting) and venereal complaints, which are exceedingly common. They are very fond of music, and have many instruments, both string and wind, but they are ignorant of true harmony. They compose verses of similar quality, and write annals. They are very fond of Astronomy, for the king trusts so implicitly in astronomers that he will enter upon scarcely any undertaking without first consulting them as to the auspicious or inauspicious character of the day.

Religion.—To turn to questions of religion and superstition · according to Texeira the inhabitants of India are divided into Mahumetans and Heathens ; but two-thirds of them really hold the same religious opinions, although almost all the Heathens follow the sect and teaching of Pythagoras : for they believe in the immortality of the soul, which they regard as receiving reward or punishment through transmigration into another body. They hold that after death the soul passes into the body of some other animal, either bad or good according to the manner of life it has led · thence again it passes to another condition either better or worse, and so on ***ad infinitum.*** This is the reason for the great veneration they show for cows. Their lawgiver Ramak [Rama] earnestly recommended them to worship cows : and so indeed they do, as if they

---

[4] Sir William Foster in annotating the corresponding passage of Terry states that the writer probably had heard Aristotle referred to as *al fallsuf, i.e.*, the philosopher. It may be that the European writers confused Aflatun (Plato) with Arastu (Aristotle).

[5] Bou Ali Sinna. The precocious and versatile genius of Bokhara who wrote on medicine, law and metaphysics. Born 370 A.H., died 428 A.H.

were divine, because they are gentle and useful beasts, which if well treated (as they believe) are destined to receive souls whose deeds have been good. In addition to these they have many other absurd opinions. Owing to this belief in transmigration they treat all living beings, birds as well as ground-animals, with the greatest kindness, never killing or eating them, because they hold that human souls have migrated into them; so much so that in the city of Cambevat which the Portuguese call Cambayet and Cambaya, there is a public hospital in which sick animals of every kind are cared for (though they care little or nothing for sick human beings). Great sums are expended in consequence of this extraordinary superstition: for instance, when I was in India (says Texeira) a certain heathen Banēan celebrated the marriage of a bull and a cow with such extravagance that he spent on it 10 or 12 thousand ducats; some indeed say 30,000; but this I doubt.

Castes, etc.—In the kingdom of Guzerat the inhabitants have various rites and sects, and you will hardly find a family, strange to say, of which all the members hold the same opinion, some eat meat, others do not; some eat meat, but do not slaughter the animals themselves; others only eat certain animals; others only fishes; others only milk and vegetables, many never eat red spinach, which is a common vegetable in those parts, because they believe that it contains blood, to shed which is sacrilege, many do not eat conserves because sugar is refined by means of the blood of sheep. They are also extremely particular with regard to times and hours, thinking it sacrilege, for instance, to take food after sunset. They show their exceptionally superstitious nature in the zeal with which they observe their diabolical ceremonies. The inhabitants of Guzerat are called by the common name of Vanean, which the Portuguese have corrupted into Banean. Their families and sects are almost infinite in number, but three are held to be more important than the others, *i.e.*, the Lonkah,[5a] Mexery [Maheshri] and Baman. The first two of these are distinguished by the fact that the Mexery worship idols whilst the Lonkah do not, but recognise one God as the beginning and end of all things, and they worship Him; but they practise intermarriage and take their food together. The Baman, whom the Portuguese and Dutch commonly called Bramenes, sacrifice to the idols in the temples and preside at marriages, etc.; some of them live on charity, but may not eat or drink in the houses of Baneanes. In the middle of the kingdom of Guzerat they have a large city called Bysantagar, around which are many villages in which about 30,000 Bramenes live. They used to be poverty-stricken, but have grown extraordinarily rich by agriculture and rearing animals. They have only one wife, though they are allowed two (which the Baneans are not allowed), but if the wife dies they may not marry a second; when the husband dies the widow may marry again; other sects have the opposite rule. None of these sects may slaughter animals or shed blood. The above is taken from Texeira.

The Reysbuth, Rasboots, or Raspoothes (for various authors spell the names in different ways) have lived for many centuries on the border between India and the adjacent regions. They are heathens. Their arms are the javelin, the sword, and a small shield made in the fashion of a beehive, so that they can carry in it drink for their camels and grain for their horses, which are very strong and agile and are never shod. They learn to ride in their earliest youth and are very warlike, brave and well-trained in fighting. When her husband dies, the widow of her own

---

5a Prof. Hodivala informs me that Lonka is the name of a Gachha among the Jainas, other Gachhas being Kharatara and Tapa (T. J. I. 437, 454). Lonkas are Shwetambaras. Bysantagar (down below) is Vishalnagar.

free will leaps upon his pyre and is burnt up, together with his corpse, as is a well-known fact.

The Hendowines [Hindus] who live to the north of Asmere in the direction of Mutta,[6] are also heathen, but their customs differ from those of others, for they eat both flesh and fish. They say their prayers naked and take their food within a ring which they think it sacrilege for others to enter. They load their women from earliest youth with rings of gold, brass and iron; they consider ivory ornaments the most comely for the arms. The heathens who inhabit the realm of Golconda receive their religion with implicit faith from their priests, whom they call Bramenes, although these can give no other account of that religion except that they have received it for many centuries from their forefathers. They believe that long ago there was only one God, who afterwards appointed certain mortals, who were distinguished for their miracles or for the sanctity of their life, to be half-gods; they dedicate their temples or pagodas to these half-gods and worship them in whatever fashion they please. They believe in the immortality of the soul and transmigration, in accordance with which superstition they refrain from slaughtering any animals They are careful not to commit theft or murder but are much given to fraud and deceit. Polygamy is permitted but is not much practised, except in cases of barrenness.

Poverty.—The condition of the common people in India is very miserable. In the first place the artisans, who are very numerous, can rarely rise to a higher station, for fathers generally teach their children the same handicraft which they themselves practise: nor is one piece of work done by a single worker, as with us, but by a number. Their daily pay is very small, perhaps 5 or 6

[6] Presumably it refers to Mata Devi of Bhawan, near Kangra.

Taccas,[7] *i.e.*, 4 or 5 Dutch stuferi. The whole family eats together of one dish, which they call Kitsery [Khichṛi]. It is made of peas and a little rice, which are mixed with water and cooked till the vegetables and grains have absorbed all the water : they eat this dish hot, generally in the evening with a little melted butter poured over it. During the day they chew these same peas or some other kind of grain. Their huts are low, built generally of mud or turf, and thatched. They have very little furniture, only a few earthen vessels ; there are two beds, one for the man, the other for the woman ; their bedding is scanty and thin, suitable enough in the great heat, but of little use when the weather is bitterly cold : however they try to combat the cold by building a fire in front of the house, of dried cow-dung, which occasions a horrible smell and intolerable smoke in their towns and villages : they never light a fire inside their houses.

Servants.—There are huge numbers of servants and slaves, for there is no one of any account who does not keep several of them. These servants are well trained to their work whether indoor or out-of-doors. They stick so closely to their own task that they think it sacrilege to touch the work of another servant even with one of their fingers. They are distinguished by their names as well as their duties. The Seluidares[8] only care for horses : the Billewani for the carriages and carts in which one travels : the

---

7 30 Taccas = 24 Stivers = Re. 1.

8 The word seems to be Silahdar, man at arms. The Silahdars formed a part of the cavalry introduced by Adil Shah (1534-1557) and afterwards adopted by the Mahrattas. Silahdars in history came to mean horsemen who supplied their own horses Here the word is used in a secondary sense. The different classes of servants are : *Silahdar*, *Bahlwan*, *Farrash*, *Sarban* and *Mahout*. Zanteles stands for Jellabdars, of whom an interesting account may be found in Monserrate, p. 212, *n*. 296. Mr. Moreland in annotating the corresponding passage of Pelsaert says that the

Frassi for the tents and curtains which are used both at home and on journeys: the Serriwani for the camels: the Mahauti for the elephants: the Zanteles or runners (who wear feathers on their heads and carry two cymbals hung from their belts, which they clash as they go) can cover 25 or 30 cos in one day. The diligence of these servants is useful to their masters, but often results in ruining their character through laziness. This is specially so in the case of the governors of provinces and towns: for if they are detected in laziness with regard to announcing what is going on in their districts, they lose the king's favour and are degraded and deprived of their posts. It would be tedious to enumerate all the other kinds of servants. Their pay is small, for they receive only 3 or 4 rupees a month. The total earnings of some are slightly larger, for they buy scarcely anything for the use of their masters without demanding a little for themselves from the seller. Their masters know all about this, but do not realise that it means that they themselves have to pay more. The merchant-class is a little better-off, except that if they have amassed any wealth, they must keep the fact quiet, otherwise they are in great danger from informers, who bring charges, either false or true, against them before the nobles, so that the wretched merchants are squeezed like a sponge, not without danger to life itself.

The Nobles.—The nobles live in indescribable luxury and extravagance, caring only to indulge themselves whilst they can, in every kind of pleasure. Their greatest magnificence is in their women's quarters (or Mahal), for they marry three or four wives or sometimes more: each

---

tsantal may represent Chandal or Santal. I differ. The remark about *tsantal* is no doubt reminiscent of a passage in Fa-hien to the effect that the Chandal, as outcaste, had to strike a piece of wood as notice of his approach.

of these wives lives separately in her own quarters with her handmaids or slaves, of whom she has often a large number according to the dignity or wealth of the household: each wife receives a monthly grant from the husband for domestic expenses, such as furniture, clothing, jewels, etc.: these grants vary according to the wealth of the husband and his love for the wife in question. The houses of the nobles are fairly large, with many halls and rooms. They are only of one storey, and the roofs are generally flat, so that the evening breeze may be enjoyed. In the courtyard they have a tank and trees to mitigate the heat. No lime is used in making the walls, which thus easily lose their uprightness and do not last long: sometimes they are lime-washed and then covered with many coats of a plaster made of quick-lime, milk, gum and sugar: this is then polished till the walls shine like a mirror. Little furniture is used except in the women's apartments, where one may see a great quantity of gold and silver vessels. In the men's rooms, especially the sitting-rooms called Diwan-Gana [Diwan-Khana], Persian carpets are spread, seated on which they receive visitors. The greeting (called the *selam*) given by an inferior is a low bow coupled with the placing of the right hand on the head: the greeting of equals is a bow only. Visitors when admitted are seated in order of precedence on either side of the host; in conversation they are very modest and polite (you would call them past masters of good manner): they never talk loudly or gesticulate: if they have to say something to one person which they do not wish the others to hear, they cover their mouth with a fold of the mantle so that they may not breathe the breath of the other. When they have accomplished the object for which they came, they go away again, except special friends and guests of the host, or members of his family, who remain till he rises or goes to a meal. The guests at a meal sit on a carpet spread on the floor: the cup-bearer (or Zattersu,[9] as he is called) places before each guest a round dish and a portion of food (this is generally very rich, cooked with a quantity of melted butter, and seasoned with a little spice). They do not use napkins, and eat with their fingers only: it is considered bad manners to use the left hand or to lick the fingers. They drink nothing till they have finished eating. The above is the most usual method of life in India.

---

9 *Safrachi* as suggested by Mr. Moreland. Prof. Hodivala suggests *Sharbatdar* which occurs in *Akbar-nama* (Vol. III, 1147) and which Beveridge renders as Butler.

CHAPTER IV.

THE POLITICAL AND CIVIL GOVERNMENT.

The Emperor of India is an absolute monarch: there are no written laws: the will of the Emperor is held to be law. Once a week [on Tuesday] he takes his seat on the tribunal, and hears patiently all causes that are brought before him, both civil and criminal, and pronounces a judgment on each, which is final. Capital punishment is generally inflicted before his eyes, and with great cruelty, whether in the capital city or wherever he is holding his court. In the provinces legal decisions are made in the same manner by the governors[1] in virtue of their delegated authority, or Firman as it is called, which gives them absolute power of life and death over their subjects. Judgments are given, both by the Emperor and by the governors, chiefly in accordance with allegation and proof, and the cases are disposed of with the greatest despatch. Those found guilty are punished with severity, being either beheaded, hung, impaled, or thrown before elephants and other wild beasts, according to the nature of their crime. The king shows himself to the people thrice every day, once after sunrise from a window called Jarneo, [*i.e.*, Jharokha] which opens to the east above the gateway of the audience chamber: he is then greeted by the people with the cry *Padsha*

---

[1] It appears from here and elsewhere that the provincial governors could not inflict capital punishment unless specifically authorized by the Emperor. Thevenot writes in connection with Surat. "The King reserves that Power to himself, and therefore when any man deserves death, a courier is despatched to know his pleasure, and they fail not to put his orders in execution so soon as the courier comes back." (Thevenot, III, p. 19). How the guilty were put to death is given in the text. Terry mentions that dogs and snakes were used for the purpose.

Salament, i.e., Long Live the King. He shows himself for the second time at midday, when he appears at the window to watch contests of elephants and other beasts. Towards evening he shows himself for the third time at another window opening westward (called the Durbar): when the sun sets he retires, amid the beating of drums and other instruments and the shouts of the people. On each of these occasions audience is given to any one bringing a written petition. From 7 to 9 in the evening he holds a private conference with his magnates in a most beautiful hall called the Guzelcan. The chief ministers of the court, and also of the Empire, are the Treasurer, the Chief Eunuch (who is also Master of the Court), the Secretary, the Master of the Elephants, the Guardian of the Tents and the Guardians of the Wardrobe and the Jewels. There is also a Governor of the Palace called the Cutwall. There are similar officers also in all the chief cities and towns, who perform the duties of city-governors. There are also governors of prisons, called Cadeae [Kazi], who imprison all bankrupt debtors and sell their goods and even the debtors themselves and their children into slavery. Other princes carry on the business of government in private, but in India all the affairs of the state are discussed in public: not even that which is decided in secret council can be kept quiet, for all that the curious need do is to give a small bribe to the secretaries of the council. No one who has a request to make from the Emperor can gain audience without a gift, which he accepts whatever is to be his decision on the case in question. He frequently even returns such gifts when he does not like them or in order to extort large and better ones.

For the rest, the government is purely tyrannical, for the king is the sole master of the whole kingdom, and gives estates at his will to his subjects, or takes them away again. He often also compels the magnates to change their place of residence together with the lands allotted to them. Those of smaller fortune, and the common people, are plagued by being compelled to change the land they hold often every half year, for the king will either resume their land itself, giving them poorer land instead, or will take land from one man and give it to another. Hence it comes about that the whole country is carelessly cultivated.

The condition of the peasants is such that they have to approach the chief man of their village (who is appointed by the king) and declare to him what land, and how much, they intend to sow, or where they will pasture their flocks and herds. When the crops ripen and are reaped, the royal officials are called, who take for the king's use about three quarters of all produce, leaving for the wretched peasant only one quarter, so that sometimes they get no advantage from their labour and expenditure. Nothing, or very little, is paid by the peasants for the right of pasturage.

CHAPTER V.

THE ROYAL COURT AND THE CITADEL OF AGRA.

The citadel of Agra, a most magnificent work, and easily the first amongst the buildings of the East, is situated on the bank of the river Gemini or Jemena. It is three or four miles in circumference and is surrounded by a very fine and strong wall of hewn stone, with broad ditches and drawbridges. It has also an earthen rampart, with redoubts, within which are the excellently-fortified walls with their gateways. The entrance to the citadel lies through four gateways: one of which looks to the north, and is defended with huge guns: the second looks to the west towards a public market which they call the Basar (this is called the Cichery [Kachahri] gate); within this, and opposite to the gate, is to be seen the Casi or tribunal of the Emperor, where he hears all cases: near to this are placed three bronze mortars of huge size. Opposite this tribunal is the Cuchery or hall of the Emperor in which the chief Wasir resides, who superintends all revenue work, all imperial permits and diplomas, and all other documents of that kind; of all of these he keeps copies. Within this gate is a street, bordered on either side by buildings and ramparts, about a quarter of a leuca long. At the end of this street is the third gate, which leads to the king's Darbar, and is always closed and secured by chains: no one is allowed to enter by it on horseback except the king and his children. This is the southern gate, and is called the Drowage [Darwaza] of Achabar. within it are the quarters of the prostitutes, of whom some hundreds live here and are supported by the king: they have to be ready in their due order to dance and sing before the royal family whenever they are bidden to do so by the king or his concubines.

The fourth gate looks down on the river: it is called Dersone [Darshana or Gate of Vision], and leads into a most beautiful courtyard on the bank of the river: the king looks down into this every day when the sun rises, and himself greets the sun: the nobles gather here to greet the king, and take their stand on some rising ground: the other Hadys, *i.e.*, horsemen, and the common people, stand in the courtyard. The king shows himself here also at noon, when he looks on at the Thamasha, *i.e.*, the contests of elephants, lions, buffaloes and other wild beasts, which take place every day except Sunday. On Thursdays[1] the king not only looks on at these contests, but also at the cruel executions of condemned criminals.

But to return to the third gate. This leads on to a most spacious courtyard, surrounded on every side by open halls, in which the generals and captains keep guard, according to a certain order, for a week at a time: these halls are called the Atescannæ [Yatash-Khana] and the order of mounting guard is called Chockees [Chauki]. A little farther on one enters, through a barrier, into an inner courtyard, to which none except nobles and other distinguished persons are admitted, the common people being kept out by the guards by means of cudgels. On passing the barrier one sees opposite the king's Durbar, or throne, before which is a small area enclosed by railings and roofed with canopies to keep out the sun's rays: above this is a balcony in which stands the king's throne; no one can approach this unless summoned, except the royal princes and the chief Vezir and two servants called Punkawas who fan the king and keep off the flies. No one is readily admitted within these railings

1 Terry says that their day of rest is Thursday. I think it should be Tuesday, the day of Mars. Thursday was Jahangir's lucky day.

except the leaders of 400 or more horsemen. On the opposite side of this courtyard hang small golden bells[2] which are set in motion by those who complain that the king's subordinates have failed to do them justice: they thus gain audience of the king himself and bring their complaints before him: but such a proceeding is attended with great danger, lest the said subordinates' decision be adjudged well-justified. The king daily comes forward to this place

---

[2] This was the famous Chain of Justice of Jahangir: "I ordered them to make a chain of pure gold thirty *gaz* in length and containing sixty bells. Its weight was six Indian maunds. . . . . One end they made fast on the battlements of Shah Burj of the fort at Agra and the other to a stone post fixed on the bank of the Jumna." (T.J., I, 7) It may be admitted that only in cases of grave and palpable injustice were men found plucky enough to pull the chain; but it would be doing injustice to the Emperor to dismiss this expedient as 'a piece of silly make-believe.' Very adverse comments have been passed on the Mughal administration of justice in the 16th and 17th centuries. Penalties inflicted were no doubt severe and, in some cases, inhuman. But in all accounts, indigenous and foreign, royal anxiety for securing justice can be perceived (Monserrate, 209-10; Bernier, 263); the machinery provided for the same is not open to much criticism; the judicial procedure had more than one good feature. Bernier concedes that injustice was due to abuse of royal authority (p. 225) and to corruption of judges; and that this corruption was not possible in all cases (p. 237). Those who abused royal authority seldom escaped punishment (H.J., p 117).

Institutions and their working must be judged by the ideas of the time. A comparison with England, a country advanced for the 17th century, does not leave an unfavourable impression. The apparatus of justice—*e.g.*, the Jury System—certainly differed. But when it is remembered how judges used to intimidate the jury (*e g.*, Scroggs, CJ., in Carr's Case, 1680) the system suffers a good deal in practical utility. The vivid pages of Macaulay have made us familiar with the doings of the Bloody Assize after the revolt of Monmouth. Compare them with the actions of Jahangir after the parallel rebellion of Khusrau—both are equally horrible.

between 3 and 4 p.m. Many thousands of people enter the courtyard and take up their position according to their dignity and precedence. He stays here till evening hearing cases and listening to despatches from the various provinces, which the Wazir reads to him. His horses and elephants are here brought before him and are tested by certain servants, to see if they are in good health.

In the inner citadel are two high towers which can be seen from a great distance : they are sheathed in the purest gold : one of them stands above the women's apartments, the other above the treasury.

On leaving the Durbar the king repairs two hours later to another gallery which looks down into the inner courtyard and adjoins the women's apartments (or Mohol, as they call it). None but the magnates are admitted here, and these only on giving the password, which is imparted to them each new moon. Here the king drinks a certain number of cups of wine, of a certain definite size. Not infrequently he becomes inebriated, and sometimes decrees horrible punishments against condemned criminals when in his cups. From this courtyard a pathway leads to a most lovely garden, and to a barge in which he crosses the river to a garden on the opposite bank.

Into the inner halls of the palace none enter but eunuchs. here the emperor's concubines have each her apartments: they are protected by a strong guard, and if any of these guardsmen does anything amiss, the royal concubines decide how he shall be punished and see that the punishment is duly inflicted.

The Nauroz.—There are two annual festivals which are celebrated by the court with special pomp, *i.e.*, the New year and the Emperor's Birthday. The first of these is kept on the new moon before the beginning of the year (in India the year is held to begin in March) : they call this festival Nourous or Norose[3] in imitation of the Persians: this word means 'the Nine days' although the festival now lasts for 18 days. In the middle of the courtyard before the king's Durbar a throne is erected standing four feet above the ground: this is enclosed on all sides with very valuable curtains, so that a square space is formed 56 feet long and 43 feet wide, which is roofed with costly awnings: the floor is covered with precious Persian carpets. Into this enclosure are admitted all the magnates and persons of high dignity, except the chief ministers of the court, who occupy another enclosure close to the throne. The throne itself is square, and is of wood skilfully inlaid with pearls; a most costly canopy protects it, hung from four columns covered with silver, and adorned with a fringe on which are strung the most splendid pearls. From this fringe hang apples and pears made of pure gold, hollow within. The king sits on cushions adorned with many pearls and most precious gems: the rest of the courtyard is filled with the tents of the magnates, who rival each other in wealth and magnificence, and display here whatever treasures they possess. The emperor is in the habit of going to the tent of each in turn and of taking thence whatever he likes best. Then he takes his seat and awaits the presents which each must give him. There are also certain places prepared for the queens, from

[3] Nauroz was a much-enjoyed festival introduced from Persia by Akbar and abolished by Aurangzeb But his successors revived it, and Shahzada Ali Gohur did not omit to celebrate it even during his luckless Behar expedition in March, 1759. It was New Year's Day, and not Nine Days festival. The number of days for which it was observed was not the same at all times. Jahangir observed the 19th day with the greatest pomp. Vivid descriptions may be found in many books (T.J., I, 47-49, Manrique, J.P.H.S., Vol. I, 92-94). The fancy fair, when the Emperor and the inmates of his harem haggled with the ladies of noble houses who kept stalls, is sometimes omitted (Bernier, p. 272).

which they can see what is going on, but without being seen. On these days the emperor shows himself to the common people from the Durbar, and receives gifts from everyone. At last near the end of the feast he distributes small gifts and pensions to the courtiers and magnates who have deserved them well: and he increases the dignities[4] of some.

The Emperor's Birthday.—The king celebrates his birthday[5] as follows. A good part of the day is spent within the palace in jesting and play: the king then proceeds to his mother's palace (if she be still alive) attended by a retinue of the highest nobles, all of whom offer splendid gifts to the queen-mother according to their wealth and position. The king then comes back to the court for a drinking-bout, after which he proceeds to a beautiful room where he weighs himself in a golden balance against gold, silver, precious stones, all kinds of grain, and so on. His weight is carefully noted and compared with that of the previous year. On the next day the king distributes all the above things as alms to the poor (or as others say, to the Bramens), but the gifts which he receives from his courtiers far exceed in value these against which he is weighed, though they are estimated to be worth £10,000 sterling. In the evening of the same day he scatters amongst the crowd of principal courtiers hollow almonds made of a mixture of gold and silver, and amongst the inferior courtiers newly coined rupees.[6] For a good part

---

[4] e.g Jahangir conferred on the Prince of Mewar the rank of 5,000 *zat* and *suwar* (March 1615)

[5] He was weighed twice—once on his lunar and for the second time on his solar birthday Roe describes the solar weighing of 1617, Sept. 1 (See *Ain.* I, 266, and J.P.H.S., Vol. I, 95-98).

[6] Presumably *nisar*. Jahangir says in T.J., that the *nisar* was equal to one quarter of a rupee, and the commonest specimens are of that value; others are half the value of a rupee and others only one-eighth.

of the night he drinks, till sleep and wine overcome him. Sir Thomas Roe, Ambassador of the King of Great Britain to the Mogol, thus describes this weighing of the emperor:—"I was led into a spacious and beautiful garden, in the middle of which a tent had been pitched: in this there was hanging a pair of scales made of gold and adorned with various kinds of jewels around the edges of the pans: the chains by which the scales were suspended were of gold, with silken bands besides. all around were the nobles seated on precious carpets and awaiting the king. He arrived weighed down, rather than adorned, with a great number of jewels and most precious ornaments, he seated himself with crossed legs in one of the pans of the scales. In the other pan were placed first of all several bags of silver: and his weight was observed to be that of 9,000 rupees, which is about £1,000 sterling. Then bags were brought full of gold and jewels. Next various pieces of cloth-of-gold and silk and cotton pieces, together with spices and other goods also, tied up in packages Lastly grain, melted butter, etc. They say that these food-stuffs, and also the fabrics, are afterwards given to Banianes, but I saw nothing [7] like this done. However all the silver is kept for the poor, and is bestowed upon them by the king himself every evening of the following year in a very gracious manner. Having been weighed in this fashion, the king ascends his throne, and scatters amongst the magnates and nobles, from great basins, nuts, almonds and other fruits so cunningly made of thin sheets of silver that I should think a thousand such gifts would not weigh 60

[7] Manrique gives the reason when he says: "All the things used in the last weighment, so they say, are presently distributed among the Bramenes and poor Baneanes, but so secretly that no one sees it, except those who give it and receive it, because although Heathen Barbarians, they understand how necessary it is that charity, which is done for the love of God, should be made in secret in order to be meritorious." (J.P.H.S., Vol. I, 96.)

rupees. Certainly a number of these gifts which I kept for myself, and which weighed 20 rupees, filled a large basin; so that I do not reckon that the king distributed that whole day more than £100 sterling. He spent the night in drinking with the nobles."

All the nobles of the empire owe their titles to the emperor and receive promotion from him alone. The nobles and magnates take precedence and have their income reckoned in accordance with the number of their horses: the highest number allotted is 12,000 horses: of this grade there are 4 nobles, in addition to the sons of the emperor and the empress: there are other grades ranging from 12,000 horses to 20. Not that the nobles must actually keep so many horses, but the king assigns to each noble an estate large enough to enable him to obtain from it an income sufficient to support so many horses, at a rate of £20 sterling annually for each horse. So that the total amount of income granted by the king amounts to a very great sum. When these nobles die, everything granted to them by the emperor, and also all that they have acquired by their own industry, is given back to the emperor, just as all rivers discharge themselves into the sea. The king generally confers the horses and furniture of the dead noble upon his widows and children, together with some title of dignity. Suppose the husband or father has held the post of commander of 5,000 horses or more, the emperor will perhaps confer 1,000 or 1,500 on the son, giving more later, or taking some away, in accordance with his deserts. The favour of the king can be gained best by rich gifts, and the nobles rival each other in trying to please him in this way.

CHAPTER VI.

MONEY, THE METHOD OF COUNTING, AND WEIGHTS.

The following are the different coins:—the pice or Peysa is of copper, each weighing 12 drams: three of them are equal to an English penny: the rupia is of silver, and is generally worth 2 shillings and nine pence in English money, but sometimes only 2/2. Large amounts are reckoned in Lacks or Lecks, which word signifies 100,000; the Crou or Carora is 100 Lecks and the Areb 10 Crous. A silver massa is 14 rupiae [?]; and 1,150 massae are 100 Toli; 10 Toli of silver make one Tolus of gold, according to Hawkins. Thirty copper Tackae make one rupia. In the port of Surate Spanish coins are in common use, eight regales being there reckoned equal to five mamudie: these mamudie are silver coins of the province of Guzarat, made of very impure silver: each one is worth 30 copper pice. Full-weight English shillings are there worth 33½ pice. The Batman is a weight of 55 pounds or 82 English pounds. The Maune is 55 English pounds or 50 Dutch pounds: smaller than this is a weight called a Ceer or Keer, which weighs 30 Persæ or 1¼ Dutch pounds. It must however be noticed that these weights are sometimes changed by the emperors, and their use varies from time to time In the days of Achabar the weights and measures were one-fifth less than in the time of his successor Selim, and both standards are still in use.

NOTE

De Laet's remarks on coins and weights are rather brief and may be supplemented so far as space permits. A Paisa or pice or dam or fulus was a massive copper (or brass) coins (copied from Sher Shah's issue) weighing normally 323·5 grains, for according to the *Ain*, one dam weighed 1 tola 8 mashas and 7 ratis. De

Laet is approximately correct in fixing the weight of a paisa at 12 drams. But a Gujarat pice was half a dam or pice of N. India (*i.e.*, 40 dams = 80 Gujarat pice = Re. 1). When De Laet says that the Peysa = 12 drams (Avoir.), he means the full Dam; but when he says Pice 3 = 1*d.* he means half Dam (Re. 1 = 27*d.* = 81 Peysa). Akbar fixed the exchange rate between rupee and dam at 1 = 40. The rate remained practically unaltered till 1626 Mr. W. H Moreland writes: "Neglecting minor fluctuations, the rupee, which, at any rate up to 1616, was worth 80 pice (or 40 dams), from 1627 onwards was worth 60 pice (or 30 dams) or a little more or less" (*From Akbar to Aurangzeb*, p 184) The standard weight of a rupee was 175 grains or so, Jahangir for some time increased it to 220 grains. Rupees of several denominations (and weight also) were in circulation of them, chalani (*i e*, current) was accepted as the standard, older issues were worth less as also worn coins. In L.R, Vol II, p 87, we read "Roupies Jangers (Jahangiri) of 100 pisas which goeth four for five ordinary roupies of 80 pisas called cassanes (Khazane) and we value them at 2*s* 4*d* per piece, 100 challenes (chalani) of Agra which goeth for 83 pisas." All foreign writers have noted the purity of rupees, and even foreign impure silver coins on their arrival in India were melted and re-issued in pure form (Thevenot, III, Chap IX, p 18) Terry writes. "This coyne is more pure than any I know, made of perfect silver without any allay They call their pieces of money roopies, of which there are some of divers value Their silver coin is either made round or square but so thick that it never breaks or weares out." De Laet has mentioned copper Tackae, 30 of which went to a rupee Tanka is a denomination employed by Akbar in his *Ilahi* copper coinage after the 40th year. Prof Hodivala is of opinion that De Laet's Tackae must be dams and not real Tankas or double dams. Lane Poole says that Tanka is used vaguely for dams of 315 to 327 grains as well as for double dams

The normal relative value of copper to silver was 72·4 to one; of silver to gold 9 or 10 to 1 Hawkins notes: "A tole is a rupia challany (*i e.*, current) of silver and ten of these toles are the value of one of gold" Gold coins are not mentioned by De Laet; and consequently the question need not be raised

Of local coins of S Gujarat, Mahmudis (Pers *Mahmudi*, 'fortunate') are mentioned (*vide supra*, Note on Mulher) Five Mahmudis made two rupees; and later when the price rose, nine were exchanged for four. Terry writes: "Both the former (rupees) and these Mahmudis are made likewise in halves and quarters; so that three pence is the least price of silver current in the country." Of Spanish coins, rials of eight were equivalent to two rupees

Regarding weights and measures, a few remarks will suffice. Apart from local variations, the usual scale of goldsmith's weight was: 8 ratti is equal to 1 masha, 12 masha is equal to 1 tola; and 1 masha is equal to 15·5 grains The batman is a Turkish weight used by some as equal to an Indian maund But the Indian maund varied widely Prinsep in his *Useful Tables*, p 77, notes four different species of the genus of Indian maund Akbar fixed the seer at the weight of 30 dams, that is to say, Akbari maund (of 40 seers) weighed 1,200 dams, each of 323 5 grains, or about 55 lbs. English. But in 1620 Jahangir, on the advice of a religious mendicant, ordered that a seer in future was to weigh 36 dams. When De Laet wrote (1631) this still prevailed, and that is why he says that in Akbar's days the weight was ⅛th less

I do not know what De Laet means when he says, in this as well as in the next chapter, that a masha was 14 rupees

CHAPTER VII.

THE WEALTH OF THIS PRINCE.

The wealth of this prince can be estimated : firstly, from the size of the territories which he controls (these form an empire larger than that of Persia and equal to, if not greater than, that of Turkey) ; secondly, from the fact that no one in his empire has any possessions at all except what he holds through the prince's liberality and at his pleasure, and that he himself inherits the property not only of all dead magnates, but also of inferior persons, taking for himself as much as he pleases of what they leave : and thirdly, from the immense gifts which are bestowed upon him every day not only by his subjects but also by foreign princes. Sir Thomas Roe gives a noteworthy instance of this latter source of wealth. When he was acting as ambassador from the King of Great Britain to this prince [Jahangir], 36 most beautiful elephants were sent to the prince by the king* of Bisampor (or Visiapor) : two of them were adorned with gold chains weighing 400 pounds of pure gold : two of them had similar chains of silver, and the rest of brass. He also sent 50 sumptuously caparisoned horses, and necklaces of pearls and Balas rubies estimated to be worth ten lacks of rupees. In brief, no one can approach him without some present.

On the death of Achabar, grandfather of the prince now reigning [Shah Jahan], his treasures were carefully counted, and were found to amount in all (including gold) silver and copper, both wrought and unwrought, together with jewels and all manners of household commodities to 34 Carores, 82 Lacks and 26,386 rupees (*i.e.*, to Rs. 348,226,386$\frac{3}{4}$) : of this total Rs. 198,346,666$\frac{2}{3}$ was in specie of all descriptions.

---

* See *Tuzuk* Vol. I, pp. 400 *et seq.*

As regards, first, the gold specie : the king had struck some coins of a weight of 100 Toli (1,150 massae) each, and some of a weight of 50 and 25 Toli. The total of these reckoned in massae, amounted to 6,970,000 massae : and at a rate of Rs. 14 to each massa were worth in all Rs. 97,580,000¾.

In the second place, the silver coins, rupees of Achabar, amounted to Rs. 100,000,000.

In the third place, the copper coins (Peysa* or pici) numbered 230,000,000 and (reckoning 30 tacki per rupee) were worth altogether Rs. 766,666.

Thus the total comes (as given above) to Rs. 198,346,666¾. The jewels of all kinds, together with the wrought gold and silver and the Chinese vessels (known commonly as Porcellane), were reckoned at Rs 93,820,068 — namely : Diamonds, rubies, emeralds, sapphires, pearls and similar gems, Rs. 60,520,521 · wrought gold, for example beautifully worked necklaces, of all kinds, Rs 19,006,745 : golden furniture, all kinds of gold plate, golden images of elephants, horses, camels and similar animals, Rs. 9,507,992 : wrought silver (cups, discs, candelabra, columns, and other plate and utensils of all kinds), Rs. 2,225,838 · dishes and all kinds of furniture made of brass, Rs. 51,225 , fine porcelain vessels of all kinds, Rs. 2,507,747 total Rs. 93,820,068

Cloth of gold and silver, from Persia, Turkey, Guzerat and Europe : various kinds of silken goods muslins from Bengala and other provinces, were estimated at Rs. 503,252 : pavilions, curtains, canopies, carpets and whatever is needful for adorning a palace and for travelling, Rs. 9,925,545 : Woollen cloth from Europe, Persia and Tartary Rs. 503,252 : Books written by great authors beautifully bound, to the number of 24,000, estimated at

---

* De Laet means Dams; Paisa = ½ Dam. Elsewhere (pp. 150, 172) De Laet says Re. 1=20 Tackas; but here 30 Tacki.

Rs. 6,463,731 in value: cannon and bombards, cannon-balls and gunpowder, and other munitions of war, Rs. 8,575,971: Armour, shields, swords, daggers, bows, arrows, etc., Rs. 7,555,525: Horse-trappings, golden and silver bridles and other equipment of cavalry, Rs. 7,555,525 · Cavalry tunics decorated with gold and silver, cloaks of all kinds and royal armour, Rs. 5,000,000: total Rs. 56,059,649.

If the whole of this treasure be estimated in our coinage (reckoning one and half florins or a thaler to a rupee) it comes to 522,339,579 gold carolines or florins.

William Hawkins, the Englishman who lived for some years in this prince's court, thus estimates the treasure of Selim who succeeded his father Achabar.

Gold specie.—There are 60 Lecks of Serofins [Ashrafi] of Achabar, each of which is worth Rs. 10: there were 20,000 coins of another type, each of which is worth Rs. 1,000, 10,000 of another coinage, worth Rs. 500 each: 30,000 of another, each weighing 20 toli; 20,000 of another, each weighing 10 toli: and 50,000 of a coinage issued here by the king's order, each weighing 5 toli.

Silver specie.—There are 13 Crou (1,300 Lecks) of rupees of Achabar · 50,000 coins of silver, each weighing 100 toli: one Leck of coins weighing 50 toli each: 40,000 coins weighing 30 toli each: 20,000 weighing 10 toli each: 25,000 weighing 5 toli each; two Lecks of the coin called Savoy, each of which weighs 1¼ toli: one Leck of the coin called Jagaries, five of which weigh 6 toli.

Gems and necklaces.—One and a half Batman of uncut diamonds of different sizes (none of which however weighs less than 1½ carats), a Batman is equal to 82½ English pounds*: 2,000 Balas rubies of different

* The meaning is this: 1 Batman = 55 lbs., so 1½ Batman = 82½ lbs.

sizes and condition: 12 Batman of pearls of all kinds: 2 Batman of rubies of all kinds: 5 Batman of emeralds: 5,000 gems from Cathay, called Eshime, [Jade], and greatly valued: corals, topazes and other less precious gems, an almost infinite number. There are 2200 swords, with handles and scabbards adorned with most precious jewels: 2000 daggers (of two kinds): 500 drums used by persons of quality when hawking (some of them of pure gold, adorned with jewels): 2,000 very valuable decorations for the head, in which feathers are fixed: 1,000 golden and silver saddles, studded with jewels: 25 very long lances (called Teukes) covered with gold and with jewelled points (these are carried in front of the prince when he goes forth to war, instead of banners): 20 umbrellas or canopies for protection from the sun (the prince alone may use these): 2 golden thrones: 3 silver thrones: 100 silver chairs: 5 golden chairs: 200 most precious mirrors: 100 wine-jars, very beautiful, and richly jewelled: 500 cups, all made of precious jewels. 2,000 Batman-weight of silver plate (dishes, bowls, jugs, etc.); 1,000 Batman—of gold plate: an uncertain number of rings containing all kinds of precious stone.

This is the total amount of the treasure kept in the one fortress of Agra: the king has other treasures at the fortresses of Gualiar, Narvar, Ratambor, Hossier and Rougtaz [Rohtas]: but by far the biggest is in the fortress of Lahore.

The same person narrates that, whilst he was at the court, the king inherited the property of a certain Hindu prince called Roga Goginat, whose treasure included 60 Mauns of gold, in addition to gems and necklaces (a Maun weighs 55 pounds).

The daily outlay at the court of Agra amounts to Rs. 50,000 spent on feeding the elephants and other beasts, and on the royal food and dress, etc.: in addition to this Rs. 30,000 are spent daily on the royal Harem.

No surprise should be felt at the fact that the prince possesses such huge treasures, when it is remembered that his ancestors seized the property of so many rulers, who had held power in India for so many centuries: and that they handed on these treasures to their descendants very greatly augmented. Also, although there are no gold or silver mines here, yet great quantities of both gold and silver (especially the latter) are imported: and re-exportation is prohibited.

Sir Thomas Roe, who has already been frequently mentioned, says that he heard from the Governor of Patan that a certain fixed amount of treasure was sent every year by the Governors of provinces or towns to the royal treasury: the Governor of Patan himself contributing in this way 11 Lecks of rupees each year Dutch writers record that the royal tribute from Surat, when Cancanna was governor, amounted every year to 2 million mamudei, though it afterwards fell to 900,000 (or according to others to 1,400,000). The same writers record that the annual tribute of the town of Brochia amounted to 1,260,000 mamudei (672,000 carolines): and that of the town of Brodera to 400,000 mamudei (213,333 florins). The Dutch also say that the total tribute of the kingdom of Guzerat amounted to 150 tons in gold, the chief part of this being derived from agriculture.

NOTE.

The inventory of the treasure of Akbar is an unique contribution of De Laet. It agrees with the later accounts of Mandelslo (1638) and Manrique (1649). So far no doubt has been entertained about the veracity of the account, on the other hand Vincent Smith fully endorses it (J.R.A.S., 1915, 231-43). There is a minor slip: 230 should be 23 millions of copper or bronze paisa. De Laet is sometimes careless about zeroes.

The Agra treasure calculating at 2*s.* = Re. 1, amounts to £19½ millions and at 2*s.* 3*d.* to £22. There were six other treasure-cities: Gwalior, Narwar, Rantambhor, Asirgarh, Rohtas, and Lahore. Smith assumes that these cities had some 18 millions sterling between them. The total comes to 40 millions. The purchasing power of money was six times greater than the pre-war rate, say, in 1914. In other words, the total brings us to the huge figure of £240 millions sterling Henry VII (who died in 1509) left £1,800,000 in bullion and was considered rich. Henry VIII debased the coinage and Elizabeth left behind a debt of £400,000 and a huge number of farthingales!

The Mughal treasure must have increased considerably during the peaceful reigns of Jahangir and Shah Jahan Mandelslo says that Shah Jahan had a store of about 3,000 millions of rupees. This is not credible, but it can safely be assumed that the treasure of Shah Jahan vastly exceeded that of Akbar

The most interesting item in the stores other than coins, kept at Agra alone, is the large number of books of great authors, 24,000 volumes. Each volume cost Rs 270 or £27 to £30 The calligraphist's charge was very high

Regarding the tribute from Gujarat, my friend Mr. S. Kumar of the Imperial Library suggests that De Laet means 150 gold tons, one of which is equivalent to 100,000 guilders. A guilder is a silver coin worth about Re 1-4 as

CHAPTER VIII.

THE MILITARY FORCES OF THIS PRINCE.

A list of all the Ommerauwı and Mancebdari who after the death of Achabar became the servants of king Selim Ziahaengier :—

	Horses	Total horses.
8 Ommerauwı supposed to provide (though they very rarely do so)	5,000	40,000
9	4,500	40,500
25	4,000	100,000
30	3,500	105,000
36	3,000	108,000
42	2,500	105,000
45	2,000	90,000
51	1,500	76,500
55	1,000	55,000
58	700	40,600
80	500	40,000
73	400	29,200
58	350	20,500
72	300	21,600
85	250	21,250
150	200	30,000
242	150	36,000
300	100	30,000
245	80	19,600
397	60	23,820
298	43	11,900
240	30	7,000
232	20	4,640
110	10	1,100
741	4	2,946
1,322	3	3,966
1,428	2	2,865
950	1	950
7,281	Total	1,068,248

The king also himself owned in all 32,234 elephants, horses, camels, dromedaries, mules and oxen as follows :—

Elephants (great and small, male and female : amongst them 100 of very great beauty) . .	6,751
Arab, Persian and Turkish horses of every kind	12,000
Dromedaries and camels	6,223
Mules and oxen for drawing carts	7,260
Total . .	32,234

I have obtained the above information from a fragment of an Indian history.

The following draught-animals belonged to Selim while the Englishman Hawkins was at his court—

Horses	12,000	(4,000 Persian, 6,000 Turkish, 2,000 Kissimenan or Tartar).
Elephants	12,000	(5,000 full-grown males, the rest females or young males)
Camels . .	2,000	
Draught Oxen . .	10,000	
Mules . .	1,000	

Hawkins makes no mention of dromedaries: hence the total of draught-animals comes to 37,000.

Among the elephants are 300 of exceptional beauty, which the prince himself makes use of. These are adorned with precious housings, and are looked after with the greatest care by the nobles, to whose keeping they are handed over, together with a yearly sum for their maintenance. They are fed on flour, sugar and butter, and the food of each costs Rs. 10 per diem.

In the year 1609 [?], when the king's son set forth for the war in the Decan, his army contained 20,000 cavalry and 300 elephants, which the prince himself had brought. Asaph Caun brought 3,000 cavalry and Emersee Rostein, king of Kandahar, 1,000 picked troops. Raja Mamsengo brought 10,000 cavalry, all Raspoots, and nearly 1,000 elephants.

In the year 1610 the royal army in the Decan consisted of at least 100,000 cavalry, with a huge number of elephants and camels · the whole number of the force then engaged on the campaign was estimated at 500,000 or 600,000 men. Further statistics might be given, some of which the reader may find in the Fragment of History below

The royal forces have very many guns, though (as it seems) these were made long ago; many of them are of exceptional size and are drawn by elephants. They make skilful use of bombards, which they light with matches: they themselves manufacture excellent gunpowder. They also use javelins, shields, swords, bows and arrows. Their swords are curved like a sickle, but are so badly tempered that they break rather than bend Hence there is a great demand for European swords They have some horsemen who are armed with sword, bow, quiver, shield and bombard, all at once, and also carry a javelin in the right hand. Yet they have scarcely courage enough to attack a stranger equipped with only one of these weapons, for the Mogols themselves are said to be an effeminate race. Amongst the Hindus the Raspoots are famed for their martial prowess, an instance of which you shall read in the Fragment of History. They lead out to battle the greatest number of men they can possibly gather together. They advance furiously to the attack; but owing to their ignorance of military discipline and tactics, they either become victorious or are routed very quickly, and battles generally result in immense slaughter. They are called to battle by a brazen drum or trumpet.

When the king himself goes on a campaign, his personal camp, which they call Leskar, covers an immense space of ground. The speed with which this camp is pitched is extraordinary. In a space of four or five hours so many tents are pitched that a town seems to have sprung up. They are arranged so as to form various broad streets in which everything needful for human life is sold The gradation of rank is so rigidly enforced that everyone in these camps, from the greatest to the least, knows precisely at what distance to pitch his own tents from those of the king (which are called the Atasykanna). No one may come nearer than the range of a bombard-ball to the royal tents, and no one is allowed inside except by special summons. Sir Thomas Roe says that in 1616 he saw a royal camp which stretched over a space of not less than 20 English miles in length, and in places three cos in depth.

They are almost powerless on the sea , and hence the Portuguese exact tribute from them in their own ports for goods which they take from those ports : and compel them (including even the magnates and the king's sons) to purchase for huge sums safe-conducts from the Spanish king, commonly called *pasports*

For these *pasports* 3,000, 4,000, 5,000, and sometimes even 8,000 mamudei are demanded.

NOTE

It is gathered from the *Ain-i-Akbari* that there were 66 grades of mansab on paper, and half the number in practice. Of these, the first three from 10,000 to 7,000 were reserved for the princes Officers of exceptional merit were sometimes promoted to the coveted list, *e.g* , Raja Man and Mirza Shah Rukh. For the remaining 30 commands, we may compare the list of Abul Fazl with that of De Laet.

Grades of Mansab in the *Ain*	Number of Officers according to the *Ain*	Number of Officers according to De Laet.
5,000	30	8
4,500	2	9

Grades of Mansab in the *Ain*	Number of Officers according to the *Ain*	Number of Officers according to De Laet
4,000	9	25
3,500	2	30
3,000	17	36
2,500	8	42
2,000	27	45
1,500	7	51
1,250	1	0
1,000	31	55
900	38	0
800	2	0
700	25	58
600	4	0
500	46	80
400	18	73
350	19	58
300	33	72
250	12	85
200	81	150
150	53	242
120	1	0
100	250	300
80	91	245
60	204	397
50	16	0
40	260	298
30	39	240
20	250	232
10	224	110

The list of Abul Fazl from 400 downwards includes only the officers living at the time of completing the *Ain*, whereas the list from 500 upwards includes all the officers dead or alive who were ever promoted to the commands during the reign of Akbar. De Laet's list includes the officers holding the mansabs at the time when the book from which he copied was written The total number according to Abul Fazl was 1,800 and according to De Laet, 2941. The one refers to the reign of Akbar and the other to the reign of Jahangir The difference in the number is well explained by this quotation from the *Ain* "But scarcely a day passes away on which qualified and zealous men are not appointed to mansabs or promoted to higher qualities. Many Arabians and Persians also come from distant countries and are honoured with commissions in the army whereby they attain the object of their desires" (*Ain*. I p. 527).

There was no grade below ten De Laet gives a list of Ahadis, *i.e.*, gentleman volunteers. It may thus be expressed in technical terms :—

Chaharaspahs	741
Sihaspahs	1,322
Duaspahs	1,428
Yakaspahs	950
	4,441 Ahadis.

CHAPTER IX.

THE KINGS OF INDIA

(A list of Indian kings, taken from D. Garcia's Treatise on Aromatic Plants. Book II, Chapter XXVIII.)

About 300 years ago a certain powerful ruler of the kingdom of Dely conquered a great part of India within the Ganges, and took from its Hindu chieftains the realm of Balaguate or Balagate About the same time certain Moors drove out the rightful Hindu rulers of Camboya, who are called Reisbuts, and occupied that region.

Those who are now called Venezaræ are believed to be descended from the chieftains of Balaguate: other inhabitants of that region are called Colles: these, together with the Reisbuts, still maintain themselves by plunder and rapine . the former extort tribute from the Decan, and the latter from the kingdom of Camboya, as the price of immunity from their raids: the neighbouring kings have never been able to subdue them, for they are very bold and warlike: though indeed the said kings, being greedy of money, permit them to plunder to their heart's content and with impunity, so long as they hand over a part of the booty to themselves

The kingdom of Dely lies far from the sea to the north it extends as far as Corason, quite a cold region, not less subject to frost and snow-storms than our (part of) Europe. This kingdom was conquered, more than thirty years ago, by the Mogors, whom we call Tartars (I have seen the brother* of that king of Dely welcomed with great honour at the court of Sultan Bhadur, king of Cambay). But some

* Sultan Alam Lodi.

time afterwards the same kingdom was reconquered from the Tartars by a knight, who having become enraged with the king of Bengala because he had killed his brother, made a plot against the said king, killed him and then conquered the kingdom of Dely and many other kingdoms, so that he came to be esteemed the most powerful monarch of his time. This knight was at first ruler of a mountainous region near the kingdom of Bengala: his name was Xaholam, *i.e.*, king of the world. A more exact historical record can be compiled concerning his exploits than concerning those of Tamirlan, whose name has been corrupted by Europeans to Tamberlane, or Tamilangue (the latter is the more correct form, for Tamir was his own name, and 'langue' means lame, which he was).

When the king Xaholam conquered the Decan and Cuncam, being unable to maintain control of so large extent of territory, he returned to his own part of the country and committed the government of the newly-acquired regions to a relation of his own, a man who always took great interest in foreigners, for instance in Turks (inhabitants of Asia Minor or Natolia, as it is now called), Rumes (inhabitants of Thrace), Corasones (who are supposed by many to be Arii) and Arabs. He divided his kingdom into provinces which he put under governors. The coast-district which extends from Angediva to Cifardam (a distance of 60 leagues) was given to Adelhan (called by Europeans Idalcam). The district from Cifardam to Negatona (a distance of 20 leagues) was given to Nizamalue. These two were the only governors set up in the Cuncam, which is a coast-district reaching back to the mountain range called Guate. This range is of a considerable breadth and in many places very high: beyond its top is, strange to say, a very beautiful plain. In Persian *Bala* means a peak and *Guate* a mountain: hence the province beyond the mountain is named Balaguate, *i.e.*, the district at the top of, or beyond, the mountains. The Governors of Balaguate are Imodmaluc (who is called by Europeans Madrumalue), Cotalmoluc, and Verid. All these governors, except Nizamaluc who is said to have been born in the Decan, were foreigners by race. Nizamaluc is said to be the son of a Tocha [Tujjar, merchant] of king Daquem this king had relations with the Tocha's wife, and hence it comes about that Nizamaluc declares that he himself has royal blood in his veins, while the other governors appointed by the king are slaves bought with the royal treasure.

In process of time all these governors became weary of serving the king, and hence concocted a plot, in accordance with which they seized the provinces they governed, captured king Daquem, and handed him over as a prisoner to Verid, one of the governors, at Beder, capital city of the kingdom of the Decan

Certain Hindus also were concerned in this plot, for instance Mohadum Coia, and Veriche* they gained large districts with several rich cities Mahadum for example became master of the city of Visapor (now the capital of Idalcan), Solaporr and Paranda (though Nizamaluc afterwards took these away from him) Veriche retained his own province which is contiguous to Camboya and the province of Nizamaluc

One of the conspirators was an ancestor of the present Adelham he was by race a Turk he died in the year 1535: he was always very powerful, yet the Portuguese twice captured from him the city of Goa, which is 200 leagues distant from the mouth of the river Indus, which the natives call Diul

* Makhdam Khwaja (?) and Bharju, Raja of Baglana (T. J I. 221, 411) The Rajas of Baglana had the title of Baharji (Bharju of T. J.). Often their personal names are not mentioned (*Supra* p 10.)

16

The grandfather of the Nizamaluc now reigning (the father of my friend and pupil who has bestowed upon me more than 200,000 *pardavi*, and offered me a salary of 40,000 a year if I would stay with him for a few months every year— but I refused the offer) died in the year 1509.

Imadmaluc or Madremaluc was by race a Circassian and by birth a Christian he died in the year 1546.

Cotalmaluc, by race a native of Corason, died in the year 1548. Verid, by race a Hungarian and by birth a Christian, died in the year 1510

GENEALOGY AND LIST OF THE KINGS OF INDIA BELONGING TO THE LINE OF TEYMUR LANE (FROM PETRO TEXEIRA'S '*Persians*').

The Great Mogoles who at present rule India boast that they are descended from that most renowned of all Tatars—the Emperor Teymurlane, who himself was a descendant of Chinguis Kan, king of Tartary, and was not of low birth, as some writers have wrongly reported.

The exploits of Teymurlane are well enough known, but Texeira in his account of Persia gives an account of the descent of Teymur Lane from Chinguis Kan and also of the descent of these kings of India, who are commonly called Mogoles from Teymur Lane.

Chinguis Kan died in the year 1228 [1227] and left four sons, of whom the eldest was called Tuxy Khan [Tushi or Juji Khan] and had been given by his father the kingdoms* of Dast Kapecha, Ross and Abulgar; but he died six months before his father. To his second son, Chagotay Khan, Chinguis Kan had given control of the kingdom of Maurenahar, Aygot and Koarrazm. He died in the year 1242 [1241]. The

* Dasht-i-Kipchak, Russia and Bulgaria.

third son, Oktoy Kahon [Oktai Khan] succeeded his father [at Karakarum]. The fourth, Tuly Khan, received from his father, together with some provinces, the whole of the royal treasure. He died in the year 1232. Hence Oktoy Kahon was the only one of the sons of Chinguis Khan who survived for long, although the others also had children, some of whom afterwards became kings.

Oktoy Kahon, who was a kindly and very generous prince, died in 1242. He was succeeded by his son Gayuk Khan in 1246 [in the interval the young prince's mother Turakina had been Regent], who only ruled for one year [three years] and died without issue. He was succeeded on the throne of Tartary by his relative Manchu Kahan, son of Tuly Khan, who gave to his brother Kablay Khan the provinces of Ketoo Kotan Kublay Kahon is said to have founded the city of Kanbaleck, capital of Tartary. To another brother, Vlakuh Khan [Hulaku Khan], Manchu Khan gave the provinces of Persia, he died in the year 1260 and was succeeded by his brother Vlakuh Khan, who ruled with great vigour in Persia and died in the year 1266, he divided his dominions amongst his three sons, giving Hyerack, Mozandaran and Karason to the eldest Habkay Kahon Aro (*i e.*, Armenia, Aderbaion and Tandon) to the second, Hyaxemet : and to the third Dyarbet and Rabyan (*i e*, Mesopotamia). He also had two other sons, Nicudaroglan and Targahe Khan, to whom he gave no dominions, though afterwards one of them, and the children of the other, became rulers.

Habkay Khan succeeded his father as king of Persia, and died in the year 1282. Although he had children, he was succeeded by his brother Nicudar Oglan, who after he became a Mahumetan was called Hameth Khan. He died in the year 1233 (?), and was succeeded by Argon Khan, son of Habkay Khan, who reigned for seven years and was succeeded by his brother Ganiatu Khan, who was killed by his uncle. Baydu Khan, son of Torgahe Khan, then came to the throne, but was soon also murdered, and was succeeded in the year 1296 by Gazun, son of Argon Khan, who died in the year 1305, and was succeeded by his brother Alyaptu or Sultan Mahameth ben Argon, who died in 1317 and was succeeded by his son Sultan Abusayd Baheder Khan who died in the year 1337

On the death of Abusayd the Tartar empire was divided amongst a number of petty rulers, until Teymurlan again united it Teymurlan is declared to have been a descendant of Chinguis-Khan because Carachar, who is reported to have been his ancestor, came from Tartary together with Chinguis-Kan, and was appointed by the latter Wazir to his son Chagatay Khan This position he handed on to his descendants, so that Teymar Lan was Wazir to Soyorgat Mexkhon, king of Chagatay, on whose death in the year 1370 Teymar Lan himself succeeded to his dominions by general consent

Teymur-Lan had four sons- - (1) Joon-Guyr [Jahangir] who died before his father and left two sons Mahamet Sultan and Pir Mahamet, the latter of whom Teymur wished to succeed himself in the kingdom of Gaznehen and India he was afterwards murdered by Pir-Aly : (2) Hometh-Xeque [Umar Shaikh] who died before his father (3) Mirunxa [Miran Shah] who was murdered in the year 1408 by Kara Issus the Turcimann . (4) Murzah-Xarok [Mirza Shah Rukh] who succeeded to his father's empire.

The third son of Teymur, Mirunxa, had a son Mahameth, and his son was Mirza Sultan Abusaya [Abu Said] who reigned over Badaxon, Gaznehen, Kabul, Sistan, Koarrazon. He was killed by the Persians in the year 1469, and was succeeded by his son Mirza Sultan Hameth, who lived till the year 1495. His near relative [nephew]

Mirza Babur governed under him the realm of Maurenatian, but in the year 1500 was driven out of his dominions by Xaybeck-Khan [Shaibani Khan] the Usbeq, and fled to India, where he seized power and reigned over both lands till the year 1532, when he died, leaving two sons Homayon Mirsa and Kamaron Mirsah Homayon conquered the greater and richer parts of India : his Wazir (chief general) was Xir-Khan, who turned against his master, and compelled him to fly to the king of Persia, Xa-Thamas, who gave to Homayon 12,000 picked soldiers under the leadership of Beyran-Khan. By the valour of these troops he slew the rebel and recovered his kingdom. He was succeeded by his son Gelaladin Akbar, who was still alive when Texeira wrote the above in the year 1600

From Indian Writers.

Indian writers declare (and the portraits in the palace of Lahore bear out their statements) that Babur together with thirty of his nobles came to the court of Secander, king of Delly, disguised as Kalenders (a monastic order amongst the Turks). After some time he was recognised by the king, and though his guile was manifest, was allowed to depart to his own country on condition that he undertook no enterprise against the kingdom of Delly so long as Secander was alive Accordingly Babur made no further attack till Secander was dead, but then sent his son Homayon (or as others call him, Hamoune) who drove Abram, the successor of Secander, from his kingdom.

However, not long after, there arrived from Bengala a brave warrior belonging to the royal family of Delly, who joined battle with Hamaune not far from the bank of the Ganges, defeated him, and compelled him to take refuge in Persia, whence he obtained fresh forces (under the command of Beyram), and returning not only regained his kingdom, but also greatly increased it. When this king died he left his son Achabar, who was still a youth, under the care of Beyram ; but when Achabar grew older he is said to have made away with his guardian by treachery ; his son was Caun-Canna, by far the most powerful feudatory of the Indian Emperors within recent years—so much so that he was able to bring together 100,000 cavalry However, more about these matters in the Fragment of Indian History.

The Indian writers also relate (as I find recorded in my Dutch sources) that Seer Sha, or Salim Sha, ruled over the kingdom of Hindostan after Babur He was by birth a Patan. He succeeded Himmoen Banean [Himu Bania ?] and was succeeded by Hamaun, the father of Achabar. Achabar reigned over India for 60 years and some months : and died in A.D. 1605 He conquered the kingdom of Gusurat in the 27th year of his reign, after the death of Sultan Momed the younger (who was the son of Latiff Sha, grandson of Badur, and great-grandson of Sultan Mohmed Begera, whose second son Rahia D'gie [Muzaffar II] is said to have founded the city of Brodera) The conquest of Gusurat was carried through as follows . Sultan Mamed the younger on his death left his son Modafar, who was only eleven years old, under the tutelage of Ethamet Chan [Itimad Khan] who could not control the magnates of the kingdom, and being in fear for his own life and that of his ward wrote secretly to the king of India, who then lived at Agra, setting forth at great length how he himself and the young king were in great peril, beseeching Achabar's help, and promising to hand over Amadabat, the capital of the kingdom and other towns which were under his control as a pledge of good faith. Seizing this unexpected opportunity, Achabar marched with a very large force as quickly as possible into Gusurat and occupied the capital and the other towns, placing his own men as garrisons in them, and carrying off Modafar and his tutor as captives to Agra. When Modafar was thirty years old, he grew very tired of captivity, escaped, and took refuge with a Rahia whose territory adjoined his ancestral kingdom. By his help he recovered many of the towns which were rightfully his own; but before he could consolidate his position in his kingdom, Can Canna came up with the royal forces of Achabar, expelled him without difficulty from his recovered kingdom, which he had only held for a year, captured him, and imprisoned him once more. Modafar could ill bear the disgrace, and cut his own throat, thus leaving his kingdom undisturbed in the hands of the Mogol.

PART II.

A FRAGMENT OF THE HISTORY OF INDIA, GATHERED FROM DUTCH SOURCES AND RENDĔRED INTO LATIN

BY

JOANNES DE LAET

(*Antwerp*, *1631*)

PREFACE.

Kind reader, before you begin to peruse this fragment, be good enough to notice the following points :—

Firstly : We have freely translated it from the Dutch,* believing it to be an extract from a genuine chronicle of the Mogol Empire, and have everywhere maintained historical truth

Secondly : With regard to titles, the appellation Scach [Shah] which is frequently pronounced Xa, belongs either to kings or to great princes, and is especially used by the Persians . derived from it is the title Padischach, which means supreme Prince or Scach Those whom the Turks called Emirs were chieftains and military conquerors in the empire of Mahomet, the word means "eminent persons" The title Chan or Han [Khan] (with a strong aspirate) is extremely common amongst the Persians and Tartars, who call the kings and princes even of small tribes Chan This title is rendered here sometimes by Chan, sometimes by Chanus or Ghanus.

Thirdly : With regard to the Mahometan era,† my Dutch authority declares that the year 962 of the Mahometan era corresponds to the year 1552 of our own , but this does not agree with the reckoning of Leunclavius, who declares that the year 958 of the Mahometan era corresponds to the year 1552 of our own I do not know whether the discrepancy is due to error or intention on the part of my Dutch authority

---

* Mr Moreland has recently, in *Jahangir's India*, shown that the Fragment was probably written by Pelsaert

† The Muhammadan era began in 622 A D But it is easy to convert A H into A D Three mechanical methods have been worked out The simplest is that of Dr Burgess "From the Hijra date deduct 3 p c and add 622 for the date A D." (Codrington's *Musalman Numismatics*, p 203) 962 A H began on Nov 26, 1554, and 958 A H. on January 9, 1551 Joannes Leunclavius is nearly correct. His book *Neuwe Chronica Turckischer nation* was published in 1590, *Franckfort am Mayn*

I. SHER KHAN DEFEATS HUMAYUN.

[1538-40.]

Hamayon, king of the Mogols, set out with his army from Agra for Bengal, where he soon put to flight the forces of the Pathans, and occupied the province, whose name he changed to Senethabad.[1] However he did not long enjoy the fruits of victory, for one of the Pathan kings, named Ferried Khan[2] (or T'zeer-Chan, as he preferred to be called) advanced from Nau[3] with very large forces. It is recorded that he had 65,000 Pathans in his army. He recovered the province of Bahar and the fortress of Radja Rattas,[4] and compelled the Emperor to retreat headlong

---

1 Jannatabad or City of Paradise—a name given to Gaur by Humayun when he occupied it in 1538 He remained in the 'far-away country of Gaur' for nine months (Gulbadan's *Humayun Nama*, p 134)

2 Farid Khan or Sher Khan was son of the *jagirdar* of Sasaram in Behar By a mixture of cunning treachery, praiseworthy valour and administrative talents, he revived the Afghan power in N India How he achieved this and why he changed his name to Sher Khan are facts too well-known to need repetition

3 It is difficult to identify this place. If Shahr-i-Nau, a mint town in Bengal, be meant, the acceptance of the view of Thomas and Codrington who identify it with Gaur, becomes obviously inconsistent with De Laet's statement. This can be obviated by identifying Shahr-i-Nau, the new city, with Tanda which was a big city at this time and which, a quarter of a century later, became the capital of Suleiman Kirani For Tanda *vide supra*

4 Rohtas Sher Shah took it by a ruse which has been attributed by De Laet to Akbar's officer, Muhibb Ali Khan (*vide infra*, Section XII). The Raja from whom Sher Shah captured the fort, was Hari Kishen Birkis (Erskine, II, 147) Many references to the two forts of Rohtas in Behar and in the Punjab will be found in De Laet's *Descriptio Indiæ* See also Monserrate, 71, *n.* 111, 116-117.

from Bengal to Pathana. When he reached Tziocha,[5] Tzeerchan caught him up and attacked him with such violence that he was compelled to fly to Agra, where he rallied his forces, summoned his Ommerau [Umara, pl of Amir] and magnates from the various provinces, gathered a new army, and hastened towards the Ganges. When Tzeerchan heard of this, he sent 20,000 cavalry fifteen cos ahead in order to prevent Hamayon crossing the river In the Mogol army no guard was kept, either through contempt of the enemy or through innate laziness and the night was spent in dancing and drinking. Tzeerchan, learning through spies of the carelessness of the enemy, sent on Chawas-chan,[6] with 10,000 light-armed troops. These performed a forced march of ten miles, and at the break of day fell upon Hamayon's army, which was sunk in a drunken sleep. The Mogol camp was filled with horrible din and tumult Hamayon was wakened from sleep, and finding himself unable to rally his men, who had mounted their horses and were already scattered in flight, began himself to think of escape He arrived almost alone at the bank of the river, and was guided across, swimming, by a certain water carrier [7] On the opposite bank he was lucky enough to come across the horse of some soldier who had been drowned in the river, upon which he made good his escape to Agra The enemy captured all his elephants and horses and an immense treasure. His

5 This is the battle of Chaunsa near to where the Son falls into the Ganges, on June 27, 1539 It may properly be called the battle of Chupat Ghat

6 Khawas Khan was the ablest general of Sher Shah Probably Tanda-Khawaspur was named after him

7 Gulbadan and Jauhar inform us that after the battle of Chaunsa Humayun was helped across by a water-carrier, Nizam by name; whereas after the battle of the Ganges (May 17, 1540) the Emperor swam the river on the back of an elephant (E. D. V, 113, 144). Here he was helped by Shamsuddin Muhammad of Ghazni whose wife, Jiji, became Akbar's nurse.

concubines also, together with his own and his nobles' daughters and all his other women, fell into the hands of Tzeerchan, who used his unexpected victory with great moderation, committing no outrage himself against the wives and children of his enemy, and allowing no one else to do so. He advanced however as rapidly as possible upon Agra, taking possession of numerous towns on the way.

II. HUMAYUN'S FLIGHT
[1540.]

Meanwhile Hamayon, having lost his whole army, took with him Zimlebegem,[8] one of his wives, who was pregnant, and fled first to Asmeere [Ajmir] and thence to the province of Siermel[9], where in the fort of Ammer [Umarkot] his wife bore him a son, who was afterwards named Achabar. Finding himself still in danger, Hamayon fled to Lahor, the governor of which city was his brother, Mirza-Kamerhaen [Mirza Kamran]. This man sternly reproved the timidity and cowardice of his brother, and asked him if he was in such terror of the enemy, to allow himself to advance against the Pathan army, which was now reported to have reached Tzerhind [Sihrind]. His brother's words struck shame to the heart of Hamayon. He left Lahor and fled to Cassimere, whose governor had been one of the royal Ommerau. However (unknown to Hamayon) this man had recently died, and the towns-men were plotting a revolution. They fortified not only

[8] The only possible explanation is that it is a corruption of Chuli or Juli) Begam, mother of Akbar. Her original name was Hamida Bano, her official title was Mariam Makani. But she was married to Humayun later (1541). De Laet confounds Bega or Haji Begam with Chuli Begam (Humayun-Nama, p. 218).

[9] I do not know exactly what De Laet means unless it be a corruption of Sind which was the kingdom of the Sumeras Siermal may mean territory of the Sumeras.

the city but also the mountain-passes (commonly called the Cothel[10]), so the access to Cassimere was rendered exceedingly difficult. Here the king, finding himself excluded, turned back, intending to retreat towards Kabul or Multhan. His brother Kamraon had however himself been compelled to fly from Lahor (for Tzeerchan had by now captured not only Lahor but also Multhan), and was even more enraged than before against Hamayon. He had reached Triulbeg by forced marches, and was thus ahead of the king on the route to Kabul. Moreover he had sent a letter to another brother of his, Mirza Assary [Mirza Askari], who was then governor of Kandahar, asking him to prepare his citadel for a siege and to prevent the king from entering The governor of Tatta, Chah-Hassen [Shah Husain], showed similar treachery; for when the king asked him for permission to pass through his province, he replied that if the king was thinking of going to Persia the route through Kandahar would be more convenient to him Thus perceiving that he was deserted by all his friends, the king marched towards Kandahar, but not being permitted to enter that town by his brother Assen [Askari], was compelled to leave his wife Zimlebegam and his little son, who was now a year old, together with all his baggage, servants and women, at the town of Tziauwhaen,[11] whence he himself proceeded to Persia and reached Sebistgan [Siwistan] accompanied only by Beyram-Chan [Bairam Khan] who had just brought him some picked reinforcements. When Assary learnt of his brother's flight, he shut up Hamayon's wife and little son in the citadel of Kandahar, and appropriated to himself his baggage and treasure.

The king of Persia, Sha-Thomas [Shah Tahmasp], proved to be of a very different character; for on hearing

10 Kotal or Kutal, a pass.

11 Sehwan on the right bank of the Indus

of the defeat and flight of Hamayon he wrote to the governor of his city of Herath bidding him, in case the fugitive king happened to come thither, to treat him with all possible kindness.[12] Hence when the king arrived within 12 miles of Herath, the governor himself went out to meet him, with all his Mancebdars and officers, and conducted him into the city with great magnificence, bestowing on him many horses and much valuable equipment, and ordering the other Persian officers to receive him and send him on his way with the greatest honour, wherever he might go. When Hamayon was not far from Chasbin, where at that time the king of Persia was residing, Sha-Tamas sent his own brother Mirza Beyram to meet him, together with all the Ommerau and courtiers. These conducted Hamayon to the Persian king, who embraced him, offered him his condolences and ordered his brother Beyram to serve the exile at table Beyram obeyed with the greatest goodwill, whereupon Hamayon uttered words which nearly proved fatal to him , for noticing the obedient behaviour of Beyram, he said that the Persian king was fortunate in having a brother of whose obedient loyalty he could be confident ; for he himself, although he had loaded his brothers with riches and honours, had found no bitterer enemies in his adversity than those same brothers. Hamayon's words bitterly offended Beyram ; and raging with hatred and anger he reminded his brother that when Sha-Ismael was king of Persia, Babur, the father of Hamayon, had been nothing but a gardener.[13] He even urged the Persian king to make away with the Mogol , and no doubt the advice would have been followed, had not the

12 The governor of Herat was ordered, among other things, to prepare for Humayun's use five hundred trays of meat of different kinds, besides sweetmeats; and the total number of trays of every description for him and his suite was never to be less than 1,500 daily ! (Erskine II, 278).

13 Gardening was one of the hobbies of Babur

sister of Sha-Tamas, Begem Sultana, taken pity on the exiled king, and succeeded in persuading her brother, by her remarkable eloquence and prudence, to give up his intention, reminding him that Hamayon was a descendant of Teymur and thus of kings from whom the ancestors of Sha-Tamas had received the greatest benefits. She urged him also to use his power in such a fashion as to hand it on unstained by ingratitude. The speech of his sister greatly moved Sha-Tamas, and he gave orders that Hamayon should be supplied with everything he needed for his journey, camels, horses, tents and other equipment for a campaign He also ordered Khan-Tramman, Badorgan, Khan-Couligan Narenzyn (father of Hassen Coulighan), Ismael Coulighan Wattebel, and other Ommerau and Mancebdars, to accompany Hamayon to India

With these reinforcements Hamayon marched from Chasbin direct on Kandahar, and laid siege to the city Having summoned his brother Assary to surrender, but in vain, he ordered his guns to be laid against the walls of the citadel However Assary exposed to the fire the little son of Hamayon, who was now two years old, and the siege was therefore abandoned, the king finally swearing to his brother upon the book of Mahumet that he would permit him to march out free and unharmed Assary went to his brother Kamraon, who was at Kabul, but the king followed hastily to Kabul, captured his brother Kamraon without difficulty, blinded the poor wretch [Dec 1553], and sent him into exile at Mecha, where he soon afterwards died

III. HUMAYUN'S RETURN TO INDIA
[1554]

In the year of Mahumet 960 (*i e*, 1550 A D.) Tzeerchan (or Tyechmecha), the Pathan king, died[14] in the

---

[14] Sher Shah died in May 1545 A D (952 A H) at Kalanjar. It was Sher Shah's son Islam Sbah (Jalal Khan) who died at Gwalior

fortress of Gualer, leaving a son Phero-chan who was only 12 years old. The magnates of the kingdom wished to place this boy on his father's throne, but his uncle Adelghan [Muhammad Shah Adil or Adali] who was blinded by the ambition of himself becoming king, made away with him and usurped the throne, greatly to the indignation of the magnates, who in consequence immediately rebelled in almost all the provinces. Adelghan, wishing to anticipate the revolt, set out with a very large army from Gualer to Tzhilnar [Chunar] which was then a great and wealthy town

The death of Tzeerchan and these disturbances in the Pathan kingdom quickly became known to Hamayon, who was still at Kabul Thinking that the chance had come for recovering what he had lost, he hastened with his army into India, and, no one daring to offer resistance, recovered all the towns and provinces he passed through, until he reached Tzerhind [Sihrind] where Recander-Chan Affega,[15] an old and faithful servant of the dead king, was governor Recander at once threw himself in Hamayon's way, with 10,000 horse, and offered battle However he was defeated after a long and doubtful contest, and fled with only 1,000 horsemen into the mountainous district of Changera [Kangra] Having won this battle Hamayon handed over his son Abdul Fetta Gelaldin Mahamet, who was afterwards called Achabar, to Beyramghan Ganna as

in 960 A H (Oct 1553 A D) His son Firuz Khan was set aside by Mubariz Khan or Muhammad Shah Adil, Sher Shah's nephew and Islam Shah's brother-in-law

15 Sikandar Sur Afghan His original name was Ahmed Khan Like Adil, he was also a nephew of Sher Shah His defeat at Sihrind took place on June 22, 1555. In the same year Akbar was formally made governor of the Punjab and the office of *ataliq* was conferred on Bairam Khan in place of Munim Khan appointed the year before

tutor, to whom also he entrusted the command of the whole army, ordering him to pursue Recander at speed with 10,000 cavalry. Meanwhile he himself advanced to Delli, and despatched Allan Couly, Semaran-Ghan[16] and Badurghan [Bahadur Khan] to recover the province of Do-Ab, which lies between the Ganges and the Jeminus or Semena rivers. Both enterprises prospered well, for Recander was utterly destroyed, and the Do-Ab was conquered

IV. THE DEATH OF HUMAYUN.

[Jany. 1550]

The king had resided for barely three months in the city of Delly, where he had begun to build a magnificent palace, when he lost his life For as he was descending the stairs of his palace one afternoon, he heard the voice of someone calling to prayer. He sat down, leaning on his staff ; but having recently taken a dose of opium, he was overcome with sleep. His staff slipped on the smooth steps, and he fell headlong, rolling down some 40 steps, and injuring[17] himself so severely that three days later he died. This happened in the year of Mahumet 962 (*i e.*, 1552 A D)

V THE DEFEAT OF HIMU.

[Nov. 1556]

Abdul-Ghan [Adali] heard of the sudden death of Hamayon at Tzilnar, where he was still in hiding, and

16 Ali Quli Khan-i-Shaibani who was created *Khan-Zaman* for capturing Hemu's artillery Samaran Ghan or Zamaen of De Laet refers to the title

17 This accident took place on Friday, January 20, 1556 (963 A.H) 962 A H corresponds to 1554-5 A D.

sent the commander-in-chief of his army, Couligan Hemou,[18] a Hindu of humble birth, but an energetic soldier, with 100,000 cavalry, 500 elephants, and a large amount of treasure with which to pay his men, to Delly ordering him to attack the Mogols. The prince of the Mogols, Abdul Fetta Gelal-Eddin Mahmet Achabar, who was pursuing his father's enemies amongst the mountains of Khoestan [Kohistan], together with Beyranghan and Chanchanna and most of the royal army, immediately on hearing of his father's death turned his march towards Kalanor, where he was proclaimed king by Beyranghan. Thence he hastened to Delly Meanwhile Hemou had put to flight Tourdichan [Tardi Beg Khan] who had ventured out of Delly against him In his flight Tourdichan fell in with the prince. He was received with a pretence of friendship, but was stabbed to death by a slave after a drinking-bout, by the order of Beyranghan Next the prince and his tutor summoned Alla-Koulichan and Badurghan with their forces from the Do-Ab, and ordered them to march ahead to Panipat in order to meet Hemou, who in the meantime had captured Delly The prince followed with the rest of the army, Alla-Koulighan and Badurghan met Hemou at Tilleputh [19] about half way between Paniput and Delly, and without delay offered battle. However the troops of Hemou were discontented owing to their pay being in arrears, and hence deserted their general and dispersed, so that the Mogols captured all the baggage and elephants. Hemou was wounded in the eye by an arrow during the fighting, and was forced to

---

18 He is simply known as Hemu—for some time at Delhi as Raja Bikramjit. Quli Khan is significant (Quli = slave) In spite of his being a Hindu of low origin (a grocer), he rose by dint of sheer merit He was made Superintendent of Markets by Salim Shah and Administrator-General by King Adil.

19 I am unable to identify this place According to Lethbridge it is Sonpat.

fly, but was captured and brought back by Couli-Gan Marem [Kuli Khan Mahram]. He was brought before Achabar, who had hastened up on hearing of the rout of the Pathans; at the request of Coulinghan he cut off the head of the prisoner with his scimitar, and ordered it to be fixed on the gate of Delly, a crime unworthy of a prince.

After this Alla Coulighan, Zemaen and Badurgan were despatched with a strong army into the province of the Do-Ab, to follow up the remnants of the Pathan army. They advanced to Ziaumpore [Jaunpur], along the bank of the river Thatsan [20] and reconquered the whole of that region. The prince, together with Beyramghan hastened to Agra, whence news had arrived that Allan Couligan and Badurgan had routed, with immense slaughter, the Pathans near the Sambel, where they had rallied their forces They fled first to Lachnou, where they tried the fortune of war once more, but were again severely defeated They suffered a third disaster, the worst of all, near Ziaunpore In this manner the aforesaid two generals speedily recovered the whole of Indostan between the rivers Ganges and Tziatsom.

VI EXILE AND DEATH OF BAIRAM KHAN [Jany 1561]

Meanwhile Achabar was spending his time at Agra in hunting and amusement. He learnt, however, either from his own observation or through information received from others, that Beyrangan, whom his father before his death had appointed his tutor and guardian, was plotting to seize the supreme power, and was already in great favour with the whole army. This greatly incensed the prince, who was moreover goaded on by his old nurse Maghem Anega [Maham Anaga]. Accordingly he made the following scheme in order to free himself from the power

20 The river of Chaunsa or the river on which Chaunsa stood. See below Note 27. Lachnou, as Lethbridge points out, is Lakhnor in Sambal.

of his tutor. With the permission of Beyranghan he went on a hunting expedition, attended by a numerous retinue, across the river Simmena to Ko-Heb,[21] whence his nurse, who had followed him by easy stages, conducted him swiftly to the city of Delly, in which the kings of India had for long been wont to assume the crown. Thither all the magnates were summoned from the country round; and in their presence the prince assumed the crown, and was acclaimed king by the whole of the assembled concourse On hearing of this Beyranghan sent to the king without delay the Ommerau and Mancebdars who lived near Agra, and wrote to him saying that he had never done anything except what he believed to be profitable to Achabar's kingdom he had taken no emoluments for himself, but had merely been fearful lest the prince's youth (on account of which Hamayon had given him his authority) should lead him into rash action and expose him to evil counsel: now however, seeing that the prince was wise enough to conduct things for himself, and that everything at home and abroad was in good order, he besought only one boon in consideration of his old[22] age and the health which he had lost in the service of the state, *viz*, that he might be permitted to retire to Mecha and to spend the remainder of his days there The required permission being readily granted, the good old man, with his servants and women, left Agra and took the road to Guzarat through Meuwat However on reaching the town of Pathan [Patan] he was there mortally wounded by a Pathan servant [23] of his in revenge, so it is said, for the execution of the man's

21 Mistake for Koel or Aligarh.

22 Bairam Khan was a young man in his thirty-seventh year He was born about 1524.

23 Mubarak Khan, a Lohani Afghan, whose father had been killed in the battle of Machiwara (1555). Another version is that the Kashmiri wife of Islam Shah with her daughter had attached herself to Bairam's suite and it had been arranged that the daughter

father by Beyranghan. Shortly afterwards he died. His servants, together with his son Mirza Abdul Rachiem [Abdur-Rahim] who was then 12 years old, returned to the king at Agra, who took care that the boy should receive an education befitting his station in life.

VII. THE BUILDING OF AGRA FORT.
[1565-79]

The citadel of Agra had in former days been surrounded by the Pathan kings with a brick wall, but this was now dilapidated and ruinous from age Hence king Achabar wishing to leave some striking memorial of his name, had it reconstructed in hewn stone The person placed in charge of this work was Cassemghan Mierbar,[24] a most skilful and experienced architect, who brought the stone from Tziekerrye [Sikri] (the city now called Fettipore), summoned master-builders from all the country round, and pushed on the work so diligently that in a short time it was finished.

VIII. THE SIEGE OF CHITOR.
[Oct. 1567–Feb. 1568.]

Meanwhile it happened that a certain Rasboot, named Zimetpatha,[25] relying on his courage and energy,

was to marry Abdur Rahim, Bairam's son This is said to have annoyed the Afghans

24 Kasim Khan, *Mir Barr-u-Bahr*, the head of the Admiralty and the First Commissioner of Works Muhammad Kasim was the best engineer of Akbar, he is known in history for building the Agra Fort, bridges of boats across the Jumna and some rivers of the Punjab and a road across the mountains to Srinagar. He fell under suspicion of treason with Mirza Hakim (Monserrate, pp. 80-81, *n.* 126). It was in 1565 that the order was given to construct a new fort at Agra and it was not completed till 1573. There had existed an old Hindu and Afghan fort at Badalgarh. According to Jahangir it took 15 years to construct the new fort (T J, I, p 3)

25 This disguises the names of the two leaders of the gallant defence of Chitore Jaimal and Patta Jaimal Rathor of Bednor

revolted against his master Rahja Rana, seized his fortress of Cittor, together with several neighbouring towns, and even invaded the provinces which were ruled by Achabar. (This fortress of Cittor is very strongly fortified, both by nature and by art: it is situated on a high mountain, and the kings of Delly were never able to capture it: Soltan Alaudin besieged it for 12 years, but was finally compelled ignominiously to abandon the siege.) When Achabar heard of this, he was in no way terrified by the difficulties ahead, but hastened thither with many guns and other warlike equipment, and a strong army. The siege made no progress for several months, and heavy losses were inflicted on the Mogol forces by the besieged. Hence the king, being determined to make a desperate venture, ordered the Turkish mercenaries in his army to undermine the chief tower of the fortress. This having been done, the mine was filled with a vast quantity of gunpowder, on firing which the tower was shattered to its foundations, and thus an entrance into the fortress was opened to the storming party. Tzimel Patha, perceiving that death threatened himself and his men, devised a cruel crime;

---

took command when the cowardly Rana Udai Singh fled. He was not in revolt against the Rana Neither did he devise the cruel crime of burning the women to death: it was the horrid sacrifice of *jauhar* Abul Fazl estimates that some 300 women thus perished Some scholars are of opinion that the elephants and riders (mentioned below) were not carved at the same time Akbar utilized some old black elephant statues (possibly Hindu work) and mounted upon them the sandstone effigies of Jaimal and Patta. In passing it should be mentioned that De Laet has often either jumbled two proper names into one or has separated the personal name from the title and mistaken them for two persons Thus 'Beyram Ghan and Chan Chana' refer to the same amir, Bairam Khan Khan-i Khanan, so too 'Gan Ganna and Munim Khan'. On the other hand, Zimetpatha or Tzimel Patha stands for Jaimal and Patta, Mia Soliman Lodi for Suleiman (Kirani) and Miyan Lodi Khan, his Vizier.

for he shut up his wives and the wives of the rest of the garrison, together with their children, in one place, and burnt them to death. Then he fell upon the storming parties of the enemy with the most desperate courage, till he himself and all his men were killed. As a memorial of this great victory the king had two elephants carved, on one of which was seated an effigy of Tzimel Patha and on the other an effigy of another of the enemy's generals. These were placed on either side of the gateway into the fort at Agra.

IX. VARIOUS REBELLIONS.
[1566-7.]

After this the king was informed by letters from Lahor, written by Saffetghan [Sa'id Khan] and Rajha Bagwander that his brother Mirza Mahamet Hackim had come down from Kabul and the surrounding regions, and was already besieging Lahor, hence the king must come as swiftly as possible with a strong force Without delay the king advanced to Lahor with a very great army. When he reached Tzerhind his brother, terrified by his unexpected advance, took to flight and returned to Kabul, leaving behind his camp with a vast amount of baggage and plunder. The king marched through and subdued the province of Pang-Ab, and then returned to Lahor, where he received a letter from his mother at Agra saying that Alla Coulighan Zamma[26] and Badorghan, whom he had left

[26] Ali Quli Khan Zaman and his brother Bahadur Khan were defeated at Sakrawal or Mankuwar, ten miles from Allahabad (June 1567). The village, after the victory, was christened Fathpur (Fettipore) Ali Quli had been appointed governor of the Jaunpur territory. He had also rebelled in 1565. The text refers to the fourth revolt in 1567. The invasion of Mirza Muhammad Hakim and the rebellion of the Uzbegs were inter-related: both were aimed against the Emperor with pro-Persian proclivities. It may be noted here that the revolts of 1580-81 were directed against the pro-Hindu or rather anti-Moslem tendencies of the Emperor.

in command at Lackno, had revolted and were plundering his provinces in all directions and destroying towns and villages. They even threatened Agra itself. On hearing this the king returned by forced marches to Agra, and led his forces across the river Semmena [Jumna]. The rebels were disheartened by the swift advance of the king's great army, and fled first to Lachnou and then to Karamemecpore [Kara Manikpur]. However the king's forces caught them up between Fettipore and Karamemecpore, and attacked them with such swiftness that Alla Coulighan was killed in the battle, whilst Badorghan was captured and executed in the presence of, and by the order of, the king. Thereupon Ganganna and Mounimghan [Munim Khan, Khan Khanan] were despatched to Zianpore as governors of that province, and to keep a watch upon the Pathans; for Zianpore is not far from Tscoutsa,[27] where Mia Soliman Lodi with the Pathan army was believed to be stationed on the watch for an opportunity of attacking the Mogols. The king himself returned to Agra with the rest of his forces.

X. THE FOUNDATION OF FATEHPUR SIKRI. [1569.]

On arriving at Agra Achabar was overcome by the desire for a male heir, for so far he was without a son. Hence he vowed to go on foot as a pilgrim to Assemere, to the tomb of the prophet Hoge-Mondea [Khwaja Muinuddin]. On his return he visited a certain dervish called Scheech-selim [Shaikh Salim] at or near Tzickeri (according to Leonclavius Scheiches are Mahumetan saints or priests), and told him for what purpose the pilgrimage had been undertaken. The prophet told the king that he would have three sons, and that one of the royal

---

27 Chaunsa, the then boundary between Jaunpur and Behar. Chaunsa appears under various guises (pp 134, 142, 147, 151 and 156) and is used for the place as well as for the river on which it stands.

concubines was already pregnant. She gave birth to a son, whom Cheek-Selim called by his own name Sultan Selim. Afterwards a second son was born to the king, and was named Chan Morad; and later a third, Chan Daniel. Having thus obtained his desire the king had a splendid palace built for himself near Tzickery [Sikri] and surrounded the town with a stone wall. He also gave the name Fettipore to the city, because there God had given him what he wished.

XI. THE WAR IN GUJARAT.
[1572-3]

Whilst fortune was favouring him so well, the king learnt from Ghan Azem[28] of Guzerat that Mirza Ebreham

---

28 Khan Azam Mirza Aziz Koka, foster-brother of Akbar He was a clean fighter and a witty man But his sharp tongue, short temper and intriguing nature ill fitted him for continuous enjoyment of royal favour Foster-brother and playmate of Akbar, he, in spite of these defects, retained his influence so long as that Emperor lived. Under Jahangir he was twice disgraced, but on one occasion owing to the intercession of the Zenana headed by Salima Begam and on another owing to the appearance in a dream of Akbar's spirit to Jehangir, he was restored to favour, though he never regained his former position (T J, I, 79-81, 261-69) He died in the 19th year of the reign of Jehangir (1033 A H)

There seems to be some confusion in De Laet's account of the Gujarat campaigns, the two expeditions of 1572-3 being fused into one. Moreover the death of Khan Koka (evidently Qutbuddin and not Mirza Aziz) which occurred in the other war of 1583, has been put in here Another discrepancy, though minor and even negligible, is that Ibrahim Husain and Shah Mirza fled from the battle and were not killed there, but the former soon after died in Multan

The Mirzas belonged to that dangerous class of 'royal cousins' who committed so much mischief in medieval England. The descent from Timur of the royal line may be thus noted Timur, Miran, Sultan Muhammad Mirza, Abu Said Mirza, Umar Shaikh Mirza, Babur, Humayun and Akbar The notorious Mirza line thus descended. Timur, Umar Shaikh, Baikara (or Mankara), Mansur, Baikara (or Mankara), Sultan Vais, Muhammad Sultan Mirza The last named had six sons Ulugh Mirza, Shah Mirza,

Hossen, Mirza Chan and Mirza Mahamet Hossen, who had already made hostile attacks on Indostan, had now invaded Guzerat together with other enemies of the king, and were plundering his territories far and wide. Hossen had been joined by numerous bands of brigands from all sides and was besieging Hamadabat, the garrison being hard put to it to resist the attack. On hearing this news at Tzickery, the king had a force of dromedaries prepared as swiftly as possible—beasts which can cover 60 or sometimes 70 cos in 24 hours. Mounted on these the king and certain of his most faithful nobles and friends covered the distance of 400 cos in 7 days, and encamped not far from Hamadabat. The unexpected arrival of the king, who had outmarched even the news of his approach, struck such consternation into the minds of the rebels, who were ignorant of the size of his forces, that they immediately abandoned the siege of the city and took to flight Thereupon Chan Azem and other royal generals, who up to that time had been lying hid in remote spots through fear of the enemy, came to meet the king with their forces. Being thus reinforced, Achabar appointed Chan Goga commander-in-chief, and sent him in pursuit of the rebels with 12,000

Muhammad Husain, Ibrahim Husain Mirza, Masud Husain and Aqil Muhammad The last Mirza played no part in the history of Akbar's reign, as to the activities of the others any book on Akbar may be consulted

The term 'Mirza' is a shortened form of Amir Zada. Originally it was applied to kings and princes Babur gave it up in 913 A.H (1507-8 A D) for the more dignified title of Badshah. But the title still continued to be suffixed or in some cases prefixed to the names of princes or royal scions. But it degenerated and in the seventeenth century it was applied to the more distinguished Amirs or Amirzadas when the word Amir itself had long come to mean a noble. The strangest metamorphosis came in the middle of the eighteenth century, whence it was used for a *muharrir* or clerk. For the rules of the Code of Mirzaship in the seventeenth century, see J.A.S.B., 1913, pp. 1-13.

cavalry and the speediest elephants. He himself remained in support with the rest of his forces. The battle which followed was a fierce one. Finally Chan Goga was killed and the royal forces began to waver, much to the king's wrath. He rushed into the midst of the fray, and put the enemy to disgraceful rout. Mirza Abraham and Mirza Chan had already been killed in the battle. Mahamet Hossen was captured alive, and paid for his treachery with his head. After this the fort of Suratte was easily captured, and the whole of Guzarat was subdued, Achabar then appointed some of his most faithful generals to administer the province, and returned into Indostan.

In the same year the fort of Agra was finished, and according to the accounts submitted by Ragu Thorenne,[29] the king's Treasurer or Wasir, it appeared that the building of the walls had cost 1,050 carores of tackas, *i e*, (reckoning 20 tackas to the rupee) 2,500,000 rupees. On the walls of Fettipore 1,500,000 rupees were spent, making four million in all.

XII. THE CONQUEST OF BENGAL, ETC. [1561-76.]

Some time later Ghan Ghanna and Monim Chan, the king's viceroys in Zyaumpore, informed him that they were frequently in conflict with the Pathans. By this time Soliman Kaharamen [Sulaiman Kirani] was dead. He had been succeeded by his son, who had been killed by his own followers after a reign of two years. Douwet,[30] son of Baratghan, a lazy and cowardly creature

[29] Raja Todar Mal is meant. There is some mistake in calculating the cost of building the fort of Agra. Jahangir in his *Memoirs* says that the red stone fort cost 35 lacs of rupees equal to 10,500,000 *Khani* according to the Turan reckoning. This gives the clue to the mistake. Or, taking a rupee at 30 tackas, it may give 1050 lakhs (35 × 30)

[30] Daud was the younger son of Suleiman Kirani. Suleiman was succeeded by his son Bayazid who was murdered by Hanso

much given to drink, had then succeeded to the throne; but he completely neglected the army and the government of his kingdom; hence (his viceroys told the king) it was time that Achabar should undertake the conquest of the Pathans and add the whole of Bengal to his empire. On hearing this the king hastily assembled his forces and all the equipment for a campaign, crossed the Ganges and the Tziotsa, [Chaunsa], and advanced with his elephants against Pathana. Xa Douwet, learning through his touts of the king's approach, sent forward 12,000 horsemen to delay the advance of the Mogols, who routed them however with the greatest ease between the Ziotsa and Moheb Alypour.[31] They fled back to Pathana, which was fortified and victualled by Xa Douwet to withstand a siege, and delayed Achabar for six months, during which time he lost a large number of men. Finally the city was stormed in the seventh month. Many of the Pathans fell by the sword, a large number of nobles, with their wives and children, were taken prisoner, and a vast amount of treasure was captured. Xa Douwet was himself dead drunk at the time, but was placed by his followers in a boat, and taken a three days' voyage down the river. Disgusted by his cowardice and sloth which had brought such disasters upon them, his followers then cut off his head and sent it to Achabar, who returned to Fettipore after subduing the whole province of Bengal.

for ill-treating the nobles. Daud, his younger brother, was then installed late in 1572 or early in 1573 as king chiefly, through the influence of Lodi Khan An attempt on the part of Gujar Khan to make Bayazid's son king in Behar, did not meet with any success. These are the facts supplied to us by Stewart, Ferishta, and Salim in R S. (p. 153) In the face of these Barat Ghan cannot be identified with Bayazid.

31 Muhibb Alipur named after Muhibb Ali, Akbar's governor of Rohtas. It was near Rohtas. (*Akbar Nama*, III, p. 245.)

Shortly afterwards, by the bravery and energy of Rostanchan and Zadoch Mamet Chan, the strong fortress of Rhan Tambor was captured [32] from its Rahja after a two months' siege. The king next turned his attention to the fortress of Rotas in the province of Bahaer. This fortress has no equal as regards its situation and the strength of its defences either in India, Persia, Turkey, or Tartary. It stands on the top of a high mountain, which is ascended by a pathway two cos long. All around the mountain is a plain extending to a distance of 18 cos. Within the circuit of the fort are 14 villages, whose fields bear in abundance all kinds of crops. A stream descending from the top of the mountain fills three very large tanks, which never dry up. At the foot of the mountain the river Tzeon [Son] spreads out into a marsh three cos broad, which is useful for the purpose of bringing in supplies from the neighbouring regions.

Undaunted by these difficulties, Achabar bade Moheb Alieghan,[33] a man of remarkable prudence and valour, to attempt to capture the fortress from the Hindu prince or Radzia who dwelt there in security. Moheb set out with some chosen troops to the vicinity of the fortress, where he cultivated the friendship of the Radzia by a mutual exchange of presents. The ruse which he adopted was this:—He pretended that the king had sent him suddenly off into Bengal, and he made a pressing request from the Radzia that he might be allowed to leave his women in the latter's fortress for safe-keeping. The Radzia, suspecting no

---

32 Rantambhore (Sansk. *Rana-sthamva-pur*) was surrendered in 1569 by Rao Surjan Hada The Mughal generals named in the text are Dastam Khan and Sadiq Muhammad Khan.

33 Muhibb Ali Khan appointed governor of Rohtas by Akbar. It has already been noted that the stratagem mentioned in the text is usually attributed to Sher Khan. M. Ali Khan rendered excellent services during the Bengal Military Revolt. He was generally called *Rohtasi*.

treachery, agreed more readily than was wise, and bade his people allow no harm to come to the women. Forthwith Mohebaliеghan sent forward into the fortress 200 doulies (litters in which women are carried) in each of which were seated two of his best soldiers. As soon as they arrived inside, these men emerged from the doulies and with a sudden attack overcame the guards at the principal gate. Alieghan, who was close at hand with the rest of his troops, killed the Radzia and made himself master of the fortress together with a huge quantity of treasure, which he handed over to the king. By this piece of trickery he won eternal fame!

In another direction, at Tzarangpore [Sarangpur] Roup Mathii,[34] an extremely beautiful woman, who assumed the name of Baduris, rebelled and summoned the Pathans to arms. Adam Ghan, who was sent against her, easily put her to flight; for she accepted battle at a time when only a few of her men were at hand. She was captured alive, but put an end to her life by drinking poison in order to avoid being made a laughing-stock.

Next the king's brother, Mirza Mamet Hackim,[35] ruler of Kabul, died of disease, and Rahja Mansingh, a Raspoot by race and commander of 5,000 horse, was despatched to form that kingdom into a province. He sent the widows and children of Hackim together with his chief ministers to the king (by no means against their will). Achabar received them kindly, and committed his nephews, who were 10 and 7 years old, to faithful ministers as tutors and guardians. He bestowed annual pensions

34 Rupmati, wife of Baz Bahadur of Malwa. De Laet's version emphasises the influence of Rupmati over the king. As a piece of historical information we may not be disposed to attach importance to it.

35 Mirza Muhammad Hakim died in July 1585 It is too early to mention that event in this connection.

upon the women, and a contingent of troops (together with the needful pay) upon his brother's chief generals [36] Mamet Maxuem Ghan and Jachtbeeck Ghan. He also appointed Maxuem Ghan of Kabul governor of the Pathan province of Bengal upon the death of Ganghanna Morumghan [Munim Khan] and despatched him thither attended by many Ommerau.

XIII. REBELLIONS IN GUJARAT, ETC. [1583-91.]

Meanwhile news was brought that Masoffer,[37] who had been deprived of his principality of Guserat, had rebelled and by a sudden attack had defeated and killed Gotobdian Mahamet Ghan,[38] the commander of the royal army in Amadabat, together with several other Ommerau. The king thereupon sent Abdul Rachim Ghan,[39] the son of Beyram Ghan, with a large force against the rebel, together with Noran Ghan and Goufer Ghan, sons of the murdered Gotobdian, in order that they might avenge their father's death The campaign was of small importance, for when Rachiem, marching swiftly, reached the confines of Gujarat, he immediately put to flight the army of Masoffer, which consisted of only 12,000

---

[36] The generals mentioned were Muhammad Masum Khan and Tukhta Beg Khan The latter received the title of Sardar Khan later on (*Ain*, I, p 469; T J, I, p 31)

[37] Muzaffar III, who represented the royal line of Gujarat, fled from surveillance at the imperial capital and raised a legitimist war in his country

[38] Qutbuddin Muhammad Khan He was slain 1583 His two sons were Naurang Khan and Gujar Khan.

[39] Abdur Rahim Khan, son of the celebrated Bairam Khan. Akbar carefully trained him after the death of his father. He was created Khan-i-Khanan, by which title he is usually known in history. Though capable, he was faithless (T.J, I, 179). He joined Shah Jahan in his revolt He died in 1627. De Laet calls him by his title Can Canna or Gan Ghanna, or Chan Channa.

horse. Masoffer was taken prisoner, but committed suicide to escape the indignity of punishment. Abdul Rachiem was rewarded for this affair by the title of Chan Channa and the command of 5,000 horse.

In Bengal also there was a rebellion, led[40] by Mazenou-Chan, Gabiet-Chan, Bamo-Chan and Mamet Maxum-Chan, all of whom had come from Kabul. They defeated in two or three battles Radzia Thoramiol [Todar Mal], Wasir Ghan, who with Zuebhar-Ghan and a strong force had been sent against them , the Radzia was taken prisoner. However the rebels were finally defeated and killed in battle, with the exception of Maxem-Ghan, who fled to Hizza-Ghan [Isa Khan] the general of the hostile army in Bengal and thus augmented the resources and the daring with which that force was carrying on its campaign against the king's provinces. Zuebhar-Ghan of Kabul[41] took over the governorship of Bengal, and Radzia Thormiel returned to Fettipore

XIV. SUBMISSION OF THE RAJPUT PRINCES, ETC. [1583-5.]

About the same time Radzia Ramziend,[42] who had hitherto remained undisturbed in the possession of his principality of Bandou, was persuaded by Radzia Biermul to visit the king at Fettapore, on condition that he received transport and supplies on a liberal scale. The king received him with much honour, and sent him back to his own country. This example was followed by the other Hindu

[40] The leaders were Majnun Khan Kakshal, Niyabat Khan Baba Khan and Muhammad Masum Khan.

[41] Shahbaz Khan Kambu, not Kabuli.

[42] Raja Ram Chand of Bhatha or Riwa was a valiant chief with his citadel at Kalanjar now in the Banda district, U.P. The date of his submission is 1569. De Laet's Bandou is Fort Bandhu (C R., 1873, p. 190).

chieftains. They began to seek the king's friendship, and gave him their daughters as concubines, in order to confirm treaties of peace and alliance with him.

About this time the king set out towards the rivers Tziotsa and Beack. He was greatly pleased with the place where the Semmena, Tziotsa and Beack [42a] joins, and ordered a fort to be built at that point. The work was carried out in five years by the most skilful builders. The cost of the fort, which was called Elabas by the king, was one myriad, two hundred thousand rupees.

Having subdued the afore-mentioned revolts the king took a period of rest, and then formed the intention of going to Lahor in order to meet Abdullack-Ghan the Usbec, king of Maurhner,[43] son and heir of Tsecander-Ghan, who had announced that he wished to come to India to meet the king. Meanwhile there came to Fettipore (where Achabar had now resided for fifteen years) Morza Tsarof of Badaxan,[44] whom the Usbeq had grievously ill-treated. This man accompanied the king to Lahor. Achabar had some idea of going on to Kabul However, recalling that lower Bengal was still in the power of the Pathans, he changed the direction of his journey and went towards Ateeck. Thence he sent Zienchan and Radzia Birmuel [Birbal] with a large army to attack the Pathans. However, these Pathans, whose rulers were Zelalia Afridi[45] and

---

[42a] These words, as suggested by Prof. Hodivala, stand for Jumna, Chaunsa and Prayag

[43] Mawar-un-nahr or Transoxiana, otherwise known as Bokhara or Turan Abdullah Khan Uzbeg succeeded his father Sekandar in 1583 as king and died in 1598. Akbar moved his imperial residence to Lahore in 1585.

[44] Mirza Shahrukh of Badakshan He married Akbar's daughter Shakaru-u-nisa and was for long governor of Malwa. Jahangir in his Memoirs (T.J., I, 27) pays him pleasant tribute.

[45] Jalal the Roshani leader, who succeeded his father Bayazid to the leadership in 1585. I am unable to explain Turcost-zey.

Turcost Zey, had blocked up their mountain-passes, so that the king's forces met with a serious defeat, Birmuel with many other Ommerau being killed in the battle, and Tzienghan-Goga [Zain Khan Koka] escaping with difficulty back to the king. Larger forces were then sent; and these had the good fortune to subjugate all the provinces held by Zelalia and Turcost.

After this it was announced to the king that Mirza Massoffer Hossen and Mirza Roston Khandehari, sons of Mirza Beyram, who had been governor of Khandahar, wished to submit to Achabar on account of injuries received by them from Xa Abas, son of Godavenda [Khudabanda], king of Persia, which had caused them to rebel against him. The king seized upon the excellent opportunity thus offered of annexing Khandahar, and sent thither Chabeeck Gan [Shah Beg Khan], a commander of 5,000, whom the two brothers immediately admitted to the city, afterwards coming to visit the king at Lahor, and being received by him with the greatest kindness.

XV. THE CONQUEST OF KASHMIR. [1586.]

Tzedder-Zia Han[46] and Haekim Hamma were sent to Bochara, ostensibly to offer condolences to Abdul-Ghan on the death of his father, and to show due respect to the memory of T'Sander-Ghan [Sikandar Khan], the dead ruler; but in reality that they might spy out the region of Maurhener, which the king greatly desired to add to his empire, so that the glory of his name might be spread far and wide, and that he might rival Tamurlane,

Prof. Sarkar suggests that the word stands for Yusufzai (T=y; st=ff). According to Sir Thomas Herbert Turcost was Jalal's general.

46 Sadr Jahan Mufti and Hakim Humam. In 1586 there was sent the embassy to Turan (A.N., III, 753).

the founder of his line. The emissaries duly arrived at Bochara, offered the king's gifts to Abdulghan, and paid respects to the memory of the dead ruler by means of a most sumptuous open-air banquet, to which all the citizens were invited (this is the custom in those parts). After spending a whole year at Bochara they returned, loaded with magnificent presents, and gave to Achabar a full account of the nature of the country, the fortifications of the cities, and the strength of the army. However the king thought it best first to attack Cassimere, which was then ruled by a foreigner Cassem-Ghan Mierbar and Mirza Alle Tzily[47] were sent on this expedition, with the whole of the royal army, and with letters to Justoff-Ghan [Yusuf Khan], king of Cassimere, in which he was promised undiminished sovereignty over the country in case he would of his own free will submit to the king without fighting. On receipt of these letters Justoff-Ghan came straight to Lahor to meet the king, leaving his son Jacob Chan [Yakub Khan] in charge of his kingdom, greatly to the disgust of his subjects who thought him infatuated and bewitched.

However Achabar did not reckon that Justoff-Ghan had made a complete surrender, maintaining that he would have brought his son with him if he had really wished to come to an agreement ; for on account of his youth the lad might easily be led into rash action against the king.

Nor was this a fantastic idea, for immediately after his father's departure the prince, scorning to be ruled by strangers, put his kingdom into a state of defence and closed the passes. These actions on the part of Jacob-Chan kept the king for some time in a state of suspense ;

---

47 Mirzadah Ali Khan, who accompanied the *Mir Bahr* to Kashmir in 1586, was killed by the Kashmiris in 1587. (See *Akbar-Nama* III, 715, 752).

for it would have been a difficult undertaking to force the passes. At length he despatched Mirza Alle Tzilly and Ghassem-Chan with an army and certain Ommerau of Cassimere who were well acquainted with all the routes by which that country may be approached. Learning of this Jacob-Chan sent some Ommerau with large forces to Kotele, a pass through the Bimber mountains, to block that approach. However these Ommerau were persuaded by the promises and presents of the king's servants to desert their master and to open the passes to the enemy. Once they had crossed the mountains the king's forces easily reached Cassimere and took the city, which was unwalled, at the first assault. The king was captured, but begged Achabar for forgiveness, and was given an annual pension to share with his father, though the amount was not sufficient to support their dignity.

XVI. THE CONQUEST OF SIND: AND THE FIRST INVASION OF THE DECCAN.

[1591-99]

The king next turned his attention to Scinde, whose ruler was Mirza Sianis [Mirza Jani Tarkhan]. This man was detested by his subjects on account of his tyrannical rule. Gan Ghanna, who was put in command of the expedition, embarked his whole force, with the necessary equipment, on a number of boats, sailed down the Ravea into the Indus, and thus reached the capital Tatta, the siege and capture of which took him six months. In the seventh month Mirza Sianis surrendered and was sent to the king, who received him kindly. Sind was made into a province.

After this it came to the king's ears that Nesam Sha, king of the Decan, was dead : and Achabar was filled with desire to add that kingdom also to his empire. No one could be found more suitable for the command of the expedition than Gan Ganna, who set out from Lahor with 24 Ommerau and a very large army. On reaching Brampore he was immediately joined by Radzia Aly Chan,[48] the governor of that place, with all his forces. The army rested for six months at Brampore. The ruler of Amdanager was at this time Tziand Biebie,[49] daughter of Nizam Sha, and a wise and prudent administrator. The commander of her forces was a eunuch, Godzia Tzuhel,[50] a man of remarkable courage and energy. He advanced against Channa with 40,000 cavalry, amongst which were the forces of Visiapore and Golconda. The Mogol general had available a force of scarcely 20,000; yet, relying on the valour of his generals Radzia Alighan, Mirza Ched Gassem[51] (a descendant of Tzadat), and others, he gladly accepted battle, and stationed himself with 5,000 chosen horsemen in support, a little to the rear of the rest of his array. The battle lasted a day and a night; but no decision was reached, though the slaughter was great on both sides, amongst the slain being Radzia Alichan. The next morning the royal army began to waver, whereupon Chan Channa led forward his reserves. They attacked the enemy, who were now wearied, with such energy as to put them to flight, Godzia Tzuhel being killed in the battle. This was a very great victory;

---

[48] Raja Ali Khan, the Faruqi ruler of Khandesh (1577-97). The title *Raja* was adopted by him in imitation of the founder of the dynasty (Raja Ahmad) and was probably liked by the pro-Hindu Emperor, who had many other Rajas under him (I A., 1918, p. 144)

[49] Chand Bibi was the widow of Ali Adil Shah and daughter of Husain Nizam Shah I She came back to Ahmednagar on the death of her husband and acted as the regent of Bahadur Nizam Shah, supported by the African amirs

[50] Khwaja Suhail Khan was the best general of Ibrahim Adil Shah II of Bijapur The battle was fought at Ashti near Supa on the Godaveri in February 1597 (I.A., 1918, pp. 178-9)

[51] Saiyad Qasim was one of the *Sadāt-i-Barha*. Tzadat is Sadat

yet it did not lead to the conquest of the Decan; for the queen raised new forces, and beat off the attack of the Mogols.

XVII. DEATH OF PRINCE MURAD.
[May 1599.]

So far the king had enjoyed uninterrupted good fortune, but after this many domestic tragedies marred his prosperity. In the first place, he sent his son Sha-Morat and other magnates to the war in the Decan, in the hope of conquering that region. The prince halted for six months at Brampore, where (in spite of his former prudence and courage) he gave himself up to drunkenness in such a way as to bring on a serious illness. When the king heard of this, he was anxious for the safety of his son, and immediately sent Abdul Fazel, his divan (*i.e.*, Lord Chancellor), who had formerly been the prince's tutor, to recall him to his duty. But this remedy came too late; for on reaching Brampore Abdul Fazel found the prince's state desperate, and shortly afterwards he died. When his death became known many Ommerau and Mancebdars who were with him took flight, but Abdul Fazel summoned[52] Ganganna, Tziediustof-Chan, Tzadoch Mamet Ghan and Mirza Tzaroch to a council of war, and addressed them thus:—"I see no cause for the flight of these Ommerau; for though the king's son is dead, his decease should be regarded in no other light than the decease of any other of the Ommerau, since the king himself is alive (and I pray God that he may live long). I intend to take supreme command of the army myself. I shall distribute the treasure left by the prince to the Mancebdars and the soldiers, and shall prepare for battle."

---

52 The amirs were Khan Khanan, Saiyad Yusuf Khan, Sadiq Muhammad Khan and Mirza Shahrukh. Sadiq was *ataliq* to Murad.

After carrying out his intention Abdul Fazel advanced 5 cos towards Chapor [Shahpur], and encamped opposite to the enemy. He sent the prince's body to Delly, and having pursued and captured many of the Ommerau and Mancebdars who had taken to flight, had them trodden to death by elephants in the middle of the camp. He then wrote to inform the king that he had hurried to Brampore, found the prince on the point of death, and after his death distributed his treasure to the troops in order to prepare for the expedition against Amdanager with the greatest possible speed.

On receiving this letter the king mourned deeply for the death of his son, but wrote graciously to Abdul Fazel confirming him in his position as commander of the army.

XVIII. CONQUESTS IN THE DECCAN, ETC. [1596-1601.]

In the same year the king made another of his sons D'Haen Xa or Xa Daniel, leader of 7,000 horse, and despatched him to Elhabasse with a retinue consisting of Coutel Mametchan [Qulich Muhammad Khan], the Chancellor, and many other Ommerau and magnates. On reaching Elhabasse the prince divided his forces, in order the better to pursue the rebels in that region.

Meanwhile Fazel added to the empire the province of Barar and Chandis, and begged the king to be pleased to come as far as Agra, for an excellent opportunity would present itself of adding Amdanager, Visiapor and Golconda to the empire. In accordance with this advice the king left Lahor, where he had now remained for twelve years, and came to Agra, where he resided for a whole year.

In the year of Mahumet 1005[53] (1595 of our era) the king decided to send his son Xa Selim to subdue Radzia Rana Mardout,[54] who was by far the most powerful of all the Radzias of the whole of Hindustan, and had lately rebelled. With him he sent Tzebhaer-Chan-Cambou, commander of 5,000 horse, Cha-Couligan Mharem, commander of 3,000, Radzia Ziagenat, commander of 3,000 and many other Mancebdars, thus making the prince's army a very strong one.

XIX. THE REVOLT OF PRINCE SALIM.
[1600.]

In the year of Mahumet 1007 (1597 of our era) the king led his army from Agra to take part in the war in the Decan. However on crossing the Nerebeda he found that Radzia Bador Xa, who held the fort of Hasser [Asirgarh] had fortified it against the king and furnished it with a great store of corn gathered from the surrounding regions. The king, thinking it dangerous to leave the fortress behind him unreduced, resolved to capture it before proceeding further. The fortress consists of three castles,[55] of which the first is called Cho-Tzanin,

---

[53] The year began on August 25, 1596.

[54] Here as elsewhere (*vide post*, Section XXVII), the Rana of Udaipur is alluded to as Raja Rana Mardout or Mazdout or Mondon. All these terms are the corruptions of Mardúd or the accursed one—certainly a fit term to be applied to a Rana who had the hardihood to defy for long the royal authority ! Malik Ambar is also the recipient of opprobrious epithets in Jahangir's *Memoirs*.

With Prince Salim were sent, as mentioned in the text, Shahbaz Khan Kambu, Shah Quli Khan Mahram and Raja Jagannath The second was known as the captor of Hemu (*vide ante*), and the third was the son of Raja Bihari Mal.

[55] I am not able to explain the names of the two 'castles.' But the following quotation from the *Bombay Gazetteer* will give the real names: "Half way up the mountain to the west and slightly to the north, were two renowned outwo ·] called the Malai and

and the second Commerghar. The third is situated at the top of a very lofty mountain, and is separated from the others by a distance of six cos. Nonetheless the king besieged the whole fortress, and pushed the siege with such vigour both by day and by night that after six months he was ready to capture the place by assault. Perceiving this Badur Xa surrendered on condition that life and property were spared, and obtaining pardon from the king entered his service together with his brothers and relations.

Abdul Fazel now came to the king and persuaded him to advance at once to the war in the Decan, for he thought that if he could add the Decan to his empire, and drive out the kings of Chandeis, Visiapor and Golconda, his glory and dominions would be great enough.

However whilst he was engaged on this expedition, the king learnt that T'Zebhaergan Kambou, whom he had sent to assist Xa Selim, had suddenly died at Assemere, whereupon the prince had seized his treasures, amounting to more than a carore (ten millions) of rupees and had marched with a large force of picked troops upon Agra, with the intention of deposing his father. On hearing this news the king changed his plans, placed Xa Daniel in charge of the operations against Amnadager and Visiapor, with Fazel, Chan-Channa and several Ommerau to assist him, and himself marched back to Agra.

Meanwhile Xa Selim had reached Agra from Assemere, but finding it hopeless to attempt to capture the fort, had marched away again, and twelve days later had reached Elhabassa, by way of Rehen and Annewar. He had

---

the Antar-malai which had to be taken before Asir itself could be reached, and between the north-west and north there was another unfinished bastion called Cheena Malai From east to south-west were hills and in the south was a high mountain called Korhiah." (B.G., XII, 579.)

occupied *en route* Siaupor, Bahaer, Kalpi, Lacknou, Oude, Berage, Kersama Mekpor, Kera Gastanpor, Ghanouts and other towns.[56] He had everywhere established his own Ommerau as governors, and had driven out his father's officers, some of whom transferred their allegiance to himself, whilst others who were more loyal to the king left all their property and fled to Achabar.

On reaching Agra the king began anxiously to ponder how he might recall the prince to his duty. First of all he wrote a letter to Xa Selim pointing out the rash folly of his design and reminding him of the divine wrath against rebellious sons, but promising him pardon for his offences and re-instatement in his old position of favour if he would abandon his wicked plans and return as a suppliant to his father However Xa Selim scorned all his father's threats and admonitions. Being now in control of the whole country as far as Hassipore [Hajipur] and Pathana he asked Manzing, the viceroy of Bengal, to come over to his side and surrender that province. However the request was refused.

XX. CAPTURE OF AHMADNAGAR.
[1600.]

In that same year Prince Daniel Xa, who was in command of the operations in the Decan, advanced with his whole force on Amadanager and reached Gandetzin. However Tziand-Bebie took refuge in the fort of Amadanager, together with all the generals of her father Nezam Xa, and prepared to stand a siege. The fort is very strong, being built on high ground and surrounded by very deep ditches, in which a number of springs bubble up. None-the-less the prince, and the valiant leaders who were with him (Check Abdul Fazel Chan Channa and Tzied-Justof

---

[56] Good instances of De Laet's careless transliteration of names The last four are: Baraich, Kara-Manikpur, Kora-Ghatampur and Kanouj.

Chan), surrounded the fort on all sides with their forces, and after a siege of six months, fiercely pushed, finally stormed the place in the seventh month. Tziand-Bebie had already destroyed herself by poison, but an enormous treasure fell into the hands of the king's troops. Next Sultan Daniel, having made Godzia Beeckmyrza [Khwaja Beg Mirza] governor of the fortress, annexed the provinces of Gandes and Berar to his father's empire, and then returned to Brampore, whither there came to him ambassadors from the kings of Golconda and Visiapore, with rich presents and letters of submission. However after this the prince gave himself up entirely to drunkenness.

XXI. THE MURDER OF ABDUL FAZL.
[August 1602.]

At the same time Xa Selim sent Godzia Ziahen [Khwaja Jahan] to his father with a letter pretending repentance for his misdeeds. The king immediately replied, holding out a good hope of pardon if the prince would return to his allegiance at once. After remaining six months at Agra Ziahan was sent back to the prince and persuaded him to return as a penitent to his father. When already on the way the prince wrote to his father that he was returning as a penitent, but that, as he had an army of 70,000 fine troops, he requested that all the gifts which he had already made to his generals, and all which he might make in the immediate future, should be confirmed, and that the generals should not be regarded as rebelse

Neither of these requests being granted, the princ· returned to Halebassa, and not only began to mint money both silver and gold, in his own name, but also sent som, of it to his father, to increase his anger yet more. The king was deeply incensed, and wrote an account of the whole matter to Abdul Fazel, who replied that the king must take courage, for he would come himself as soon as he could, and he had the power and skill to bring the prince bound before the king.

Thus shortly afterwards Abdul Fazel, having obtained supplies and two or three hundred cavalry from Daniel Xa, and having given orders for all his baggage to follow him, set out for Agra. Xa Selim knew what was happening; remembering that Fazel had always been very hostile to himself, he was afraid (and with reason) lest Fazel should inflame yet more his father's anger against him. Hence he decided to intercept him on the journey. He asked Radzia Bertzingh Bondela,[57] ruler of Osseen, to lay an ambush for Fazel in the neighbourhood of Soor and Gualer,[58] and to send him his head. He promised also that in return for this service he would make the Radzia commander of 5,000 horse. The Radzia agreed, and stationed himself with 1,000 cavalry and 3,000 infantry three or four cos from Gualer. Scouts were posted in the neighbouring villages to give timely notice of the approach of Fazel.

After leaving Collebag, Fazel was advancing towards Soor when he was attacked by Radzia Bersingh and his men on both flanks. Fazel and his escort put up a brave fight, but were overwhelmed by numbers. Fazel himself received twelve wounds in the fighting, and was captured, his identity being betrayed by a slave who had been taken prisoner. His head was cut off and sent to the prince, who was overjoyed. But when the king heard of the murder of Fazel, to whom he was greatly attached, he mourned deeply and remained in seclusion for three days

---

57 Raja Bir Singh, the Bundella chief of Orchha (*vide supra*).

58 Sir Roper Lethbridge identifies them with Shadorah and Kolaras. But I think the references are to Sarai Barar and Gwalior. The former is two stages from the latter (E.D., VI, 107, 155). Collebag is Kalabagh.

Nor was this the last of his griefs; for not long after he was informed of the death of his son Xa Daniel, who died of over-drinking at Brampore. This affected the king so much that he became almost tired of life. On being comforted however by his followers, he recalled Ganganna from Brampore. He was extremely angry with him for not having taken better care of the prince. When the offender arrived, it was long before he was admitted to the royal presence. However he was finally taken back into favour through the intercession of the Ommerau, and having been promoted to the rank of Commander-in-Chief of the army, was sent back to the Decan.

XXII. SALIM MAKES SUBMISSION, [1604.]

Soon afterwards the king decided under the stimulus of great anger to move against Xa Selim. He crossed the river Semena with a large army, but was forced to return to Agra on hearing of the illness of his mother. Two days after his return she died, and was laid to rest with great pomp in the tomb of her husband Hamayon at Delly. When the days of mourning for her were ended, the king sent to his son his former tutor Miratseddera,[59] with a letter in which after severely blaming the prince, he reminded him that he alone was now left, and that there was no one who could deprive him of the throne. He must however present himself as a suppliant before the king, in which case he would be forgiven for his ill deeds and received back into favour. Other secret instructions were also given. With this letter Miratseddera went to the prince, and at length persuaded him to return to his father as a penitent.

---

59 Miran Sadr Jahan He was Akbar's agent at the Court of Salim and a great favourite of the prince who regarded the Sadr as his spiritual preceptor.

Hence in the year of Mahumet 1013[60] (1602 of our era) Xa Selim and his son Sultan Perwees left Elhabasse with their army, crossed the Semena, and two days later (on a lucky day, according to the king's soothsayers) arrived with all his Ommerau at the fort of Agra, where he was escorted to his father's presence by Mortosa Chan.[61] When he had bowed to his father's throne, in the fashion of the country, the king took his hand and drew him into the Mahael or inner apartment, where in great anger he gave him several blows in the face, upbraiding him bitterly meantime for his treatment of himself, and ridiculing his cowardice because although at the head of 70,000 troops, he had yet come to his father's feet as a suppliant. After this the king gave orders that the prince should be conducted into another room and there kept a prisoner.

The Ommerau of the prince, with the exception of Radzia Batso,[62] who had fled in time, were arrested, loaded with fetters, and thrown into jail. Xa Selim, who had been in the habit of using opium, abstained from it for 24 hours, but on the next day the king visited him, and gave him some with his own hand. On the third day all the royal concubines waited upon the king, and persuaded him to pardon the prince, who was dismissed to his own palace, whence he daily came with a large retinue to

[60] The year began on May 30, 1604

[61] Murtaza Khan, known in the reign of Akbar as Shaikh Farid, a Bukhari Saiyad (*vide supra*). Salim arrived at Agra on October 9, 1604 Farid rose to high posts under Jahangir.

[62] Raja Basu of Mau and Pathankot at the foot of the Himalayas in the Punjab. In Akbar's reign he broke out in revolt several times. Such recalcitrance fitted him to become a close adherent of the rebellious prince. On Salim's ascension to the throne, he was made as in the case of Bir Singh, a commander of 3,000. He played a somewhat conspicuous part in the Mewar campaign, died in 1613. His name has been variously spelt as Radzia Batsu, Rahja Bossu.

22

pay the customary respects to his father. However the members of the royal household had filled the suspicious mind of the old king with the fear that his son was plotting to kill him, and hence Xa Selim was in future admitted to his father's presence accompanied by four companions only.

XXIII. DEATH OF AKBAR AND ACCESSION OF JAHANGIR.

[Oct. 1605.]

The king gave orders some time afterwards that Mirza Gazia,[68] the son of Zianius, and governor of Sind and Tatta, should be made away with by poison, on account of an arrogant boast which he had uttered. To this end the royal physician was instructed to make two pills, of identical shape and weight, one of which was to be poisoned. The king proposed to give this one to Gazia, whilst he himself took the other, which was merely to contain a medicinal drug. However, by an extraordinary mistake, the king took the wrong pill, having held both in his hand for some time, and having given the harmless one to Gazia. Later when the mistake was discovered, the poison had already taken hold upon his system, and antidotes were administered in vain.

The king refused at first to believe that his hour had come. However he placed his own Tulbant [Turban] on the head of Xa Selim, who happened to be visiting him at the time, and girded the prince with the sword of his father Hamayon, forbidding him however to draw it within the precincts of the palace or to visit him again till he should be better.

---

68 Mirza Ghazi Beg, governor of Sindh and Thatta. He was the son of Mirza Jani (*vide supra*). He was a dissolute scamp. For his life, see *Ain.*, I., 363

The king died twelve days later, in the year of Mahumet 1014, after a most prosperous reign of 60 years.

The chief Ommerau who were present at the king's death-bed shut all the gates of the fortress of Agra as soon as he was dead, and set a faithful officer to guard each of them. Then the following assembled[64] in the palace of Chan Azem for urgent deliberation:—Mortazachan, Tzeysetchan, Coulie Mamet-Ghan, Radzia Raemdas and Radsia Mansingh. Chan Azem and Radzia Manzingh wished to elevate Sultan Gousro to the royal throne; but Radzia Raemdas, who had at hand 4,000 or 5,000 Raspot cavalry, was opposed to this design and occupied the treasury, declaring that he would prevent any one touching the royal treasures without his consent.

Sultan Selim, hearing at his own palace of his father's death, called his Ommerau and informed them of what his rivals were doing. Meanwhile Morteza Chan, who had been set to guard the chief gateway of the fort, went to the prince and congratulated him on attaining the dignity of kingship. This example was followed by Nabab Tzaeyiel-Chan and his relative, Coulie Mamet-Chan, and soon afterwards Chan-Azem joined them. However Radzia Manzing conducted Sultan Gousro to his own palace through the gate which opens on the river, whither he was brought in a boat. Selim, being now supported by the chief Ommerau, entered the fort and conveyed the body of his father on foot outside the fort, accompanied

64 The members of the conference mentioned in the text are Murtaza Khan, Saiyad Khan, Qulich Muhammad Khan, Raja Ram Das, and Raja Man Singh. Both Man Singh and Aziz Koka were interested in setting aside Salim in favour of Khusrau, nephew of the former and son-in-law of the latter. The plot miscarried. The opposition was led by Saiyad Khan Barha Raja Ram Das Kachhwaha held the treasury for Salim The cause of Khusrau became hopeless.

by his Ommerau. The body was then conducted by the nobles with great pomp to a tomb at Tzekandra [Sikandara], three cos from Agra. On their return to the fort they crowned Ṣelim, by the title of Mahomet Ziahaengier. Finally, three days later, Sultan Gousro was brought by Radzia Mansingh and Chan Azem to his father in the fort; and a reconciliation was effected, so far at least as outward appearances went.

When it became known that the coronation of king Zianhaengier was shortly to be celebrated, ambassadors came from Persia, Tartary, Golconda, Visiapor, the Decan, and the neighbouring Radzias, bearing rich gifts with wishes and prayers for the new king's complete happiness.

At that time the king was master of the following well-defined provinces[65] :—Kandahaer, Kabul, Cassamier, Ghassenie, Benazaed, Guzaratta, Sinde (or Tatta), Gan, dhees, Brampore,[66] Barar, Bengala, Orixa, Ode, Malouw-Agra, Delly. The annual revenue of these provinces, according to the roll of king Achabar, is 6 arebs and 98 carors of dams, *i.e.*, 3 arebs and 49 carors of tangae, or (according to the official rate of exchange which reckons 20 tangae per rupee or 1 caror of tangae to 5 lacks of rupees), 17 carors, 45 lacks of rupees The whole of this annual revenue is spent on the magnates and generals and on the pay of the army I have dealt elsewhere with the treasure left behind by king Achabar.

---

65 The provinces in the text respectively are Kandahar, Kabul, Kashmir, Ghazni, Benazaed (Bangash or Punjab), Gujarat, Sind or Thatta, Khandesh, Burhanpur, Berar, Bengal, Orissa, Oudh, Malwa, Agra and Delhi The list does not tally with that of Abul Fazl in the *Ain* The 15 provinces are too well-known to need enumeration here.

66 Burhanpur should not have been distinguished from Khandesh.

XXIV. REVOLT OF PRINCE KHUSRAU.
[April 1606.]

In the year of Mahumet 1015, A.D. 1605 (the first year of king Ziahaengier), the king being in doubt concerning the loyalty of his son Gousrou [Khusrau], asked the most prominent of the Ommerau, Mirza,[67] for advice as to what he should do with his son. Mirza advised the king to put the prince's eyes out The king hesitated and delayed, whereupon Gousrou, who had taken alarm and had gained some inkling of what was intended, plotted to escape and wrote to his old friend, Hazem Beeck Gan Badaxas[68] (whom Achabar shortly before his death had despatched to Kabul to choose and collect remounts) bidding him expedite his return and come to his (Gousrou's) assistance with all the troops he could gather; for he himself was planning secretly to leave Agra with the most faithful and brave of his followers, and to repair to Lahor.

Hazem, in accordance with the prince's request, hastened to meet him as rapidly as possible. When he had reached Achabarpor, only 24 cos from Agra, the prince, who had been informed of his approach, stole out of the fort of Agra at evening time with a body of picked troops. The Coutuwall (*i e*, commander of the imperial guard), whose name was Godzia Meleck Ali[69] had not yet left the guard-house, but did not dare to stop the prince.

67 Evidently Sharif Khan, *Amiru-l-umara*, the Grand Vizier, is meant At places he is referred to as Mirza Amir

68 Hasan Beg Khan Badakhshi Akbar had put him in charge of Kabul He had Rohtas as his fief It was on his advice that Khusrau, after the defeat at Bhaironwal, was retreating to Kabul, when he was arrested on the way (*Ain*, I, 454, T J., I, 54, 66-68).

69 Khwaja Malik Ali Jahangir (T. J., I, 53) gives the name of the *Kotwal* as Ihtimam Khan When Shaikh Farid was sent in pursuit of the prince, the *Kotwal* was made scout and intelligence officer. *Akbar-Nama* mentions (III 502) one Malik Ali as Kotwal-i-Urdu (See also Ain I. 515).

The fugitives extinguished the lights wherever they went, looted a few shops, and then left the city as swiftly as possible. Gousrou paid his respects on the way to the tomb of his grandfather, and at dawn arrived in Achabarpor with 500 troops, mostly mere lads. Hassenbeeck was awaiting him there with 2,000 or 3,000 cavalry. Gousrou proceeded with these as quickly as possible to Lahor.

On learning of the prince's flight the king ordered the Coutwall Godzia to give chase with the cavalry under his command. He started at dead of night with 300 men. The same night Mortazachan [Murtaza Khan] was despatched in support with 1,500 cavalry. By the advice of the Ommerau Mirza the king himself followed at dawn with the swiftest elephants and several Ommerau. In order to expedite his march he took no baggage at all.

The prince was at most 10 cos ahead of Godzia, 10 or 12 cos more ahead of Mortazachan, and about as much again ahead of the king. He looted all the villages on the way, carried off the royal horses from the post-stations, and compelled all the travellers and traders whom he met on the road to accompany him. Having in this fashion collected a by no means contemptible force he reached Lahor on the ninth day of his flight. However Ebram-Chan [Ibrahim Khan] a Patan, whom the king had shortly before despatched to Lahor with the authority of governor, hearing of the prince's flight, prepared with the utmost speed to intercept him, and fortified the citadel of Lahor against him.

Another unforeseen mischance happened to the fugitive. Sayet-Chan,[70] who was on his way to Bange, had just encamped with his force only three cos from the

70 Said Khan was on his way to Kashmir. (T. J., I, 62.)

city. The prince invited him in a friendly fashion to join forces with himself, nor did Sayet-Chan at first reject the proposal. However on reaching the bank of the river Ravee in company with the prince's soldiers, he cleverly gave them the slip, and caused his boatmen to land him at the fort. Meanwhile Zalaeldin Hassen,[71] whom the king has sent on ahead to catch up Gousrou, announced to the prince that the king had handed over to him Kabul and Banasoed [Bangash], and bade him leave Lahor and repair to those provinces. However Gousrou demanded for himself the whole district of Zerhind, and laid siege to Lahor.

Eight days later, on learning that the king had crossed the river [Beas] which flows by Sultanpor and that Mortazachan was about to cross the river Nackhoder, Gousrou resolved to risk a battle, collected all his stragglers, and advanced against his father's army with 20,000 cavalry. After marching 30 cos he came into contact with Mortazachan, who on learning of the prince's advance had drawn up his forces to oppose him. The weather was rainy, and a storm was raging. The battle began with a skirmish between the prince's troops and the royal cavalry, who scarcely numbered 300. The latter were caught in a net, as it were. Xachelial [Saiyad Jalal], their commander, was killed, and they were being rapidly driven off the field when Godzia Malick came up in the nick of time, with the main body of the royal army. He cried out that the king himself was close at hand, and thus so encouraged his own men and at the same time dismayed those of the prince that Ommerau Abdul-Rahiem flung away the prince's standard. On this Gousrou's troops, imagining that their master had been killed, were so terrified that they took to flight, and dispersed in all directions. Many were

[71] Mir Jamālu-d-din Husain. Jahangir mentions the pacific errand of the Mir. (T.J., I, 64.)

killed or captured by the peasants for the sake of their horses and camels. The rest of the spoil came into the hands of the royal forces, who thus gained a notable victory.

When the king came up, he named the place of the battle Fettipor.[72] The prince fled to Lahor with Hassenbeeck Chan-Badixas, and Abdul Rahiem. The last-named stopped in Lahor; but the prince crossed the Ravee with Badixas on his way to the fortress of Rautas. He succeeded in reaching the river Tzenab [Chenab] and entered a boat to cross it. However the boatmen had received instructions from the sons of Cassemchan Niemeck [Qasim Khan Namkin] who were in command of the garrison of Rautas. They ran the boat upon a sand bank in the middle of the river, and leaving the prince swam away to the bank. Thus the poor wretch, together with Hassenbeeck Chan, was captured by the king's forces, and was conducted to the king, who had already crossed the river Latir [Ravi, the river of Lahore].

In preparation for his return with his captives to Lahor (where Abdul Rahiem had also been discovered and dragged from his hiding-place) the king ordered the peasants to cut down the trees and to fix sharp stakes on either side of the road. The captives were impaled on these stakes, or were hung from neighbouring trees. When all was ready, the king, taking his captive son along with him, returned to the city. In order to increase his suffering the prince was mounted on an elephant, and Zemanabeeck [Zamena Beg] was seated behind him with instructions to call to his attention *en route* the names of his followers and the dreadful punishments which had been

---

72 Fathpur. The place was called Bhaironwal. It was bestowed on Shaikh Farid who was henceforth to be styled Murtaza Khan. Farid named it Faridabad. Bhaironwal is on the right bank of the Beas on the road from Jalandhur to Amritsar.

inflicted upon them. On reaching Lahor the prince was committed to the custody of Zemaneebeeck (or Mahobet Chan as he was afterwards called). Hassenbeeck Badaxas was sewn up in a raw ox-hide, and perished in dreadful torment. His head was cut off and sent to Agra, where it was fixed above the gate of the fort. Abdul-Rahiem, after spending some time sewn up in the hide of an ass, was finally pardoned.

XXV. SUNDRY CONSPIRACIES.
[1607.]

After this the king amused himself at Lahor for four months with hunting expeditions, and then set out[73] to visit Kabul. Sultan Gousrou was still a prisoner, strictly guarded by the royal Ommerau and Mancebdars. It happened on a certain day, when Mirza Fetullha, Mirza Charieff (son of Ethamadaulet), Mirza Mouradin (who was related through his brother to the great Assof-Ghan), Mirza Ziafferbeeck and several other Ommerau[74] were on guard, that they hatched a conspiracy to assassinate the king amongst the mountain defiles near Kabul, and to place Sultan Goufrou on the throne in his place. However the plot failed, for lack of a suitable opportunity for the crime, and the king reached Kabul safely.

---

73 Jahangir had gone from Agra to Lahore in April 1606; left Lahore for Kabul towards the end of March 1607, reached Kabul in the beginning of June, and remained there till the close of August of the same year; he reached Agra again in March 1608.

74 The amirs mentioned in the text are Mirza Fathullah (son of Hakim Abul Fath), Itimad-ud-dowlah *i.e.* Mirza Ghiyas, (father of Nur Jahan), Mirza Nuruddin (nephew of Asaf Khan) and Mirza Jaafar Beg. The eldest son of Itimad-ud-dowlah was Muhammad Sharif and his second son Asaf Khan. The eldest son was implicated in this conspiracy of 1607. The plot was to assassinate Jahangir on the way back to Lahore and proclaim Khusrau Emperor. It was detected and the ring leaders were put to death.

Meanwhile Ethamandaulat, the treasurer of Mirza Ommerau, was accused before the king by his Hindu slave Otthem Tziend[75] of embezzling 50,000 rupees, and was handed over to the custody of Dianet Chan [Dayanat Khan].

It also came to the ears of the king (in the year of Mahumet 1018)[76] that Cheer Affengan,[77] son-in-law of the captive Ethamandaulet, had murdered the governor of Bengal, Cotopdyn Mahamet Chan Gagam,[78] near Radia-Mahal [Raj Mahal]. However, Cheech-Gheassedin, the brother of the murdered Cotopdyn, and his son Kiffewerchan cut off the head of the rebel Affenchan, and sent it to the king. They also threw his brother Gommer, his son, his mother, and his wife Maheer-Metzia (daughter of Ethmandaulat) into rigorous imprisonment. All these events incensed the king yet more against his captive.

The king was preparing to return to Lahor when there came to him Godzia Vehes [Khwaja Wais] who reported to him both in speech and in writing that Mirza Mouradien, Ziafferbeech, Mahomet Zeriff (the son of Ethamandaulet), Fettula (the son of Hackiem Abdulfheet), and many others had for some time been plotting against his life. On hearing this the king flew into a terrible rage, and ordered Ethamandaulat's son, Mirza Mouradien, Abdul-fet and the other captives to be brought before him. This was instantly done, whereupon he ordered

---

75 Uttam Chand.

76 The year began on March 27, 1609 The date is wrong.

77 Sher Afkun, first husband of Mehrunnisa or Nur Jahan. His personal name was Ali Quli Istajlu He was jagirdar of Burdwan; his death occurred there in March 1607.

78 Qutbuddin Muhammad Khan Koka. "He was to Jahangir in the place of a dear son, a kind brother and a congenial friend." (T.J, I, 115) His brother was Shaikh Ghiyasuddin, and his son, Kishwar Khan, whose personal name was Shaikh Ibrahim. Kishwar was slain in the battle against Usman in 1612.

them to be beheaded and their corpses exposed on the minarets.* However Dianetchan interceded on behalf of Ethamandaulat, urging the king to allow him to be ransomed for two lacks of rupees. To this the king agreed, and the captive was led off to prison once more by Dianethchan, with every mark of disgrace. Mirza Mouradien, Mahomet Cheriff and Mirza Fettula were executed in accordance with the king's orders.

After this the king left Kabul and returned to Lahor, where in accordance with the advice of Mirza Ommerau and the other magnates he gave directions for his son to be deprived of his sight. The prince's eyes were smeared with juice extracted from the leaves of the Aeck,[79] as a result of which the sight of one eye was entirely destroyed, though he could still see dimly with the other.

About the same time, and in connection with prince Goufrou, the king became incensed against Chan Hazem [Khan Azam], deprived him of all his property, treated him with the deepest ignominy (even ordering all the Ommerau to spit on his beard), loaded him with chains, and sent him to be imprisoned in the fort of Gauler, where he lay for full two years. At length he was released and restored to favour and to his position in the court, through the entreaties of some of the king's concubines.

In the same year Mirza Ommerau was incapacitated by an attack of apoplexy, which deprived him of the use of one hand and one foot. Tzalamghan,[80] the Fausdar

* Or 'turrets' (Tr.)

79 De Laet evidently means *Ak*, the name of a plant. That is the Jesuit version.

80 Islam Khan. Some historians have Jahangir Quli Khan as an intervening governor between Qutbuddin and Islam Khan who administered the country from 1608 to 1613. His original name was Allauddin and was one of the descendants of Shaikh Salim Chishti of Sikri.

of Agra (or rather the leader of the brigands in all the district round), was promoted by the king to be governor of Bengal in place of Cotopdienchan, who (as mentioned above) had been murdered.

XXVI. MEHIRUNNISA.

[1608-11.]

Having had his fill of hunting, the king designed to return to Agra, and sent on ahead the captive Ethamandaulat, together with his jailor Dianetgan and all his household, in order that at Agra he might raise and pay into the royal treasury the two lacks of rupees which he owed to the king for his pardon. Shortly afterwards the king himself proceeded to Agra. He then wrote to Tzalamchan ordering him to send immediately to Agra the family of Cheer Affeghan, or at any rate his widow Meher-Metzia and his brother. On reaching the province of Bahaer Meher-Metzia visited a certain dervish whom she had heard to be a truthful foreteller of the future. On seeing her the dervish foretold that the king would be exceedingly gracious to her, and that her future would be brilliantly successful.

When they reached Agra the brother and son of Cheer Affeghan were handed over for custody to the Ommerau; but Meher-Metzia,[81] together with her little daughter, was committed to the care of the queen-mother, Rockia Sultan Begem [Ruqayya Sultan Begam], who received them with the greatest kindness, and could scarcely ever allow Meher-Metzia out of her sight.

---

81 Another version is that Mehirunnisa was appointed lady-in-waiting to Salima Begam and not to Ruqayya Begam. Both were widows of Akbar Daughter of Mehirunnisa was Ladili Begam, afterwards married to Shahriyar. Jahangir married Mehirunnisa in May 1611.

It happened sometime afterwards that Rockia took Meher-Metzia with her into the Mahael (*i.e.*, the king's seraglio). The king came in, and on learning that she was present, though veiled, loosened her veil with his own hand, and gazed at her face. A few days later, whilst the festival of the New Year was being celebrated after the fashion of the Mahometans, and whilst the king was enjoying himself amongst his concubines, Meher-Metzia brought to him her little daughter, then six or seven years old. Being by this time deeply in love with Meher-Metzia the king exclaimed with a smile, " I will be father to this child." Meher-Metzia replied, " Who am I that I should be numbered amongst the king's wives? Your Majesty must disregard me, who am but a poor widow. Only take pity on this child, and show kindness to her." After this the king fell so passionately in love with Meher-Metzia that he repaired in a boat every evening to the house of Ethamandaulat, and only returned to the palace at dawn. He had been in love with her when she was still a maiden, during the lifetime of his father Achabar; but she had already been betrothed to the Turk Cheer Affeghan, and hence his father would not allow him to marry her, although he never entirely lost his love for her.

After going to and fro to see her for forty nights, the king instructed Godzia Abdul Hassen[82] to demand the hand of Meher-Metzia for him from Ethamandaulat, for he was determined to make her his wife and to set her above all his other wives and concubines. Godzia Abdul Hassen was unwilling to carry out these instructions, and represented to His Majesty how ill it consorted with the

---

[82] Khwaja Abul Hasan. He should not be confounded with Abul Hasan or Asaf Khan, brother of Nur Jahan. The Khwaja began service as the Diwan of Daniyal. He made his mark in the Deccan campaigns. He was for sometime paymaster of the royal household and then Diwan (1621).

royal dignity for him to marry the daughter of a man who lay under such deep disgrace. The king received this advice with considerable displeasure, and drove Godzia Abdul Hassen away to carry the message. On receiving it Ethamandaulat came and prostrated himself before the king after the customary fashion, professed his unworthiness, and declared that he and his daughter should be at the king's disposal. Finally, an auspicious day having been selected, the king married her before the Cazi. Amidst impressive acclamations her name was changed from Meher-Metzia to Nourzia Begem ([Nur Jahan], *i.e.*, Light of the World. The king loved her so deeply that he set her above all his other wives. He made her father a commander of 5,000 horse, and bestowed various dignities and offices in the court upon all her relatives.

XXVII. CAMPAIGNS IN RAJPUTANA AND THE DECCAN.

[1608-14.]

In the year of Mahumet 1020[83] and the sixth of his reign the king despatched Nabab Mortesa Ghan with his youngest son Sultan Tzerriar [Prince Shahriyar] to Guzrat with the full authority of a governor. Ghan Zia [Khan Jahan Lodi] was sent with several Ommerau to Brampore (the province of Khor having been assigned to Gan Ganna)[84] : and Mahabatgan was made commander of the army sent to carry on the war against Radzia Rana Mondou.[85]

In the same year there came to the king a splendid embassy from Xa Abas, king of Persia. At the head of it was Zennhelbeecq [Zambil Beg] who brought most

---

83 It corresponds to March 1611—February 1612.

84 Khan Khanan, *i.e.*, Abdur-Rahim Khor is Karra. *vide infra*.

85 The epithet Mondou or Mazdout has already been explained. (See *n.* 54.) It is *mardud*.

costly presents. He was received by the king with the greatest honour, and was sent home again with many splendid gifts.

In Bengal the dominions of Radzia Cots were subdued by Tzalauchan. Moursa Chan,[86] son of Hissa Chan, made his submission to the king, together with many other chieftains. Mahabot Chan, who had been sent against Radzia Rana, after capturing sundry towns from Radzia Mazdout was recalled to Agra, his place as commander of the army being taken by Abdul-Chan,[87] with the support of other Ommerau. On reaching Sissemere[88] Abdul-Chan inflicted a heavy defeat on the army of the Raspots, or Hindus, which the Rana had led against him. They fled in rout to Oudepore, and all that district was conquered, the Hindu women and children being enslaved. The royal army then advanced to Siavend,[89] the capital of the Rana's ancestors, and a very strong place, which the kings of Delhi had never dared to attack, on account of the impenetrable wildernesses and forests by which it is surrounded. Abdul Chan gave orders that these forests should be gradually cut down ahead of the advancing

---

86 Musa or Muchha Khan, son of Isa Khan who had his capital either at Sonargaon or Katrabuh in the neighbourhood. Cots stands for Kuch (Bihar) The new Raja, Lachmi Narayan consented to pay homage (T. J. I. 269, 443-4).

87 Abdullah Khan He succeeded in 1609 Mahabat Khan as commander of the imperial forces against Rana Amar Singh. Khwaja Abdullah, an immigrant from Transoxiana, was manly and zealous. He had been a partisan of Salim but later on deserted to the side of Akbar. But for this, says Jahangir (T.J, I., 27), he would have been a faultless hero. The Padshah continued to show confidence in his abilities. References to him will be found in the text.

88 We read in other books that it was at Mihrpur that a defeat was inflicted on the Rajputs by Abdulla Khan.

89 Chavand where Amar Singh had been crowned on January 29, 1597.

army, and that pathways should be constructed through the fastnesses of the hills. On perceiving what was being done the Rana, leaving 2,000 or 3,000 Raspots in the fortress, together with a great store of provisions, fled into the trackless wilds of the forests and mountains, taking with him his family and the members of his seraglio.

Soon afterwards the forces of Abdul-Chan arrived within sight of the fortress. The moat was filled up with logs of trees, and so huge a mound was raised against the walls that at last, the garrison having been exterminated, the place fell. Thereupon all the Hindu temples (or "pagodas") were razed to the ground; some of them were over 1,000 years old. In their place the conqueror gave instructions for the building of a most beautiful mosque.

Next Abdul-Chan and his cavalry pursued the Rana with such energy through the desolate forest-tracts that he was compelled frequently to change his hiding place, and to abandon his territory to the enemy.

After this highly successful campaign the king transferred Abdul-Chan to the governorship of Gusarat, in order that he might subdue or destroy the Bielsgrati [90] and Coulyes, who infested the roads and plundered the caravans of the merchants. Many Radzias and inhabitants of the province came to welcome Abdulgan, giving him costly presents and making their submission to him; but Radzia Eder and Lael Coulie,[91] trusting to the trackless retreats in which they lived, refused to submit. However after visiting Amadabat, Abdul Chan, supported by 500 picked cavalry, attacked the stronghold of Eder (which lies 70 cos from Amadabat) with such

90 Bhils and Grassia, two hill and robber tribes. For Grassia and Kolis, *vide supra* pp. 20, 34.

91 Obviously he was a Koli chief—Lal Koli. Radzia Eder is Raja of Idar, which place was the retreat of the Kolis.

energy and speed that he preceded the news of his own coming. After an obstinate battle lasting some hours, the Radzia's forces were so thoroughly defeated that the Radzia was forced to fly with 4 or 5 followers, whilst the fort and its treasure fell into the hands of Abdul Chan

Shortly afterwards, on learning that Lael Coulie had cut off and plundered a caravan, looting all its goods, Abdul Chan moved against him Lael Coulie accepted the challenge, and advanced with a force of 2,000 or 3,000 cavalry and 10,000 or 12,000 infantry. After a fiercely contested battle Abdul Chan emerged victorious. Coulie was killed in the battle; and his head was cut off and fixed above the gate of Amadabat

Chan Ziahan,[92] who had been sent to Brampore to carry on the war against Melec Amber, king of the Decan, was by no means so fortunate. He wrote to the king ascribing his ill-success to the power of Amber and to the discord amongst his own Ommerau, and urging the king to send one of his sons to take command. Accordingly the king sent to Brampore Sultan Perves, together with Radia Ramdas. Sultan Perves sent letters to Adel-Chan

92 Khan Jahan Lodi His name has been variously spelt as Ghan Zia, Gan or Chan Ziahan Pir Khan, styled Salabat Khan and Khan Jahan (1608), was one of the greatest nobles of the court and enjoyed the much-coveted distinction of 'sonship' (*Farzand-i-Khas*) He at this time held 5,000 *zat* and *suwar*.

Parvez was sent to the Deccan in 1609 and Khan Jahan next year But De Laet says that Khan Jahan Lodi had preceded the prince to Burhanpur The double attack on Ahmednagar (1611) from the north by Khan Jahan and from the west by Abdullah Khan (governor of Gujarat) failed. The plan was that the two forces would meet at Daulatabad and attack Malik Ambar, the minister of Ahmednagar But Abdullah Khan did not keep himself in touch with the movements of the northern army, arrived early and was harassed by the guerilla bands (Bargis) of the Nizam Shahi minister Lack of concerted action was the main cause of the failure (T. J., I, 219-221).

and Gotobel Melicq asking them why they had omitted to send the customary gifts to king Ziahiangier. They replied that the presents had been ready for a long time. let the prince send a representative to receive them: and let him make the same demand from Melec Amber, and if he refused compel him by force to obey.

Thereupon Sultan Perves sent Radia Mansingh and Radia Ramdas with a strong force to Ballagat against Melicq Amber Fierce fighting took place daily in that region between the royal forces and the armies of the Decan. Finally the king sent Gan Azem with 3,000 or 4,000 Hadis to Brampore · and advanced himself to Assemere.

Soon afterwards it was announced that the Rana had emerged from his hiding place, and had regained possession of Oudepore, Pormandel[93] and the surrounding region. The king's son Sultan Grom[94] was sent with a strong force against him, and decided first to attack Oudepore, whence he sent out detachments in various directions, and reduced the Rana to such straits that he entreated the prince as a suppliant that he might be restored to the king's favour. Sultan Grom persuaded the Rana to entrust to himself his son Kharen in order that he might

---

93 Prof Sarkar is of opinion that the reference is to the two well-known places in Udaipur, Pur and Mandal.

94 Prince Khurram. The imperial army against Rana Amar Singh was commanded successively by Mahabat Khan (1608-9), Abdullah Khan Feroz Jang (1609-11), Raja Basu, Mirza Aziz Koka (1612-13) and Prince Khurram (1613-14). It was at the suggestion of Mirza Aziz that Jahangir shifted his residence to Ajmir (Nov. 1613) and Prince Khurram was appointed to the command The prince and Khan Azam quarrelled and the latter was recalled. Khurram pressed the Rana so hard that terms of peace were arranged in 1614. No war indemnity or territorial compensation was exacted; even Rana Amar Singh was spared the humiliation of personal attendance at the Mogul court. His son Prince Karan (Kharen of De Laet) was to represent him there.

be sent to the king, and undertook that this step should bring about a reconciliation between the king and the Rana. The latter agreed and sent his son to the prince together with many magnificent gifts, amongst which was an elephant named (on account of its great beauty) Alem Ghomaen,[95] *i.e.*, pride of the world.

The prince received Kharen with great honour, bestowed on him rich gifts estimated to be worth a lack of rupees, and conducted him to his father at Assemere. As a result of this the king received the Rana into favour again. He retained Kharen with himself, and gave to him Oudepore, Pormandel and neighbouring localities.

Ghan Azem, having arrived at Brampore, summoned thither also Gan Ganna, who was conducting a campaign in the district of Khoor.[96] At a council held by the strongest and most loyal of the king's magnates it was arranged that Radia Abdul Hassen, Radia Mametzing and Radia Raemdas, with many[96a] of the Ommerau, should advance towards Ballagat, and that Gan Ganna with Ganziahan should follow in support with the rest of the army. Melecq Amber advanced to meet the attack with 20,000 cavalry which he had raised himself, 20,000 which Adelghan had lent to him, and 10,000 sent by Gotobel Melicq. Abdul Can, the governor of Gusarat, was also ordered by the king to join his forces as soon

95 Alam-guman. This with 17 other elephants was captured by Khurram. At the sight of the elephants the "hearts of the loyal rejoiced." The Padshah mounted the elephant and scattered about much money (T. J, I, 260).

96 Khor or Khoor may be Korah or Karra, or it may be Shamsabad.

96a The names in the text are Khwaja Abul Hasan, Raja Man Singh, and Raja Ram Das. Khankhanan had been recalled but was reappointed next year (1612) on the failure of the combined attack of 1611.

as possible to the army in the Decan; and this order he obeyed with alacrity.

The royal forces had by now drawn near to Kerki [Khirki], the capital of the Decan, an unwalled town, but only 5 or 6 cos distant from the strong fortress of Daultabad. Melecq Amber, who had resolved to risk a battle, sent Fassen to cut off Abdulchan before he joined forces with the royal army. Fassen carried out his orders with energy, but when the royal army, which consisted of 100,000 cavalry, came into sight, Melicq Amber was terror-stricken and fled in panic with a few followers. However, Molhena Mamet Lary, the Wackhil of Adelghan, and commander of the 20,000 cavalry sent by the latter in support of the king of the Decan, remained behind in the fortress, and perceiving the greatly superior power of the royal forces, had recourse to guile. He caused forged letters to be conveyed by obscure messengers to the chief Ommerau Radia Manzing, Raemdas and Gan-Ganna, in which it was announced that king Ziahangier was dead. The Ommerau were deceived by the letters, collected their baggage, left the Decan, and retreated to Brampore. On receiving similar letters Abdulchan burnt his tents, retreated to a strong position at Thaliegieran,* and thence returned to Gusarat. Meanwhile Melicq Amber, recovering from his panic, had no difficulty in recovering all the places which had been occupied by the Mogols, and set to work to fortify them with new defences.

King Ziahiangier was greatly enraged at the silly credulity shewn in this affair by his Ommerau, and sent them letters in which he reproached them bitterly. Having advanced to Mandow he made Mahobatgan governor of

* Abdulla retreated to Baglana (T J., I, 221). The word may stand for Thalner.

Brampore and the province of Barar. Fortune favoured Mahobatgan to such an extent that in a short time he had reconquered all the country as far as Kerki.

XXVIII. REVOLTS IN BENGAL, ETC.
[March 1612.]

After staying at Mandow for 17 months the king visited Gusarat, and on reaching Amadabat transferred Abdulchan from that province to the province of Kalpi and Chor. Thence, after spending a whole year in hunting, the king returned to Agra. Chabeech [Shah Beg], the governor of Khandahaer, was now incapacitated by old age, and was therefore recalled, Bador-Chan the Usbeg being sent in his place. About the same time the king sent Tseziad-Ghan Chieck Zaden[97] to Tzalam-Ghan [Islam Khan], governor of Bengal, with instructions that he should be made governor of Odia [Orissa]. However Osman-Chan, the Pathan, who had for several years been master of the region between Odia and Daeck,[98] and had made many incursions upon imperial territory advanced with a very strong force to besiege Daeck. Tzalan-Chan sent Tzesiad-Chan against him, together with Mirza Efftager, Ethaman-Chan and many other Ommerau,[99] following himself with the rest of his forces at a distance of 10 or 15 cos, in order to give support if they were hard pressed

[97] Shujaat Khan Shaikh Zada He was a descendant of Shaikh Salim Chishti Shaikh Kabir was his personal name; Shujaat Khan was his title Jahangir speaks highly of him

[98] Dacca The capital of Bengal had been changed from Rajmahal to Dacca by Islam Khan (*vide supra*). It was called Jahangir-nagar, and Raj Mahal was known as Akbarnagar.

[99] The amirs mentioned in the text are Mirza Iftikhar and Ihtimam Khan Others were Kishwar Khan, Shaikh Achhay, and Saiyad Adam Barha

When the battle [100] began, Effager and Mierieck Zilaier [Mirak Jalayer] made such an impetuous attack that the enemy were driven back in disorder. However Osman sent against them a very fierce elephant, which killed Efftager and compelled the royal forces to fall back. Tzesiadgan, who was himself mounted on an elephant, in endeavouring to escape the attack of the raging beast, cast himself down and broke his leg, being with difficulty rescued by his followers. The royal forces had begun to retreat in disorder, and would have been destroyed, had not an unlooked for chance restored their fortunes. A certain wounded soldier, who was lying on the ground, chanced to shoot Osman in the eye as he was riding past on his elephant. Osman shortly afterwards died of the wound, and his troops were so much dismayed by his death that they immediately tookto flight. The royal forces were rallied (though this took a considerable time), and news of the battle was sent to Tzlan-Chan, who arrived on the scene of action two days later. Tzediatchan [101] had died of his wound, but Tzalanchan rapidly pursued the brother, widow and children of Osman, and captured them. He then returned to Daeck, the capital of Bengal, and despatched his captives [102] together with all their elephants and treasure to the king, who had left Agra and repaired by speedy marches to Lahor.

Abdulchan [103] who had been made governor of Kalpi and Khor, thoroughly reduced those districts, either

---

[100] Fought on March 12, 1617, at a place called Nek Ujyal, some 200 miles from Dacca

[101] Evidently the reference is to Shujaat Khan But he did not die in 1612 but lived to enjoy the fruits of the victory and was given the title of Rustam Zaman (T. J, I, 214)

[102] The captives were very well treated by the Emperor. There was policy in the generous treatment

[103] There were two disturbances round Kalpi and Kanouj. The earlier one was suppressed by Abdullah Khan in the autumn

subduing or destroying all the Radias and others who had rebelled, though many of these had never obeyed former governors. Their wives and children were enslaved, to a number which is said to have exceeded two lacks, and were sold in the region of Yran [Iran]. The strongholds of the rebels were razed to the ground.

XXIX. EMBASSY TO PERSIA. [1613-20.]

The king selected Chan Azem,[104] a prudent statesman and a noble of high birth, as ambassador to Persia. He entrusted to him the most splendid presents for king Xa Abas, *viz.*, some most valuable vases made of agate, a great variety of cotton and woollen stuffs made in India and interwoven with gold and silver, gilded and bejewelled daggers, scimitars, shields, and other articles of rare and precious workmanship. The total value of these presents was reckoned at 70,000 rupees. 60,000 rupees were allotted from the royal treasury for the expenses of the journey; and a splendid retinue, with a picked bodyguard, was sent with the ambassador, who was the bearer of most friendly letters to the king of Persia. In these the king spoke very highly of Chan Azem, the ambassador, calling him his friend and even his brother.

---

of 1606; the second one of 1611 was put down by Khan Khanan who was then despatched to the Deccan as mentioned above in Sect. XXVII.

104 His title was Khan Alam, not Khan Azam. His original name was Barkhordar. There is some confusion about the dates of the embassies and the names of the ambassadors. In 1611 came the Persian ambassador Yadgar Ali to the Mughal court. When he went back after a stay of two years, along with him was sent Barkhordar as return ambassador. In March 1615 arrived the second Persian embassy under Mustafa Beg, and in Oct. 1616 the third under Muhammad Reza (who died at Agra), and in Dec. 1620 the fourth under Zambil Beg. Barkhordar returned in 1619 and was made Khan Alam.

Chan Azem and his retinue, having reached Seraed [Shiraz ?], a Persian city, whose governor was Hassenbeecq Ommerau, were there received by the governor with the greatest honour and magnificence. The embassy then proceeded to Spahan, whence the king of Persia sent out Konstalicq Chan Ommerau with many others to meet it. Chan Azem was conducted with the greatest pomp into the city. When he was brought before the king of Persia the latter rose from his throne, came several paces forward, took the hand of the ambassador, and seated him beside himself on the throne

After this gorgeous banquets were held daily, and all kinds of sports and shows were carried on. The ambassador was also permitted to visit all parts of the province of Yraen. Finally, the king prepared magnificent gifts, 500 most beautiful Persian horses, 20 very fine he-mules, 500 she-mules, 150 excellent dromedaries of either sex, a great quantity of silken fabrics and of cloth of gold and silver, etc. All these were entrusted to Chan Azam for king Ziahaengier. Chan Azem also received magnificent presents for himself, and was warmly praised in the letters which were sent by him for his extraordinary prudence. In these letters the king of Persia asked that King Ziahaengier should consider whether it would not be just to restore to Persia the city of Khandahaer, which had been treacherously handed over by rebels[105] to his father Achabar; Xa Abas also professed that he would be ready to surrender equally valuable districts elsewhere in exchange for Khandahaer.

105 Muzaffar Husain Mirza, the Persian governor of Kandahar, unable to hold it against his several enemies, handed it over to Akbar in 1594 Muzaffar Husain implored Shah Abbas the Persian king (1587-1629) to send him aid. But no help came. Rather than be overwhelmed by the Uzbegs, he surrendered the fort to the Moguls.

Finally, after staying for full two years, the ambassador left Spahan with his retinue, in company with a Persian embassy.[106] Lahor was safely reached. At that time the king was paying his first visit to Cassemere. Sultan Goufrou, who had long remained in the custody of Assoff Chan, had recently been handed over to Chan Ziahan. Mahobet Chan was then the governor of Kabul and Banges.

XXX. EVENTS IN BENGAL, ETC.

[1613-20.]

Tzalanchan died in Bengal and was succeeded by his brother, Chieck Cassem,[107] governor of Patana. Kherram Chan,[108] the son of Tzalanchan, went to wait upon the king, taking with him all the property of his father. He had left Daeck and arrived at Radia Mahal when he met his uncle, who had long detested him, and who now took the opportunity to steal several of his elephants and some other property. When the affair was reported to the king it roused such a storm of indignation against Cassem that he was recalled after less than a year of office, and Ebraham Chan,[109] one of Nour Ziahan's relatives, who had already risen through her favour to be commander of 5,000 horse, was sent to take his place.

---

106 Reference here is to the embassy of Zambil Beg, Dec. 1620. He and Khan Alam travelled together but the ambassador was detained on the way. Jahangir's first visit to Kashmir was in March 1620.

107 Shaikh Qasim. Qasim Khan governed Bengal from 1613 to 1617.

108 Ikram Khan. His original name was Hushang. He made presents of Maghs and elephants to Jahangir (T.J., I, 236, 269).

109 Ibrahim Khan was Nur Jahan's brother. He was governor of Behar before his appointment to the subah of Bengal. (See Note 110). He was governor of Bengal from 1617 to 1623.

When Cassem received the order about his successor, he left Daeck as rapidly as possible, with his family and all his property. However he met Ebraham near Radia Com [Raj Mahal ?], and was ordered to surrender the elephants and other goods which he had stolen from his nephew. He refused; whereupon ensued first a quarrel and then a fight. Perceiving himself likely to be worsted, Cassem barbarously slaughtered several of his women in order to be able to fly the more swiftly, and leaving all his property in the hands of the royal forces escaped with a few followers. Ebrahim was inducted into his governorship with the greatest loyalty and obedience by the lesser officials. Soon afterwards the king sent an expedition against the Moeckhani,[110] who had committed various daring hostilities. Ebrahim was sent in support, and defeated the rebels with huge slaughter, many being killed in the battle, more being sold into slavery, and much valuable booty being taken. The king was so much pleased by this affair that he sent Ebrahim a present of horses, a scimitar and a dagger, and changed his name to Pherooszian Ghan.

In the same year[111] the king sent Martasachan to capture the fortress of Kangra, which is very strongly defended both by nature and by art, so much so that the kings of Delhi had never been able to capture it from the Hindus. It is surrounded on all sides by steep crags and a deep ditch. The only approach is through a forest 50 cos broad, the pathway through which is very narrow and precipitous. However, Martasa Chan was in no way terrified by these difficulties, but summoning engineers and workmen from

---

110 De Laet refers to the Zemindar (Durjan Sal) of Khokhara which was annexed in 1615. Ibrahim was made *Fath-jang*, not *Feroz-jang* (T. J. I 316).

111 In March 1615 Murtaza Khan, governor of the Punjab, was appointed to capture Kangra. He died soon after. Kangra was taken in Nov. 1620 by Raja Bikramjit. It was a proud feather in Jahangir's cap.

all sides, had the forest cut down ahead of his advance, and moving forward about half a cos a day, finally reached the fortress in the eighth month. He attacked it by means of a lofty mound and many engineering works, and pressed it so hard that it seemed likely to fall in a short time. However its commander's death cut short the expedition.

In the year of Mahumet 1028[112] (A.D. 1618) the king paid his second visit to Cassemere, and returned at once to Lahor. Sultan Gousrou[113] was still in the

---

112 It began in December 1618

113 A summary of Khusrau's career may be given here. The events of 1606-7 had sealed his fate but temporarily. He had the support of the older nobility, he was the son-in-law of Mirza Aziz and the nephew of Raja Man; and he was 'the *amor et deliciae* of the people' In course of time the memory of his revolt wore off and 'the feelings of fatherly affections having come into movement the son was allowed to pay his respects every day to the father' (T.J, I., 252). He was considered, and naturally enough, the future sovereign Prince Khurram had not power enough to dissuade the emperor from his intentions or attractiveness enough to dislodge his brother from his place in the people's affections But he was for the time being helped by a new party of upstarts that had been organising its strength and establishing its influence over the emperor ever since 1611. This was the Nur Jahan *junta* The Court thus divided itself into two parties—one for and the other against Khusrau. The latter party triumphed Man Singh was dead (July 1614), Mirza Aziz had been disgraced, Mahabat Khan, the famous general, might, with impunity, rail against the petticoat ascendancy but he could not disentangle the emperor from the web of degenerating romance that Nur Jahan was weaving round him. The emperor's kind attitude towards Khusrau did not suit her purpose, and so the prince was forbidden to pay his respects because 'his appearance showed no signs of openness and happiness.' (T J, I, 261.) In 1616 he was transferred from the custody of Ani Rai Singh Dalan, the well-known Rajput gaoler of Gwalior, to Asaf Khan, brother of Nur Jahan. It is idle to speculate how the course of subsequent events would have been affected had the empress made peace

custody of Ghan Ziahan, but Noursiahan Begem and Assof-Ghan at length persuaded the king to commit him to the charge of his brother Sultan Ghorom, whom the king loved dearly, had made commander of 40,000 horse, and had despatched to the war in the Decan, together with Godzia Abdul Hassen and other powerful nobles. For the kings of Visiapor [Bijapur] and Golconda had now for several years refused to send their gifts to the king, and Melecq Amber [Malik Ambar] had seized the provinces of Candhees and Baraer, while Chan-Channa [Abdur-rahim] with his army of Raspots sat idle in Brampore [Burhanpur].

Bador Chan the Usbec was succeeded in the governorship of Candahar by Abdul Azies Ghan. Ghan Ziahan [Khan Jahan] was made governor of Molthan. Bador Chan was put in command of the Kangra expedition; and Abdul Chan, governor of Kalpi and Radzia Bertsingh Bondela were ordered to join the army of Sultan Gorom. Sultan Perves became governor of Pathana.

---

and alliance with Khusrau At any rate it was not done, though for some time there was some talk and probability of its occurrence. But it did not materialise probably because Nur Jahan wanted a more docile son-in-law like Shahriyar (*Nâ-shudani*) or because Khusrau refused the hand of Ladili Begam, or possibly because such a strengthening union was against the interest of Asaf Khan who had his own son-in-law (Khurram, married in April 1612) to support For sometime Khusrau was handed over to the custody of Khan Jahan Lodi in 1619 or 1620; and then he was given over to the tender mercies of the "subtle, false and barbarously tyrannous" Prince Khurram in 1620 The tragic end came in January 1622, so far as we know in the manner described by De Laet (*vide* Sect. XXXI) In the process of time when Nemesis had done her work, Aurangzeb (Khurram's son) thus wrote to the captive father: "How do you still regard the memory of (your brothers) Khusrau and Parvez, whom you did to death before your accession and who had threatened no injury to you?" The Mughal history is a history of the survival of the fittest—fittest in mean chicanery and inhuman valour. Khusrau and Dara (though first-born and possessing many good qualities) had no chance in it.

XXXI. SHAH JAHAN IN THE DECCAN.
[1617-22.]

In the year of Mahumet 1029 (A.D. 1619) Radia Rana died and was succeeded by his son Kharen, whom the king sent from the court to his own province. He despatched his brother Radia Riem [Raja Bhim], with two or three thousand Raspots, to support Sultan Gorom[114] (henceforward called Xa-Ziahan), who had established the headquarters of his great army at Brampore, where he had been joined by Abdul-Chan and his brother Therder-Chan [Sardar Khan] and also by Lala Bert-Sing with his Raspots.

Having concentrated all his forces at Brampore, Xa Ziahan sent forward Abdulchan, Lala Bertzingh and Godzia Abdul Hassen with many other Ommerau to attack Melicq Amber. Ziadourayam [Jadav Rai] and Mirza Mackhey [Makki] were despatched at the same time with letters to Cotobel Melic of Golconda, and Mahamet Tachie[115] with letters to Adel-Chan of Visiapor, in which those kings were threatened with invasion and expulsion from their dominions in case they did not immediately send their customary gifts to the king.

Abdulchan and his forces crossed the Ballagatta, being followed at a distance of ten or twelve cos by the prince with the rest of the army. After some battles with Melic Amber, in which the royal forces were always

---

114 Strictly speaking, Prince Khurram was not styled Shah Jahan before the conclusion of the truce of 1617. He was styled in November 1616 Shah Sultan Khurram. After his revolt he was always called Bedaulat by his father. He arrived at Burhanpur on the same day on which the emperor reached Mandu (March 6, 1617).

115 Muhammad Taqi T.J. gives the names of Afzal Khan and Raja Bikramjit as being the men sent to Adil Shah of Bijapur (T.J., I, 368).

victorious, Kerki[116] was once more occupied, the palace of Amber was razed to the ground, and vast amounts of booty were captured. The provinces of Gandees and Barar, and the district around Amdanager, were again annexed by the king's dominions. All the booty, together with the presents which had been sent by the kings of Visiapor and Golconda, was sent to the king, who received it with great joy, and began to have high hopes of his son's military prowess.

In the year 1030[117] the king returned to Agra, where he spent his time in hunting, and resided for the most part in the garden of Sultan Perves across the river. In the same year died Ethaman Daulet,[118] the king's chief Wazir. The king bestowed all the dead man's property upon Nourziahan Begem, his own wife, and daughter of Ethaman Daulet. He appointed Godia Abdul Hassen chief Wazir in place of the dead man.

Xa-Ziahan, who was at Brampore, and was acting as jailor to his brother Gousrou, began to make a plot whereby he might be able to get rid of his brother without incurring the suspicion of having murdered him. He took into his confidence Ganganna and his most faithful Ommerau, and then departed on a hunting expedition. His slave Reza, who had been commissioned to commit the crime, knocked at dead of night upon the door of prince Gousrou's bedroom, pretending that he and the companions whom he had brought with him were the bearers of

116 Khirki, the new capital The events herein described were those of 1620-21, and not of 1617 when a truce had been concluded without any fighting

117 Corresponding to November 1620-21 A.D Jahangir stayed at Ajmir for 3 years, November 1613-1616, thence to Mandu which he reached in March 1617, thence he had his tour to Ahmedabad. He did not return to Agra before the spring of 1619.

118 Itimad-ud-dowlah died in the beginning of 1622 (*vide supra*).

robes and letters from the king, and that they had instructions to set the prince at liberty. The prince did not believe this story. However Reza broke open the door, struck down the prince, who was unarmed, strangled him, placed his corpse back on the bed, and shut the door once more. At dawn the wife of the prince, who was the daughter of Gan Azem, entered the bedroom and finding her husband dead filled the whole palace with her shrieks. There was general mourning for the prince's untimely death, and for a space no suspicion that he had been murdered.

Xa-Ziahan returned to the city, and sent letters to his father announcing his brother's death. He made all the Ommerau and Mancebdars add their signatures to these letters, in order the better to conceal his own crime. He had the body buried in a garden outside the city. Nabab Nourdien Coulie [Nuruddin Quli], who was present in Brampore at the time, wrote a full account to the king of what had actually happened. On receiving the news the king mourned deeply for the death of his son, and wrote most bitterly reprimanding the Ommerau, asking why they had neglected to inform him whether his son had perished from a natural or a violent death, and giving directions that the body should be exhumed and sent to himself, in order that it might be buried in his mother's tomb at Elhabas. He summoned the father-in-law of Gousrou, Ghan Asem, condoled with him, and committed to his charge his grandson Sultan Bolachi [Bulaqi] (who was made a commander of 10,000 horse) in order that he might be responsible for his education.

About the same time Abdulchan left Xa-Ziahan without taking leave and returned to his province of Kalpi, much to the king's anger, who recalled him while still on the way home; he then returned to Brampore.

XXXII. WAR WITH PERSIA.
[June 1622.]

At this time also it came to the king's ears that Sha Abas, the ruler of Persia, was about to attack Kandahar. The governor of that district was then Assiessghan [Aziz Khan]. He strongly fortified the citadel, concentrated his forces, and asked the king to strengthen the garrison. The king ordered Chan Siahan [Khan Jahan], governor of Molthan, to hasten to Kandahar with abundant supplies and all the men he had available. However Chan Siahan neglected to obey these orders. Meanwhile the Persians formed the siege of the city and pressed it hard night and day.

The king was for some time in doubt as to whom he should send to raise the siege, but finally, on the advice of his counsellors, he sent Abdul Chan, who had returned to Kalpi, this time with Xa Ziahan's leave. On receiving the king's orders Abdulchan betook himself to Lahore with 5,000 picked cavalry and 100 elephants. This so pleased the king, who was himself at Lahor, that he bestowed the hand of the daughter of Dhan-Xa upon Mirza Chan, son of Abdulchan.

The siege had already lasted for six months when Sha-Abas himself arrived at the head of a very large force. On hearing of this Ziahangier came to the conclusion that it was too late to send reinforcements, and wrote to the king of Persia saying that he would surrender the city of his own accord. At the same time he sent orders to Assufghan and the other Ommerau to hand the city over to the Persians. However Assufghan, suspecting these letters to be forged, refused to carry out the order, whereupon Sha-Abas had the chief bastion undermined and blown up, so that the place would have been captured by assault had not Assuffghan and the other Ommerau surrendered. They were sent home unharmed, together with their troops, by the Persians. Having in this manner obtained possession of the town and fortress, Sha-Abas made Colis Ally Chan governor, and then returned to his capital at Spahan [Isfahan].

XXXIII. SHAH JAHAN'S REBELLION. [1623.]

Shortly before this the king had sent Assofghan, brother of Nourziahan Begem, to Agra, with orders to bring the royal treasure to Lahor. However Ethabarchan [Itibar Khan], the governor of Agra, and Ethamatchan [Itimad Khan], the Treasurer, both of whom were eunuchs, at first refused to carry out the orders, and later, when they could no longer refuse, caused delays, instituted elaborate calculations, had repairs made on the bags in which the treasure was contained, and in every way hindered its despatch. Meanwhile Assofghan was urgent with them to make haste, for he had secretly sent letters to Xa-Ziahan informing him of his forthcoming journey with the treasure, and asking him to make his appearance between Agra and Delly, and to carry off the treasure.

Xa-Ziahan, who was most ambitious, had long desired to seize[119] the reins of government whilst his father was still alive. To this end he had married the daughter

119 The denouement of the reign began with the revolt of Shah Jahan early in 1623. Khusrau had been killed; Parvez had been sent away to the distant province of Behar; and Shahriyar had become the son-in-law of Nur Jahan (April 1621). The plan was to send Shah Jahan away to Kandahar on a risky expedition. So long he had been the impartial recipient of the favours of the emperor and of the empress, but now it was her interest to secure the succession for her son-in-law. Owing to the emperor's failing health, her grip over the imperial affairs was tighter and firmer than ever. But the marriage of her niece Arjumand Banu or Mumtaz Mahal (Asaf Khan's daughter) with Shah Jahan

of Assofghan, whose party,[120] consisting of himself, his sister, his brothers, and other Coratsensian [Khorasani] magnates, possessed almost supreme power at court. To this same end he had bound his Ommerau to his cause by many kindnesses and heavy bribes, so that they had even sworn loyalty to him against the king himself.

He had been placed by his father in charge of great and very rich provinces,[120a] Mandow, Brampore, Gandeers, Oudepore, Baraer, Amdanagar, Guserat (which extends from Brampore to Suratta and from there to the city of Amadabat). In all these provinces and their cities, which were very numerous, he had set up prefects or governors by his own authority, and had lavished high salaries upon them.

Finally, and to the same end, the prince had lately made away with his elder brother, by the advice of Radia Bickermanse,[121] who was supposed to possess the power of foretelling the future.

---

in April 1612, had cut athwart the solidarity of her party. Moreover the prince had grown too big to be thus trifled with. His revolt ostensibly began with the unsuccessful attempt to intercept the convoy of royal treasure from Agra to Lahore.

120 Itimad-ud-dowlah had four sons and four daughters. His sons were: Muhammad Sharif (killed in 1607 for complicity in the Khusrau plot) Abul Hasan, Itiqad Khan and Ibrahim Khan. Of these, the second was the most famous, and he is known in history as Asaf Khan, so styled in 1614. He had been styled Itiqad Khan in 1611, but soon after the title was passed on to his younger brother. Yaminuddowlah was another name of Abul Hasan who again should be carefully distinguished from Khwaja Abul Hasan (Dewan). Asaf Khan became *Vakil* in 1626 Itiqad Khan had also the name of Shapur (T. J., I, 218).

120a Udaipur is included in this list because from the Imperial point of view its Rana was merely a tributary Zamindar. Coins were struck there (Irvine's *Later Mughals* I, 42) Gandeers is Khandesh with Burhanpur as the headquarters. Under Akbar, it was called Dan-desh, after Prince Danyal.

121 Raja Bikramjit. His original name was Sundar. He had a great reputation as a warrior and was the right-hand man of Shah Jahan, whose deputy he was in the government of Gujarat.

Nothing seemed to be wanting save that he should add to the huge treasures, which he had collected from his provinces during five or six years, his father's treasures also.

On receiving the message already spoken of from his father-in-law, the prince immediately called together all his Ommerau, and also Radia Bickerman, the governor of Gusaratte, from Amadabat, and the governors of Brodora, Cambaia and Brot-Chia [Broach], all of whom came to join him at Brampore.

In the year of Mahumet 1031,[122] Xa-Ziahan left Brampore with a very strong army of 70,000 horse. He pretended that he was going towards Mandow to hunt. Such was the speed of his advance that he covered, with his whole army, 20 and sometimes 30 cos a day. He hoped to reach Assemere before Ethaberghan, the governor of Agra, should gain any inkling of his intention. Thus in 15 days from Brampore he reached Fettapore, in company with Ganganna, Mirza Darab, Radia Bickermanse, Rostomghan, Tsosshalie, Mamet Tackieck, Sayetghan and many other Ommerau,[123] both his own and the king's.

When Ethabarchan heard of this, he brought back the royal treasures, which he was preparing to hand over to Assofghan, into the fort, and sent word to the king through the post-service about the prince's advance and what he planned to effect. The king hastened to Agra from Lahor.

---

122 Corresponding to November 1621—October 1622

123 Shah Jahan's followers were: Khan Khanan and his son Darab Khan, Raja Bikramjit, Rustam Khan, Muhammad Taqi, Saiyad Khan. Others mentioned below are Bairam Beg and Wazier Khan. I am not able to identify either Tsosshali or Tsoffali (*infra*). Prof. Hodivala points out that Shighāli was the surname of two men, Muhammad Quli and Yakub (*Akbar-Nama* III. 424, 663, 1197). He may be Yusuf Ali or Shujaat Ali.

Meanwhile the prince sent Radia Bickermanse, the chief officer of his camp, Beyrambeecq, Rostomchan, T'Soffali, Deria Chan, and Wasirchan Mamet, Tackieck to seize Agra fort. However Ethabarchan, who was loyal to the king, had already fortified it, arranged artillery defences, and protected the gates by inner fortifications. Beyrambeecq entered the city and took up his quarters in the palace of Mirza Abdulla, son of Ghan Azem. However on attacking the gate of the fort he was decisively repulsed by the garrison under the leadership of Radia Baderois.[124] Soon afterwards Radia Bickermanse came up and took up his quarters in the palace of Assoffghan. He gave instructions to Rostomchan and Derria-Chan to ransack the palaces of the king's chief nobles, Nouradien Coulie, Lascarchan and others, who were holding the fortress, and to plunder their treasures. Sixteen lacks of rupees were taken from the palace of Lascarchan, ten from that of Nourdien Coulie, and more still from that of Assuff Chan. In this fashion sixty or seventy lacks of rupees were amassed in a space of three days from the palaces of various Ommerau. This done, the rebel Ommerau returned to the prince at Fettapore, without harming the inhabitants of the city in any other way.

Perceiving that he must give up the hope of carrying off his father's treasure, and despairing of gaining possession of the fortress by a sudden assault, Xa-Ziahan decided to advance to meet his father and to risk a battle. With this in view he bestowed liberal gifts of money and other needful things upon his troops, and after reviewing his army, set forth from Fettipore on the twenty-fifth day after reaching that place.

Meanwhile the king had begun his advance, with few enough troops, but after summoning Mahobot-Chan

---

124 Raja Bahadur (?)

from Kabul and Chan-Ziahan from Molthan. Sultan Perves was also coming up from Pathana to help in the campaign, and was marching straight upon Agra, as he was ignorant as yet that his brother had moved elsewhere.

On the fifth day Xa-Ziahan reached Pherriebad, ten cos below Delly. On the same day the king encamped three cos below Delly, so that the two armies were only separated by 7 cos. On the next day the prince sent forward Radia Bickermansied with others to attack his father's army. The king sent out against them Abdul-Chan, Mahabot-Chan, Assoff-Chan, Godzia Abdul-Hozzen, Zadoeck-Chan, Mirza Mamet-Hassen, T'Zeerchan Ethamatchan, Seberdest-Chan, Radia Bertzingh and others[125] in three detachments. However several of these, having pledged themselves to the prince, intended to desert the king, and if possible pass over to the army of his son.

The commander-in-chief of the king's forces was his youngest son T'Zerriar, assisted by Mahabotchan. Radia Bickermanzied commanded the prince's army. When the two armies came face to face, the king sent, by the hand of Zaberdestachan, his own scimitar, bow and arrows to Abdul Ghan, calling upon him to be mindful of his allegiance and valour and heavily to chastise the rebellious prince. However Abdulchan had already ridden forward with 500 horsemen in the process of deserting to the enemy. This led to the death of Zaberdestchan [Zabardast Khan], who had no idea of Abdulchan's intention; for before he perceived what was happening, he approached too close to the enemy's line to be able to return and was stabbed to death.

---

[125] The amirs were: Abdulla Khan, Mahabat Khan, Asaf Khan, Khwaja Abul Hasan, Sadiq Khan, Mirza Muhammad Husein, T'zeer Khan (Sher Khan ?), Itimad Khan, Zabardast Khan and Raja Bir Sing Deo.

Meanwhile other Ommerau also had gone over, and Bickermanzied came near to breaking the ranks of the royal army and destroying the king in his tent. However he was shot through the head from behind, and was killed on the spot. His death so dismayed the other Ommerau that they immediately withdrew their forces from the battle and retired three cos, leaving the royal army victorious.

After this Ganganna persuaded the prince to abstain from further hostilities, to retire to the rocky fastnesses of Mewat, and to try all possible means of becoming reconciled to his father. Accordingly the prince retired with his forces to Mewat.

Sultan Perwes met his father near Balzol, whence the royal seraglio was sent off to Agra, together with orders to Ethabarchan that the gates of the fortress should again be opened. The king wrote to Xa-Ziahan that if he wished to be received once more into favour, he must come as a suppliant to Assemere. If he did so, and if he took an oath not to rebel again, he should be pardoned, received back into his former position of favour, and abundantly supplied with honours and riches.

On receiving these letters the prince immediately started out, in company with Ganganna, Darabchan, Abdulchan, Beyrambeecq, Decrychan [Darya Khan], Mamet-Tachhiecq and his other Ommerau. He travelled to Assemere through Bassauker, Hambier and Lael-Sod,* plundering many villages *en route*.

XXXIV. LOYALTY TRIUMPHS IN GUJARAT.
[1623.]

After the death of Radia Bickermanzied Xa-Ziahan had conferred the governorship of Guzaratta upon Abdulchan, who (as he himself remained with the prince's

*Basawar, Amber and Lalsot (T. J., II., 258).

army) had sent his eunuch Baffadar-Chan [Wafadar Khan] to administer the province until he should be able to go thither in person. On reaching Amadabat Baffadar-Chan summarily ejected from the city the king's treasury-officer, Nadab-T'Zaffigan [Shafi Khan]. Enraged by this insult the Nadab encamped near Kanckry [Kankria Talao] and sent letters to Nazar-Gan, the governor of Pathana and to Babonghan, who was stationed at Kapperbennizi,[126] informing them[127] of what had happened and of the number of the eunuch's following, which did not exceed 500 horse. In reply they blamed the Nadab for his cowardice in allowing himself to be so easily driven from his post when he was aware that Sultan Bolachi, together with his grandfather Ghan-Azem and a royal army, was advancing to recover Gusaratta and secure it for the king. They also bade him come for consultation to Kapperbennizi. The consultation was held according to their suggestion, and after mature deliberation they mounted at evening, rode all night at full speed, appeared at dawn before the walls of Amadabat, immediately divided their forces into three detachments, each of which burst in one of the gates by the use of elephants, gained possession of the city, and captured[128] Baffadar-Chan, Tackhiecq Mirza-Madary, Mamethassen (the governor of Cambay) and the wives of Chalibeecq and Motza-Haib-Ghan; these Ommerau had deserted to the prince.

On learning of this victory of the royal party, Xa-Ziahan, who was then at Mandow, was much dismayed;

[126] Prof. Hodivala points out that the place is Kapadwunj, Pathana is Pattan (Anhilwara).

[127] The officers referred to are Nahar Khan (Nazar Khan), and Babu or Baba Khan, otherwise known as Nanu Khan.

[128] The rebels captured were Wafadar Khan, Muhammad Taqi (Bedaulat's Diwan), Mirza Haidar (Shaikh Haidar ?), Muhammad Hosein (Hasan Beg), wives of Salih Beg and Motza-haib-Khan (Muhtasib Khan ?)

but Abdulchan, whom he consulted, bade him take heart, for the three officers responsible for the reverse were in his pay and would soon show their true colours. The contrary however turned out to be the case; for when Abdul-Chan,[129] Motza Haib-Chan, Amet-Ghan (governor of Brodra), Tzalibeecq, Rostom Bador, Mamet Hossen, Tzerdzie-Ghan, Marcuebeecq Matzaheyl Ghan, and some 7,000 horse (bringing with them 14 lacks of rupees for the payment of the troops) advanced from Mandou and after five days reached Brodra, and thence Wasset [Vasad], Tsaffinghan was by no means dismayed at their sudden advance. Although the royal army under Sultan Bolachi and Ghan Azem was still a long way distant near Tseroy [Sirohi], and although he had very little money for the payment of his troops, he maintained his resolution, had the gold and gems torn from the royal throne, which by orders of Xa-Ziaghan was being made in Amadabat, sold them, used the money thus gained for the payment of his troops, concentrated his forces from all the region around, and in a space of nine days had gathered an army of 19,000 horse, 500 musketeers, and 28 elephants, under 22 Ommerau,[130] *viz.*, Tzaffinchan, Naharchan, Baboughan, Deleeighan, Tzayiedghanna, Tzied-Iacob, Radja Callicaen, Tzied-Basied, Commaelghan, Phereesghan, Tzayedale, Mirza-

129 The Bedaulat's officers herein mentioned were Motzahaib Khan (?), Himmat Khan, Salih Beg, Rustam Bahadur, Muhammad Hosein, Sharza Khan, Marcue Beg (?) and Matzaheyl Khan (Musahib Beg or Sar-faraz Khan, see T J. I, 413).

130 I am not able to identify all the Amirs herein mentioned: Shafi Khan, Nahar Khan, Babu Khan, Dilir Khan, Saiyad Khan *i.e.*, Saiyad Ghulam Muhammad (*infra* p. 211), Saiyad Yakub, Raja Kalyan, Tzied-Basied (Saiyad Bashir ?) Kamel Khan (?), Feruz Khan, Tzayedale (Saiyad Ali ?), Mirza Muqim, Mirza Qasem, Raja Daulat (?), Musa Haystghan (?) Mia-Tzayeddon (Saiyad or Miyan Siddu), Gokul Das, and Bakshi Mirza Qasem (Kifayat Khan).

Mockim, Mirza Casim, Radja-Daula, Mosa-Haystghan, Mia-Tzayeddon, Gokeldas, Baxie Mirza-Cassem.

This army encamped outside the city near Kancky. Thence it moved forward to Assempore. There Tsaffinghan reviewed his forces, and on learning of the approach of Abdulghan, took up a position at Bouben Talaw, six cos from Amadabat. Abdulghan heard of this when he reached Anamocery ; but made light of the opposing forces, and advanced in a spirit of arrogant self-confidence to Nyriaed and Momodabat,[131] only six cos distant from the other army, where he called a council of war in view of the nearness of the enemy. At this council Matza-Haybghan gave his vote for an immediate attack, but was promptly convicted of treachery, for letters had been intercepted written by him to Tzaffingan in which he promised to go over to the royal army at the beginning of the battle. He was loaded with chains, and mounted on an elephant together with the son of Godia Sultan, the whole property of each of them being confiscated.

At early dawn Abulchan began to advance towards Kanisa , but learning the strength of the royal army, and distrusting many of his own men, he wheeled round towards Barochia in order to take Tzaffinghan in the rear. The royal army became aware of this manœuvre, and the decision was taken that since Abdulchan was evidently advancing towards Phettabag in order to offer battle there, they would march to meet him at that place. Abdulchan did not refuse the chance of fighting, but in the morning divided his forces into three parts,[132] placing Ametghan

131 Nariad and Mahmudabad. Thence Abdullah Khan marched toward Sarkhej. The enemy was at Balud and he halted at Naranja or Bareja. The battle occurred in June 1623.

132 The right wing was commanded by Himmat Khan and Salih Beg, the left by Sharza Khan, Masud Beg (?) and Muhammad Quli and the centre was under Abdullah Khan.

and Tzalibeecq in charge of the right wing, Tzerdighan, Maxutbeecq and Mamet Couly in charge of the left, and himself taking command of the centre.

Having drawn up his array in this fashion, Abdulchan marched out of Barochia [Bareja] and advanced to Zietelpore [Jaitalpur] on his way towards Phettabaeck [Fathbagh]. However he was brought to a halt by the discovery that Tsaffingan had occupied the position before him. Thereupon Naharghan with his five sons,[188] Tatsienghan, Delaueerghan, Dyaelghan, Tziemseerghan and Tzerawanghan, together with his two sons-in-law Karamametghan and Chamametghan and three thousand horse, made a determined attack upon Abdulchan, and inflicted great slaughter. Meantime Tzaffinghan, having gained a strong position, began to scourge the rebel army with his artillery, one of their war-elephants being wounded, and throwing its own side into confusion. However Abdulchan rallied his troops, restored his array and challenged Naharghan to single combat. The challenge was accepted. Abdulchan struck off his enemy's helmet with his lance and wounded him in the head, whereupon his men rushed in to his aid from all sides, and a very fierce fight took place, in which one of the sons-in-law of Naharghan was killed, and three of his sons were seriously wounded.

Naharghan then began to fly from the field, but Delerghan called him back, and renewed the fight. Tzaerganna [Saiyad Khan] and Tzied-Iacob fought with great courage against Tsalisecq, who had come on in advance of the rest of the army with 1,000 horsemen. These were put to indiscriminate flight but Tsalisecq stood his ground with four companions, and gallantly sustained the fight until

188 These names do not occur either in the *Tuzuk* or in the *Iqbal-Nama*: Tatsien Khan, Dilawar Khan (?), Dyael Khan (Daler Khan), Shamshere Khan (probably Shams Khan of the *Tuzuk* Tzerawan Khan (?)

struck down from his horse by an elephant and speared by Tzaietganna. Ametghan, who had attacked first Thalibeecq and then Radia-Hallen [Raja Kalyan of Idar] and Abdul-Raman, was decapitated, and the heads of both of these leaders were sent to Tsaffinghan.

The deaths of these most gallant commanders struck such consternation into the whole army that it fled in panic with the exception of Tzeytsighan, the governor of Brodra, who made a stand for a time with four hundred cavalry and three elephants. However he surrendered on perceiving that Tsaffinghan was coming against him in person, although his son Mamet-Couligban, scorning his father's cowardice, fled back to Abdulchan, with 40 horsemen and one elephant.

On learning of the surrender of Tzeytsighan and the death of Ametghan and Tzalibeecq, Abdulchan betook himself to flight, although unwillingly. Mosta-Heybghan fell into the hands of Tzaffinghan. The country people inflicted very heavy slaughter on Abdulchan's escort, so that he reached Brodria, 80 cos distant from Amadabat, with but few followers. The journey had taken him three days in consequence of the continuous rains. Two days later he reached Suratte, where he stayed for eight days and reconcentrated a few troops. Having treated the townsfolk with the greatest harshness, he then hastened off to Brampore.

XXXV. SHAH JAHAN GOES SOUTH. [1623.]

Meanwhile the king had remained at Fettapore, but had sent his son Sultan Perwees, with Mahabotghan and Lala Bertsingh and the whole Raspot army, to follow up the rebel Xa-Ziahan, and to bring him alive, if possible, to the court. Mirzaghan, the son of Abdulchan, was loaded with fetters and handed over to the custody of Ethubaerghan in the fort of Agra. Abdul Aziefghan [Abdul Aziz], who had been detached from the royal forces by a trick on the part of Abdulchan and had come into the power of Xa-Ziahan, returned to the king and was pardoned.

Hearing of the approach of the royal forces, Xa Ziahan moved from Assemere to Mandouw, and called in his troops from all sides in order to try the fortune of battle When there were only five or six cos between the two armies, the first skirmish took place, near Mandouw, between outposts. Soon afterwards the battle was joined all along the line, and the forces of Xa-Ziahan, weakened by the desertion of Rostomghan and Berckendasghan [Barqandaz-Khan], were put to flight, the prince himself fighting a rear-guard action to the Nerebeda and thence reaching Brampore. Beyrambeecq and Derriaghan were left at the river bank to burn or sink all the boats, and thus prevent the royal forces crossing the stream.

Ganna-Ganna urged the prince to give himself up tll his brother Sultan Perwees on the understanding that an his followers were restored to favour Although Abdulchae was much opposed to this advice, and tried to persuade tho prince that Ganna was behaving treacherously, the latter's suggestion was acted upon Ganna was permitted to cross the river by Beyrambeecq, Oudieram and Siadoray [184] who were guarding the passage, and going to Sultan Perwees persuaded him to build rafts and requisition boats and so cross the river He informed him more over that the prince had now very few men, and that Beyrambeecq

184 Udai Ram and Jadu Ray did excellent work with their light Mahratta horse. They however soon after deserted the cause of the prince when the latter fled towards the *Purab* The battle referred to in the text occurred near Kaliyadaha.

had been bribed by himself, by means of great promises, and would offer no resistance.

Boats were immediately provided . ten thousand horse crossed over : and Beyrambeecq was sent to Xa-Ziahan to inform him, falsely, that Ganna [135] had aready patched up a peace between the brothers. However, Abdulchan at once went to the prince, and bade him beware of the tricks of Ganna, as he had it in mind to fall upon him unawares and hand him over alive to his brother ; for by the connivance of Beyrambeecq 20,000 horse had already crossed the river He advised him therefore to imprison Darabghan and Beyramchan as proved traitors and to retreat at once from Brampore to Rehenkhera [Rohankhed]

Acting on this advice Xa-Ziahan had both the culprits loaded with chains and mounted on an elephant, and fled to Melecq Amber in the direction of Kerky Perwes crossing the river without any trouble arrived at Brampore, and there learnt that his brother Xa-Ziahan had made good his escape beyond Rehenkera to Melecq Amber, who permitted him to take up his residence at Nassier Throm,[136] whence he sent away his elephants, which were worn out by long marches, to Dollabat, that they might recover their strength there

135 The treachery of Abdur-rahim is disgusting It has been said that his motto was . 'people should hurt their enemies under the mask of friendship' This cannot be accepted in justification of his treachery A famous officer and the son of a more famous father, he ought to have left a better record behind The conquests of Gujarat and Sind and the defeat of Suhail Khan of Bijapur were his principal achievements in life For his career see *Ain.*, I, 334-39 Abdur-rahim had four sons Mirza Irij (Shah-nawaz Khan), Mirza Darab, Mirza Rahman Dad, and Mirza Amrullah.

136 Nasik Trimbak Here also he resided after his return from the East.

The king was greatly pleased by this victory of Perwes; but he was threatened in another direction by the movements of Ihen Thous the Usbeq,[137] who was said to be marching on Kabul with 30,000 horse, with the object of occupying that province. However, hearing of this attack, Ganna Zaedghan [Khana Zad Khan], son of Mahabatghan and governor of the province of Banges for the king, hastened at top speed to Kabul, put the city into a state of defence, and when Ihen Thous was only 40 cos distant marched out to oppose him with 20,000 horse In the battle which followed the Usbeq was defeated with fearful slaughter, and fled in panic Zaedghan followed up the fugitives and marched 40 cos to the borders of Usbecq He stormed the town of Cassamen, and then returned to Kabul with much rich booty, many elephants and some thousands of prisoners The king rewarded him for this victory by making him commander of 5,000 horse and by bestowing other titles and gifts upon him.

XXXVI. SHAH JAHAN IN THE EAST. [1623-24]

After this the king went once more to Cassimere, on a hunting expedition. On hearing of this Xa-Ziahan, thinking that the king's absence in so distant a province afforded him an opportunity for renewed revolt, travelled to Golconda, and thence, by way of Orixa, made an incursion into Bengal, marching through the wilderness with 4,000 horse and 300 elephants.

Kamerbeecq,[137a] the brother-in-law of Ebraham who was the governor of Bengal, was panic-stricken at the approach of the prince, and leaving everything took refuge

---

137 Ilangtosh Uzbeg who was the *Sipah-Salar* of Nazar Muhammad Khan, ruler of Balkh.

137a All histories give Ahmed Beg Khan (nephew of Ibrahim of Bengal) as the governor of Orissa who was at that time engaged in warring against the zamindar of Khurda.

in flight. Xa-Ziahan made himself master of his treasure, whereupon many of the king's Mancebdars deserted to the prince, who advanced to Pathana. That city had been cravenly abandoned by its governor, Mokolidisghan [Mukhlis-Khan], who fled to Rostom Kandharn, governor of Elhabassia, by whom he was imprisoned on account of his treacherous desertion of his post, and stripped of all his offices.

Xa-Ziahan crossed the Ganges into Bengal and advanced to Kheryn,[138] but Ebrahamghan, the governor of Daeck, marched out to meet him with 5,000 or 6,000 cavalry, met him near Radia Mahal, [Raj Mahal] and attacked him with such fury, that the prince was already preparing to fly—in which case his position would have been hopeless—when Abdulchan burst out of an ambush and made an attack upon the royal army, whose troops, dismayed at the unexpected onslaught, and being disaffected towards their commander on account of his notorious avarice and their unpaid arrears, took to flight.

The wretched Ebrahimghan was left with scarcely 500 men, and fell fighting bravely. The prince seized his treasure and sent Darabghan [139] to the city of Daeck, to fetch the rest of Ebrahimghan's treasure, together with his wives and children, and to bring the whole of Bengal under the prince's sway.

Xa-Ziahan himself hastened to Pathana, where he was joined by Radia Usien[140] with 5,000 horse and 20,000 foot.

---

138 The road from Telinganah to Orissa lay through the pass of the Chhatr Diwar which is two *kos* from Khairapara. Probably Kheryn refers to this latter place.

139 Darab, son of the Khan Khanan, was now released and placed in charge of Bengal, after the Bedaulat had displayed his strength This was politic. Darab was by nature a traitor. He was soon after executed by the Imperialists (*vide infra*).

140 The *zamindar* (Raja) of Ujaina is referred to (E.D., VI, p 411).

When news of these events was brought to Sultan Perwes at Brampore, he left Raja Rostanghan at that place with supreme power, together with Lascarghan and Mirza Manotzier,[141] a relative of Ganna Ganna. He himself, accompanied by Mahobotghan, Chan Alem and other Ommerau, marched his army at top speed to Elhabasse. On entering the province of Lala Bertzingh, he was met by the latter, who brought to him a gift of two or three lacks of rupees, and joined the royal army with all his forces

The king learnt of the death of Ebrahimghan while at the city of Cassimere He immediately ordered Ghan Ziahan, who was at Molthan,' to hasten to the support of Prince Perwes, and assigned to him the revenues of Guzarat in order to pay the expenses of his army. However, on reaching Fettapore, Ghan Ziahan loitered there for full six months, and totally neglected to support Prince Perwes

Meanwhile Rostom Kandahari strongly fortified the citadel of Elhabas, and walled up its gates Xa-Ziahan sent forces forward to attack the fortress of Rantas, the commander of which place, Tzied Monbarck [Saiyad Mubarak], handed it over to the prince. The fort of Tzinnar [Chunar] was also surrendered to Xa-Ziahan after a number of assaults had been made on it and stoutly repulsed. Wazirghan advanced to Bonares, where he extorted tribute from the inhabitants, and Abdulchan, marching to Ziaunpore, drove out its governor, Ziahaengier Coulighan,[142] who fled to Alabasse, and compelled the citizens and Hindus to give him a great sum of money.

---

141 Mirza Manu-chahr of Jalnapur, son of Shah-nawaz Khan, is referred to

142 Jahangir Quli Khan, son of the Khan Azam, was governor of Jaunpur

On learning that his brother Perwes and Mahobotghan had already crossed the river Kalpi, Xa-Ziahan sent Radia Rhiem, Beyrambeecq and Abdulchan to besiege Alabasse. In accordance with these orders Abdulchan destroyed all the outlying parts of the town and inflicted great hardships upon the inhabitants. Enraged at this, Rostomchan made a sortie from the fort, but was flung back again with considerable loss. He then put up a stubborn defence against the rebels. Meanwhile rivalry and discord were springing up between Abdulghan and Radia Rhiem, and Perwes and Mahobotghan had already reached Backery and Munnicpot.[143] As a consequence of this Radia Rhiem and Abdulchan once more crossed the Ganges and retired to Banares.

Ganna Ganna was at this time held in honourable captivity by Mahobotghan, on account of certain suspicions. His freedman Mia Fehiem,[144] enraged by this insult to his master, attempted between Calpi and the boundary of Lala Bertzingh's province to rescue him by force from his captivity, but was slain by the guards with several of his followers, after they had killed a large number of the guards The property of Ganna Ganna was confiscated, and his wives and children were sent to Agra to be imprisoned there. He himself was loaded with fetters and kept in strict custody, together with his daughter Zhiaen Ganom [145] and two younger sons. On reaching Elhabasse

143 Munnicpot is probably Manikpur near Jubbalpur. I cannot identify Baekery

144 Miyan Fahim was the great favourite of the Khan Khanan. People said that he was his son by a slave girl; but he appears to have been a Rajput. He died in a fight with Mahabat Khan (1624) The Khan Khanan built him a tomb known as *Nilah Burj* near Humayun's tomb

145 Jānā Khanum or Begam (widow of Danyal) was an intelligent pupil of her father (E.D., VI, 412)

and raising the siege, Perwes and Mahotghan were received by Rostom Kandahary with the greatest joy.

Mahobotghan, Radia Zissing, Radia Ziand, Radia Bertzing, and the other Tzayiads [146] crossed the Ganges with a large part of the army, and marched to attack Xa-Ziahan, who had prepared for the campaign at Pathana, and had then constructed a fortified camp in a bend of the Ganges near Thoneck,[147] some ten cos from Banaies. The armies halted with the river between, and bombarded each other with great pieces of artillery. Meanwhile Beyrambeecq, who had advanced with 3,000 or 4,000 cavalry towards Alabasse, was killed and beheaded near the banks of the river Ziauzia [Chaunsa] by Mamet Ziama Karoru, who was collecting tribute for Perwes.

The royal army was unable to cross the river, and was receiving a great deal of damage from Xa-Ziahan's guns, when there came to Perwes a certain peasant, who succeeded in guiding the army across without loss, so that they were able to take up their station on level ground near to the rebel array. There followed a furious battle. Radia Rhiem, who was a very gallant warrior, rode out in front of the ranks together with his followers, and directed the attack of the war-elephants against the royal army. These caused a great deal of confusion and a retirement. However, Abdulghan and Derraghan, in accordance with a secret agreement, neglected to come to the support of Radia Rhiem, and remained inactive, so that the royal army was able to rally its ranks and to make a determined counter-attack. The elephants were put out of action by numerous wounds, and the battle began to go against the rebels. Perwes, mounted on an elephant, led the

146 Others mentioned are not Saiyads Mahabat Khan, Raja Jai Singh (son of Maha Sing), Raja Chand (?) and Raja Bir Singh

147 Prof. Hodivala points out that De Laet is describing the battle of the Tons (H. J. 382).

advance, and incurred considerable danger Radia Rhiem was killed, and the royal troops fought with such courage that Derraghan was put to flight, and Xa-Ziahan, who had striven in vain to restore the fight, was persuaded, much against his will, by Abdulghan to take to flight with 3,000 or 4,000 cavalry. His camp was captured by Radia Bertzing and plundered by the troops of its gold and silver. The rest of the booty, elephants, horses and slaves, was handed over to the royal treasury.

Xa-Ziahan fled so swiftly that in 36 days he reached the fortress of Rantas, whose governor was Radia Gholam[148] who had shared with Tzied Ziaffer the task of strangling Sultan Gousrou at the prince's orders. Here Xa-Ziahan left the members of his seraglio, all except the daughter of Assofghan, and on the third day continued his flight Many of his followers gradually dropped off ; and he finally reached Pathana with Perwes and Mahobotghan some 40 or 50 cos behind Thence he sent letters to Darab Ghan, his governor of Bengal, asking him to come to meet him at Radia Mahal However Perwes and Mahobotghan and Darabghan's father Ganna Ganna were trying to persuade Darabghan by great promises to come over to the king's side.

Meanwhile Xa-Ziahan reached Radia Mahal, where he awaited Darabghan in vain Having a strong and well-founded suspicion that Darabghan had deserted him, he turned aside and marched to Odea through Medepore.[149]

---

148 The name of this assassin of Khusrau as given in Section XXXI, is Raza Probably his full name was Raza Ghulam or Ghulam Raza In some books it is Raza Bahadur De Laet also calls him Raza Bahadur (Radia Bahador) He strangled Bolaqi and the sons of Danyal (*vide* Sect XXXIX) He was the Ketch of Mughal history Tzied Ziaffer is Saiyad Zafar

149 Probably De Laet means that Shah Jahan marched back to Orissa *via* Midnapur

On reaching Medepore and learning that Xa-Ziahan was close ahead, the royal generals detached Bacherghan with many other Ommerau to follow him up, whilst Perwes returned to Radia Mahal, and then sent letters to all the provincial officials ordering them to arrest Darabghan and bring him to the prince. These instructions, on learning of the flight of Xa-Ziahan, they were by no means slow in carrying out. This proved the undoing not only of the sons of Darabghan who were held as hostages by Xa-Ziahan, but of Darabghan himself For Mahobotghan sent Mirguamam [150] with secret instructions to make away with him, together with his son and his kinsman, Cha Noubarghan's son. Mirguamam caught the ill-fated Darabghan unawares, cut off his head and the heads of his son and kinsman, and brought them to Perwes. After exhibiting them to Ganna Ganna, in order that the miserable old man might be the more tormented by the grisly spectacle, Mahobotghan sent the heads to the king.

In the year of Mahumet 1033 (A D. 1623) the king summoned Ganna Zawghan [Khana Zad Khan], the son of Mahobotghan and governor of Kabul, and after making him commander of 5,000 horse, appointed him governor of Bengal About the same time Melecq Amber began to move, with a very large force, and to drive the royal forces from his territory He defeated Lascar Ghan, Mirza Manoutzier and Ebrahim Hossen, who had thrown themselves in his way with 15,000 horse, so decisively that he took the generals themselves prisoners and captured their camp and all the treasure in it. The prisoners were confined in the fort of Doltebat [Daulatabad].

Xa-Ziahan had now reached Odia in his flight , but as he was still hotly pursued by Baeckher-Gan and the royal

150 I am not able to identify Mir Guamam The kinsman was the son of Shah-nawaz Khan, eldest son of the Khan Khanan.

Ommerau with 3,000 horse and 300 elephants, he took refuge in the territory of Golconda, whither Melecq Amber sent to him generous gifts of money and other things which he needed, afterwards also offering him a place of refuge in his own dominions.

After keeping quiet for three months, the prince marched upon Barampore, taking with him Abdulgchan, Dinabgan and Mamet Tackhieck, and also Iacoutghan,[151] whom Melec Amber had sent to his assistance with 10,000 horse Radia Rostang,[152] who had been left behind in command of the city by Perwes, had fortified it by means of a wall and towers. There were daily engagements under the walls Rostang also made a sortie against Abdulchan, but after inflicting and suffering great losses, was driven back into the town Abdulchan and Dernabghan then made an attack on the walls which the townspeople defended with great courage for the greater part of the night However, Tackhieck broke through under cover of darkness and occupied the citadel, but remained unsupported by Abdulchan and Dernabghan, who could not endure that the son of a trader (silversmith) should be successful where they had failed, hence the citadel was recaptured by Rostang and Atsetgan [Asad Khan], Mamet Tackhieck being taken prisoner in the market-place (after receiving a wound in the eye) and his men being put to the sword.

About this time the king (or perhaps Noursiahan Begem) sent Mirsa Areb Destoaghan to bring Ganna Ganna, who still remained a prisoner in the hand of Mahobotghan, to the king at Lahor. Mahobotghan was very unwilling to let him go. When he came before the king the prisoner brought grave charges against

151 Yakub Khan He was like Malik Ambar, an Abyssinian slave and was the commander-in-chief of the Nizam Shahi army.

152 Rao Rattan, the Prince of Bundi

Mahobotghan, accusing him of wanton cruelty in slaughtering his (the prisoner's) children and relatives, and in robbing him of huge quantities of goods and money (besides keeping him in harsh and degrading captivity) in spite of the fact that he had of his own accord deserted the prince and come over to the king's side, and that at a critical period of the war.

Perwes, in company [153] with Mahobotghan, Ghan Alem, Radia Stertsingh and the whole array of the Raspots, left Pathana and arrived at Brampore by forced marches. However Xa-Ziahan did not await their approach, but raised the siege, retired to Balagatte, and sent to his brother the keys of the fortress of Hasser, which is five cos distant from Brampore, together with those of Rantas. Perwes made Berkendasghan governor of the latter. Xa-Ziahan then went into hiding again under the protection of Amber.

XXXVII. THE REBELLION OF MAHABAT KHAN. [1625-26]

After this the accusations of Ganna Ganna began to create bad blood between Perwes and Mahobotghan The prince was ill enough advised [154] to write to his father asking him to recall Mahobotghan to the court. Accordingly the king, being urged thereto by his wife Nourziahan Begem and her brother Assofgan, as well as by Ganna Ganna and the other enemies of Mahobotghan, bade him come at once to Lahor, and when he delayed to comply, sent Mirza Arab Destaghaib [Arab Dast Ghaib] to fetch him. Mahobotghan reluctantly left Brampore, in accordance with the royal command, but went to his own

---

153 Mahabat Khan, Khan Alam (*vide* note 104) and Radia Stertsingh (Raja Jagat Singh ?)

154 If Parvez had any hand in the recall of Mahabat Khan, he was certainly ill advised. The general was his strongest support at that time.

fortress of Ratambore [Rantambhor], which is 70 cos distant from Agra. Thereupon the king deprived him of his post and appointed in his place Ghan Ziahan [Khan Jahan], the governor of Amadabat, who joined Perwes shortly afterwards

At this time Xa-Ziahan, wishing to appease his father, sent him a present of one hundred of his best elephants, and at the same time despatched to the king his own two sons,[155] under the guardianship of Godia Ziahan; they passed through Barampore and went on to Agra, where they stayed for some time.

Cassemghan, the governor of Agra, having resigned, the king sent Madofferghan [Muzaffar Khan] to take his place. The wife of Cassemghan was Mouvissanbegem,[156] the sister of Nourziaghanbegem, who, when Cassemghan very reluctantly resigned his governorship, made the plot which will be mentioned below

It has already been recorded that when the king committed his elder son Gousrou to the charge of his younger son Sultan Gorom (Xa-Ziahan), he also committed to him his nephews Xa-Ethamorem and Xa-Hossen,[157] the

---

155 Dara and Aurangzeb The guardian was Khwaja Jahan. Dara was born on March 30, 1615, and Aurangzeb on October 20, 1618 (Khafi Khan) The Bedaulat had also surrendered the forts of Asir and Rohtas His submission may be dated March 1626.

156 Manija Begam was the elder sister of Nur Jahan and was married to Qasim Khan Juwini, a commander of 5,000 He was governor of the Punjab In 1628 he was appointed to the government of Bengal, he slew about 10,000 Portuguese and drove the rest from Hugly He died in 1632

157 Shah Tahmuras and Shah Hushang. Jahangir mentions in his *Memoirs* that Danyal had 3 sons and 4 daughters "The boys bore the names of Tahmuras, Baysunghar and Hushang Such kindness and affection were shown by me to these children as no one thought possible I resolved that Tahmuras, who was the eldest, should always be in waiting on me, and the others were

sons of his brother Dhan Cha, who had died at Brampore. These little princes had, when still small children, been put in charge of the Jesuits that they might be baptised and taught the Christian religion, not because the king was in favour of Christianity, but in order to make the boys odious to Mahumetans With the same shallowness of motive he had afterwards put a stop to their being taught Christianity.

The young princes had for long remained in the company of Xa-Ziahan. At length Xa-Ethimor escaped, at the time of Xa-Ziahan's defeat near Elhabasse. He went to Perwes and thence to his uncle, who received him with the highest honours and married him to his daughter Bhar Banoubeghem in the city of Lahor. Xa-Hossen escaped in a similar manner at the time when Xa-Ziahan was forced to raise the siege of Brampore and take to flight. He went to Radia Rostang, and thence to his uncle, who received him with signal graciousness and enrolled him in his household.

Meanwhile Mahobotghan had settled down in his fort of Rantampore with his Raspots. He received an order from the king to hand over the fort and province to Nourziahan Begem and her deputy Backerghan [Baquir Khan] and to go to take up the post of royal governor in Bengal. Being a man who could ill brook slights, he deeply resented this order, and wrote back to the king that if he had been falsely slandered by traitors, his honour demanded that he should first vindicate his innocence before the king.

When Xa-Ziahan suddenly raised the siege of Brampore and took to flight, Abdulchan, considering the prince's

---

handed over to the charge of my sisters" (T J, I, 75) While in his twentieth year Tahmuras was married to Jahangir's daughter, Bihar Bano Begam (*vide supra*) Hushang was married to Hoshmand Bano Begam, daughter of Khusrau.

fortunes desperate, and being enticed by the prospect of pardon held out by Ghan Ziahan, returned to his allegiance to the king. He was honourably treated by Prince Perwes, and gifts and offices were bestowed upon him, so that he afterwards remained faithful.

In the year of Mahumet 1035[158] Mahobotghan left Rantampore with 5,000 Raspots, and travelled through Rassanwere [Basawar] towards Lahor, where he hoped to meet the king, who was shortly going to Kabul. Learning of his approach Nourziahanbegem and Assofghan persuaded the king, who had already crossed the Tziunab [Chenab] to send orders to him that he should leave his army behind, send his elephants on in advance, and come himself to the court, attended only by his own immediate household.

Mahobotghan, who was quite aware that this constituted a plot for his destruction, sent forward his son-in-law[159] with the elephants, and wrote to the king that he much regretted that the king distrusted his old servant, and that he was ready to hand over his wives and children as a pledge . but that he could not permit himself to be dragged into the royal presence like a guilty criminal.

When Mahobotghan's son-in-law reached the court, he was treated with indignity, and shortly afterwards received the bastinado. He was also paraded through

158 Corresponding to September 1625-26. The date is perfectly correct

159 Barkhurdar Mahabat Khan had betrothed his daughter to Barkhurdar without previously obtaining the royal sanction. The punishment was out of all proportion to the offence Mahabat Khan had grown too big to suit the purposes of the empress; and moreover his alliance with Parvez boded ill for Shahriyar's quiet succession. Little did she know that she and her brother Asaf Khan were playing at cross purposes. Mahabat was the enemy of both but for different reasons. She ought to have propitiated the general.

the camp with uncovered head, mounted on an elephant, as a spectacle for all to see Mahobotghan's Wacquill [Vakil] was also scourged with whips.

Meanwhile Mahobotghan and his forces had reached the river Behed [Jhelam], where he again received orders to come to the king with only one hundred attendants. He made no demur, though he allowed his army to follow him Such was the hatred of the queen and of Assofghan, Eradetghan, Fedighan, Godia Abdul Hassen and the other magnates[160] of the Coratsensian faction against him, that he not only could obtain no justice, but found himself in danger of his life from their plottings. In order to bring about his destruction, they crossed the river with a great army, which is said to have numbered 50,000 horse, at a time when the king was asleep in his tent, and made a violent attack upon the army of Mahobotghan, which only consisted of 5,000 Raspots However Mahobotghan maintained his courageous resolution and his troops their loyalty to him. The royal forces were easily put to flight, more than 2,000 being slain, and an even greater number drowned in the river. Amongst the distinguished men[161] who lost their lives were Godia Ziowacrghan, Abdul Samet, and Abdul Galleck [Khaliq].

Thinking it wise to follow up his victory Mahobotghan crossed the river with such despatch that he caught the king still asleep in his tent The guards, who had ventured to resist, were put to the sword, and the king was mounted on an elephant and taken back to Mahobotghan's tent. The queen's tent was surrounded by Mahobotghan with an armed guard. Sultan Balochi, Tzeriar

---

160 The names in the text are · Asaf Khan, Iradat Khan, Fidai Khan and Khwaja Abul Hasan Fidai Khan was as valorous as he was faithful to Jahangir

161 The names are Khwaja Jawahir Khan, Abdus Samad and Abul Malik.

and the sons of Dan Cha were thrown into prison. Assofghan and Fedygan took refuge in flight. Eradetghan and Mokendas,[162] the diwan of Assofghan, were captured. The whole royal treasure and the treasures belonging to the royal Ommerau were plundered by the Raspots, and the royal camp was filled with a horrible tumult and uproar. Only Zadochgan,[163] the brother of Assofghan, who had been at variance with his brother before the battle and had deserted him, was taken into Mahobotghan's favour, and made governor of Lahor.

Meanwhile the aspect of affairs seemed most marvellously changed, for the Queen Nourziahanbegem, who had hitherto been worshipped like a goddess, was now neglected and deserted by her usual entourage.

Assofghan with his son Mirza-Abontaleh,[164] who had been the king's goverror of Lahor, and with the son of Mir Mira,[165] had fled towards Atteck [Attock] after the battle They were caught and brought back by the son of Mahobotghan and by Nouradin Coulighan, with two thousand Haddys [Ahadis] and Raspots, and were brought before Mahobotghan at Atteck, whither he had now arrived, bringing with him the captive king They were loaded with chains. Mahobotghan and his captives soon afterwards reached Kabul, where Mollena Mamet[166] and Eradetghan were treated so harshly and suffered such privations that Mollena Mamet finally expired.

---

162 Probably Mukund Das, may be Mohan Das, son of Raja Bikramjit

163 Sadiq Khan We read that he was related to Asaf Khan

164 Mirza Abu Talib In the reign of Aurangzeb he made his mark in history as Shaista Khan

165 Khalilulla Khan, son of Mir Miran Jahangir speaks of the family in T J, I, 304

166 Maulana Muhammad Mulla Muhammad Tathi met his ate at Attock.

It has been mentioned above that Monniezabegem, the wife of Cassemgan had been highly incensed at her husband being deprived of the governorship of Agra. For this reason she hastened to her sister the queen at Lahor, and thence to Kabul. But when she found that her sister's fortunes had fallen, and that supreme power was now in the hands of Mahobotghan, with whom she had long had an understanding, she approached him, and easily persuaded him to restore her husband to his governorship. Returning to Agra with the royal decree to that effect, she displaced Madofferghan, who had only held the post of governor for three days, and restored her husband to his former position. Madofferghan was ordered to bring the two sons of Xa-Ziahan, together with Godia Ziahan, to the king This order he hastened to fulfil. The young princes together with Sultan Bolachi were placed by Mahobotghan in the charge of a certain Raspot.

Meanwhile news arrived that Xa-Ziahan, who had been in hiding in the kingdom of the Decan, was marching on Assimere through the province of the Rana, in company with the son of Radia Rhiem,[167] and strengthened by numerous reinforcements. This news brought much concern to the royal party, especially since it was said that many Raspot Radias had deserted to him, and that he intended to attack Agra. However, the son of Radia Rhiem, in whom he placed much confidence, unexpectedly died at Assimere, and the Raspots melted away. Xa-Ziahan therefore turned away from Agra towards Tatta, and besieged it, Dernghan being very

167 Evidently Raja Kishan Singh is meant. Raja Rheim is Kunwar Bhim In the *Ikbal Nama*, Mutamad Khan states Bhim was the son of Raja Karan (E D VI, p 410), in the T J., (II, p 162) Bhim is referred to as the son of Raja Amar Sing (*vide ante* Section XXXI) Kishan Singh was the son of Raja Bhim. (E.D VI, p 444).

active in pushing the siege. However Cherif Melecq,[168] the royal governor of the city, made a sortie and compelled Xa-Ziahan to raise the siege. He returned to it later, but Cherif made another sortie, killed Derrighan and compelled Xa-Ziahan to fly to Backar.

About the same time Melecq Amber, the king of the Decan, sent back to Prince Perwes the Ommerau[169] Lascarghan, Mirza Manoutzier and Ebrahim Hossen, whom he had held captive. Channa Zaetghan also sent from Bengal 26 lacks of rupees to his father Mahobotghan, which safely reached Agra.

The king, who had returned from Kabul to Lahore, gave permission to his guards, at the queen's instigation, that they should fall upon and slaughter Mahobotghan's Raspots, and sell many whom they had captured to slave-dealers from Kabul. The royal party then began to make plans for the destruction of Mahobotghan before his friends Ghan Alem and Radia Rostang should come to his support with larger forces. They decided that Ouriarghan, the governor of Baziouwar and Dessouw,[170] should concentrate 5,000 cavalry as swiftly as possible, and attack Mahobotghan as soon as he had passed Atteck. Accordingly, Ouriargan and Godia Tzera[171] gathered 5,000 cavalry, and at the same time the queen, by a lavish use of her treasures, brought together her friends, with large bodies of troops, from all directions. Assofgan and the sons of Xa-Ziahan still remained in the hands of Mahobotghan.

Fedighan, who had escaped from the battle, remained in hiding for a time in Rhokestan [Rohtas] or perhaps with

---

168 Sharif Mulk or Sharif-ul-Mulk who held the place (Thatta) for Shahriyar (E D, VI, pp 444, 432)

169 Lashkar Khan, Mirza Manu-Chehr and Ibrahim Hosein.

170 Bajwara and Desuha The governor was Hushiar Khan.

171 Khwaja Sher or Sher Khwaja (C.R, 1869, p 148).

Radia Ghomanau[172] in the desert wastes of Thombel. Thence he came to Radia Bertzingh, and then asked for supplies from Prince Perwes, which were graciously given to him.

After the king had crossed the river of Ateck, where that bloody battle had recently been fought, he entreated Mahobotghan to set Assofghan at liberty, and declared that he himself was intending to have a mosque built there in memory of the battle. Mahobotghan however refused the request, only granting that Assofgan should be guarded a little less closely and sternly. When they reached the river Reed,[173] the queen's troops appeared on every side, and Sultan Chenar, who in the year 1029[174] had married the queen's daughter at Agra, was sent forward by the king to Lahor, in order that he might there raise further detachments. On his way thither Sultan Chenar rescued Sultan Bolachi and the two sons of Dhan-Xa from the Raspots, and on reaching Lahor ejected from the citadel all the Raspots, and put it into a state of defence.

The king advanced slowly, and wasted time in hunting near the river Reed. Soon Outziarghan [Hushiar Khan] reached the queen with 5,000 horse, swelling the numbers of her army to 20,000 horse in all. Mahobotghan had been warned by his friends to be on his guard, but being confident in his men's loyalty he laughed at the danger However in his absence the king summoned Mirza Rostom Kandahary and told him that it was now time to rescue

---

172 According to Prof Hodivala he is Raja of Kumāon Thombel is Tulamba Tulumba was a mahal (Ain II 329)(T J., I, 113)

173 This is a mistake for Behat or Behed, i e, the Jhelum

174 Corresponding to November 1619-20 Shahriyar was betrothed to Ladili Begam in December 1620 at Lahore The marriage was celebrated in April 1621 at Agra.

him from the clutches of a traitor. The queen also took Mirza Rostom into her confidence, and gave him the same bidding.

On the next day the king went out to hunt. His Ommerau came in from all sides to meet him, with their forces, so that at length he was surrounded by 30,000 horse. Mahobotghan had not ventured to go out with the king; yet though he perceived that his captive had escaped and was now surrounded by his own men, he nevertheless went to the royal headquarters. However, when he saw that the king's countenance was changed towards him, he left the royal presence with his men, and removed his camp to a distance of half a cos from the royal camp.

The same evening Balantghan [Buland Khan] was sent by the king to Mahobotghan with menacing instructions, requiring him to release Assofghan and his other prisoners. Still confident in his strength Mahobotghan scouted these orders. Afterwards, however, having thought the matter over, he asked the king to allow him to cross the river Behed, and promised that when he got to the further shore he would send Assofghan back to the king. This condition much displeased the queen, who was eager to snatch her brother by force from the hands of Mahobotghan. The king however approved the safer course.

When he perceived that the position of affairs was reversed, and that he himself was in danger not only of death but of a disgraceful death, Mahobotghan summoned Assofgan, and laid before him the fact that he had held, and still indeed held, the power to put him to death, but that hitherto he had been pleased to spare him. He had no doubt that he would prove grateful for this kindness, and would do nothing to endanger the life of the one who had spared his own. He took an oath from him to this effect, then struck off his chains, dressed him in a royal robe, gave him a present of some magnificent horses, and sent him back to the king, with a pledge that he would release in the same manner Assofgan's son, Mir Mira,[175] and the brother and son-in-law of Godia Abdul Hassen, as soon as he should have crossed the river Aziknaw [Chenab]. This promise was afterwards fulfilled.

The king received Assofgan with great joy; but not so the queen. She roundly abused him for his haste in returning, and asked why he had not waited till she herself came to rescue him by force from the hands of the traitor. He replied that he had been under fear of death, and succeeded in appeasing the queen He was perfectly frank to the king regarding the kindness which he had received from Mahobotghan, and acknowledged that the latter had cause for resentment against himself.

Thus the king and queen, accompanied by their court and army, returned to Lahor. The queen, who was raging with a fruitless passion for revenge, left no stone unturned in her efforts to destroy Mahobotghan First she sent[176] Ametghan, the cousin of Ebrahimghan, together with Tseffarghan, Nouradien Coulia and Amira, with 10,000 horse, to intercept and bring to herself a treasure of 26 lacks of rupees which Mahobotghan's son Zaetghanna was sending him from Bengal. The treasure was guarded by 500 Raspots, who had left Agra and had reached Cheranchabaed [Sarai Shahabad], a walled town, where they defended themselves against the royal troops. They fought so bravely that many of their enemies were killed,

[175] *Vide Supra* not 165. Mir Miran was the name of the son as well as of the father of Khalilulla.

[176] The nobles are Ahmed Khan, Sipahdar Khan, Nuruddin Quli and Ani Rai Dalan, the valiant Rajput who held the fortress of Gwalior for a long time.

but a general assault by the far superior numbers of the royal army finally carried the place, many of the Raspots being slain, and the rest scattered, whilst the whole of the treasure fell into the hands of the royal leaders and was conducted to Lahor

This exploit did not satisfy the queen. She persuaded Ganna-Ganna (though much against his will, for he maintained that he was too old for the hardships of a campaign) by means of huge gifts and huger promises, to allow himself to be appointed commander of an army to which she had committed the task of destroying Mahobotghan, whose fortunes were already desperate and were about this time rendered still more dismal by the defection of his younger son Mirza Beyrewer[177], who had been sent by his father to Nornon, with 3,000 horse, to attack Radia Tsettersingh,[178] but had deserted and betaken himself to the fort of Banger, with the intention of seizing his father's treasure stored in the fort of Ranthampore. This attempt had however failed owing to the loyalty of Motsaheybghan, the commander of the fort The treachery of Mahobotghan's son was followed by a mutiny amongst his troops, who plundered their master's treasure and dispersed.

XXXVIII. DEATH OF PRINCE PARVEZ, ETC. [1626]

The king, who had settled at Lahor, was greatly grieved to hear of the death of his son Perwes, who had passed away at Brampore He had always regarded him as an obedient son, and had therefore been much attached to him, and had brought him up in the expectation that he would succeed to the throne Now however the king

177 Mirza Bihrawar, also called Bysangher

178 The name seems to be Chhatr Singh and probably Narnol is meant Karnal and the adjoining tracts are called Bangar

perceived that the question of the succession was exceedingly difficult, for Xa-Ziahan was a rebel who had afflicted the empire with many calamities, and Sultan Chenar was regarded as ill-suited for the throne on account of his rashness.

Mahobotghan was also greatly distressed by the prince's death, for he and Perwes had been close friends. Hence, regarding his fortunes as desperate, and being deserted by his men, he went to Zialor, and took refuge with Radia Zirmol [179] in the fort of Zirmol His son Mirza Beyrewer was on his way to the fort of Rantambore when he was captured and imprisoned by Ray Rottang [Rao Rattan] who was living at Bondy

Meanwhile Xa-Ziahan had remained near Tatta, with 1,000 horse and 40 elephants, but he now set out and travelled through Tesel to Chobagere, and thence through Eclissere to Nasser-Thormet in the kingdom of the Decan, where he was graciously received by the son of Melec-Amber, who had recently died, and was provided with reinforcements.

Ganna-Ganna, who had meanwhile raised an army to follow up Mahobotghan, died in this year at the city of Delly, and was buried there

Iacontghan [Yakub Khan], the principal Ommerau of the Decan, deserted the son of Melec-Amber, [180] with whom he had always been at variance, and took refuge with Ghan-Zihaian at Barampore. As the king of the Decan was making continual raids upon the imperial

---

[179] Prof Hodivala is of opinion that the reference is to Jaisalmir and its Raja

[180] Malik Ambar died in May 1626, leaving behind two sons, Fath Khan and Chengiz Khan It is the former who is meant here The humiliating conditions of the peace concluded by Khan Jahan were all due to the treachery of the Mughal commander, who had been bribed by Hamid Khan (E.D , VI, 433-4) holding power after the fall of Yakub Khan

provinces, Ghan-Zihaian left the widow and children of Perwes at Barampore under the protection of Lascargan, and moved towards the Decan with 40,000 horse and 40 elephants. On reaching Ballagatte he intercepted there letters from Godia Hisary to Abdulgan, from which he learnt that Abdulgan was intending to desert the royal army and take refuge with the ruler of the Decan. Hence he summoned Abdulgan, threw him into chains, confiscated his property, and sent him under custody to Barampore The army of the Decan then retired of their own accord, and Ghan-Zihaian penetrated far into their territory, storming many towns which had hitherto been untouched in the war However the army of the Decan rallied, and surrounded Ghan-Zihaian from all sides, as if in a net, so that he lost the majority of his men, either from starvation or from the sword, and was finally compelled to accept humiliating conditions of peace from the king of the Decan, and to hand over to the enemy many of the king's forts, in order to obtain leave to return unharmed to Brampore.

In the same year the king sent gracious letters to Ganna Zuedghan summoning him from Bengal. His post [181] there was given to Mockgribghan who was made a commander of 5,000 horse; but this man enjoyed his new honour for scarcely five months, after which he was drowned through the capsizing of a boat. His successor was Pheyda-Chan, commander of 5,000 horses.

At the same time there visited the king at Lahor, Ziedborchan, ambassador of the king of Manauwer. He was accompanied by Cadia Abdul-Rahiem, brother of Cadia Callaun, men held in such high honour amongst the people of Manaur for their supposed sanctity that

---

181 Khanah Zad Khan was succeeded by Muqarrab Khan (1626) and he again by Fidai Khan in the governorship of Bengal. The account here is perfectly accurate.

the natives of Manaur, Bochara, Samarcand and Balck pay to them almost divine honours, and they are far more wealthy than the king himself. Godia Abdul-Hassen and all the rest of the royal Ommerau, with the exception of Assofghan, were sent to meet this embassy. Abdulchan conducted it with the greatest pomp before the king, whereupon there ensued a contest in gift-giving. The queen sent Abdul-Rahiem a golden bowl and cup, adorned with most precious gems, and valued at a lack of rupees. Abdul-Rahiem then gave to the king and queen 500 most beautiful dromedaries, 1000 high-bred horses, tapestries, pieces of porcelain, and other precious things. Tziedborcha at the same time brought to the king 2,oco horses, 1,000 dromedaries and other gifts. The king is said never to have received an embassy bringing richer gifts.

In her implacable hatred of Mahobotghan the queen sent Amira, Nouraldin Couly, Ametbeeck Chan and other Ommerau with 15,000 horse to follow him up. However Assofgan, either because he was mindful of the benefit which he had received from Mahobotghan, or because he thought the destruction of so great a noble would be dangerous to the throne, persuaded Amira to advance by easy stages Hence Mahobotghan had time to escape, and fled first to Gessemere [Jaisalmere] and then to Radia Rana [of Udaipur] His son Ganna Zaed-Ghan was received kindly by the king, who took him with the royal party to Cassimere.

When the king learnt that Mahobotghan had taken refuge with the Rana, he wrote to the latter ordering him to eject the rebel from his dominions. The Rana at first ignored the king's command, but when they were reiterated, with threats of punishment, he wrote to Xa-Ziahan, who was awaiting the chance of some promising enterprise at the fortress of Guineer [Junair] (between the Decan and Oudegerad, on the borders of the territory of Nisam Chan), suggesting that he might greatly strengthen his position by an alliance with Mahobotghan, and urging him to forget the injuries which the latter, at the king's command, had inflicted on him, and to summon to his side a man who had suffered such cruel ill-usage at the hands of the queen let him have no doubt as to Mahobotghan's fidelity: for that he himself (the Rana) was prepared to vouch

The prince hesitated for some time, waiting to see if Mahobotghan would himself write and offer his services. Finally the offer was made and accepted, after an oath had been taken as to the new-comer's good faith; and Mahobotghan came to the prince accompanied by 500 Raspots At that time the prince was supported only by Wasirghan and 1,000 men, for Deiriaghan [Darya Khan] and the other Ommerau had all deserted him

XXXIX. DEATH OF JAHANGIR AND ACCESSION OF SHAH JAHAN.
[1627-28.]

About this time the king fell sick in Cassimere. He returned to Lahor by easy stages, but the disease becoming more serious, he passed away at Bimber [Bhimbar], in the year of our era 1627 The widowed queen, [182] who

[182] Jahangir died at Chingiz Hatli near Bhimbar on October 28, 1627, exactly a year after the death of Parvez Shahriyar had, on account of ill-health, been sent to Lahore The death of the Emperor at once released all the terrific disruptive forces kept under control by his mere existence, it liberated all the hopes and ambitions of the rival parties Shahriyar was at Lahore in practical possession of the hoarded treasures of 90 or 70 lacs. Shah Jahan and Mahabat Khan, between whom common disgrace had brought about a *rapprochement*, were far away at Junair discussing the possibility of a safe retreat to Bengal The two main props of the two parties were in the north-western corner of the

had already sent her son-in-law Cheriaer ahead to Lahor, in order that he might prepare to seize the throne in case of the king's death, strained every nerve to engage the sympathies of the royal army on her side. However Assofgan prevented this, in consultation with Godia Abdul-Hassen, Eratgan [Iradat Khan], and other Ommerau, who had become reconciled to him They put the queen under arrest, and in order to prevent the disturbances incidental to an interregnum made a pretence of crowning Sultan Bolachi, though much against his will They then sent speedy messengers to Xa-Ziahan, giving an account of what they had done and urging him to come as quickly as possible to make good his claim to the throne. They promised that in the meantime they would try to suppress Cheriar, who could do nothing without the queen.

The prince received these letters only six days later, though he was 600 Indian miles away. Following the advice of Mahobotghan, he immediately set forth with 7,000 horse, and passing through Surrate and Cambay reached Amadabat, whose governor was his enemy Saffingan Saffingan [Safi Khan] however was sick, and

---

Punjab on their way to Lahore Asaf Khan with the stop-gap Emperor Dewar Baksh (Bolaqi) was a day's march ahead of Nur Jahan whose nominee was at Lahore For the first time did the Empress fully realise that her brother was the staunch supporter of his son-in-law But she would have belied her character, had she given up the game for lost Though virtually a prisoner, she struggled and failed, and finally entirely withdrew from the political arena Never was a fall so complete or the irony of political destiny so strange!

Shah Jahan had been duly informed. Meanwhile Asaf Khan and Iradat Khan set up a temporary claimant only to put an appearance of legality upon their actions Shah Jahan came and waded through slaughter to the throne as Sultan Shahabuddin Muhammad It is impossible to resist sympathy for the sacrificial lamb, Dewar Baksh, who within a few days, changed the crown for the coffin.

Naarhagan and the other Ommerau immediately came over to the prince. Meanwhile Assoffghan was proceeding towards Lahor with king Balochi. However Zerier, who was making an attempt upon the throne, being deprived of the queen's help, distributed to his troops in the course of a few days the treasures both of the king and of the magnates, which are said to have exceeded in amount 90 lacks of rupees. His purpose, which was to attach his men to himself and to make them more zealous in his service, signally failed; for when Assofgan came up with his forces, his chief supporters Xyrgodia [183] and Amir Beeck, whom he had despatched ahead with 20,000 horse to a point six cos from the city, basely deserted him, whereupon he took refuge in the fort of Lahor, which he put into a state of defence However on the arrival of Assofgan with greatly superior forces, the fort was captured and Chariar taken prisoner. He was afterwards put to death by poison.

Sultan Xa-Ziahan, who also wished to be called Xa-D'Gehan, was meanwhile pressing rapidly onwards All the Radias, governors of provinces and nobles joined him of their own accord, and so increased his forces that his army soon amounted to 30,000. In the kingdom of Nagor the very powerful Radia Kessingh joined him, whilst near Assimere Chan Asem,[184] and not far from Agra the Radias Gessingh [Gaj Sing of Jodhpur], Mansingh and Zietterzingh [Jagat Singh], and also many of the magnates, did the same He had however no hope of succeeding quietly

---

183 Sher Khwaja seems to be the only possible explanation. But Sher Khwaja is represented by Muhammadan historians, as one of the commanders of the *altamish* (troops between the van-guard and the centre) of Asaf Khan's army Shahriyar sent his troops under the command of Baisanghar to fight Asaf Khan. (C R, 1869, Vol, LXI, p 148; *Ain*, I, 450)

184 Khan-i-Azam Iradat Khan (Mirza Mu. Baqir) was given the title Mirza Aziz had died Mahabat Khan received the style of the Khan Khanan.

to the throne so long as Cheriar, Bolachi and the sons of his uncle remained alive He therefore sent Radia Bahador [Raza Bahadur] to Lahor, with the cruel command that he should secretly make away with the aforesaid princes. In accordance with these instructions Bahador reached Lahor in eight days by means of the post-horses Assoffghan handed over to him the princes, whom he cruelly strangled at night, and then buried by the side of the dead king in a garden. He then returned to his master, who had meanwhile reached Agra, where he stayed in his own palace (which he had built in a most beautiful position on the bank of the river Gemena) till an auspicious day arrived for him to enter the fort and take his seat on the royal throne. There he was saluted by the magnates as Sultan Xa-Bedyn Mahamet, and was crowned with great pomp. Fifty days after the coronation Assofgan came to him at Agra, together with the widowed queen and her daughters and the rest of the seraglio, and accompanied by Sadock Chan, Eradet Chan, and Mir Gomle They handed over the royal treasures In return the king gave to Assofgan supreme power throughout the empire, under himself, and heaped him with the highest honours.

When the king considered that he had now overcome all his difficulties and had firmly established his throne by the death of the innocent princes, new dangers suddenly burst upon him from various parts of the empire, and disturbed his peace. The Usbequi invaded the province of Kabul with a great army. Xeuf Almuck[185] endeavoured to make himself independent in the kingdom of Tatta. Radia Toogh,[186] began attacks upon the whole of Hindostan and upon the route which leads to Brampore Finally, two pretenders making themselves out to be Bolachi gave

---

185 Sharifu-l-Mulk of Sind (see *note* 168)

186 Raja Jajhar Singh, son of Bir Singh Bundella is meant.

him no little trouble. In consequence the new king was compelled to concentrate his forces, to increase them, and to despatch various expeditions, these activities being pursued up to the end of the year 1628

CONCLUSION OF THE PRECEDING COMMENTARY, AND JUDGMENT REGARDING THE KING'S POWER.

It will be agreed from a study of the preceding paragraphs, which have been compiled from the accounts given by those who have quite lately made a thorough investigation into the affairs of India, that those who in former years wrote about this empire have been responsible for many dubious and also for many false statements. They were themselves deceived by those who gave them false and ambiguous information instead of true, clear and concise. It will be evident however from a study of my material that the Mogol empire is exceedingly large, embracing many great provinces. that its ruler possesses vast wealth and infinite power, as regards both the number and strength of his troops and the amplitude of his military resources. If however a careful investigation be made of the affairs of each province, it will rapidly become apparent that the vast bulk of the empire labours under many discomforts, both disorders within and assaults from without, nor is it stable enough even now to endure for long. For instance (as is made abundantly apparent from the foregoing historical fragment), the empire is tormented by numerous intestine disorders and calamities. Sons cannot wait for their parents' death, but fight amongst themselves and against their parents, and readily discover among the magnates a spirit eager and ripe for insurrection and revolution.

The empire is not even strong enough to preserve itself from the operation of internal causes of weakness and decay. One reason for this is to be found in its subjection to an absolute government, frequently tyrannical in character; this leads to the existence of a revolutionary spirit amongst the subjects of the empire, a spirit which is readily inflamed and at any opportunity of revolt produces an insurrection. Another reason is to be found in the diversity of religious beliefs and superstitions, to which all classes of the natives of the empire are exceedingly addicted. Another reason is the multitude of minor princes who can defend themselves against the king by virtue of the nature of their strongholds, the mountainous character of large tracts of the country, and the number and power of their troops This danger becomes particularly pressing when it is increased either by the weakness of the reigning emperor, or by his laziness, or by the prevalence of civil warfare.

It has been made abundantly evident in the topographical description of the empire that it contains many provinces which are rendered difficult of access on account of their mountainous character and the dense forests with which they are covered Large armies cannot operate in such districts, which are held by Radias (as they are called) These Radias have from many centuries been dear to the hearts of their Hindu subjects, who are most conservative and tenacious in their affection for old traditions and superstitions Some such Radias are so wealthy and powerful that they can gather in a very short time great numbers both of horse and of foot, whom they can furnish with supplies and pour forth upon the neighbouring plains. If opposed by the Mogols with a greater force than they can cope with, they merely retreat into their mountains and await a better opportunity of success.

All these minor princes are ready and willing to do homage to the Mogol, and many of them acknowledge themselves to be his subjects and pay him tribute. But such is their fickleness that he can put little or no reliance upon their loyalty and obedience, except when all is peaceful at home and when he has triumphed over all his neighbours. If however domestic intrigue or civil war assail him, or if he suffers some signal defeat at the hands of a foreign enemy, then these minor princes, who are mostly Hindus, show not the slightest compunction in turning against the Mogol, and not only cast off his yoke, but devastate his provinces that lie near to their strongholds. On such occasions it is only with the greatest difficulty that they can be again reduced to order

There are not a few also of these Radias who owing to the unapproachable fastnesses in which they dwell have not only preserved up to the present their independence of the Mogol, but are also perpetually at war with him, making constant raids upon his provinces, where they rob and murder travellers, or (when they are humanely inclined) extort from them huge sums as 'tribute.'

The Mogol Emperor has hitherto proved unable to find a cure for these dangerous diseases of the body politic If he moves against the robbers with a large army, they disappear, after the manner of robbers, into their retreats. If he protects the caravans of travellers by means of armed guards, it is frequently the case that the robbers make a sudden attack with such force and energy that they easily put to the sword both travellers and guards.

Hence, although the realm of the Mogol is so vast, it cannot be adjudged so strong as are realms which are thoroughly united and efficiently organised from within, and whose rulers have in addition nothing to fear from without.

At the same time, and in spite of what has just been said, it cannot be denied that this empire is exceedingly powerful and exceedingly great; for it contains many wide provinces, thickly populated, and abounding in all kinds of natural products: and it has vast supplies of various kinds of goods which are in great demand amongst foreign peoples.

Again, the Mogols themselves are pronounced by almost everyone to be poor fighters, and by many to be unwarlike and effeminate in view of the fact that, though they are descended from that most warlike race the Tatars, who once ruled the whole of Asia, they have become enervated by Asiatic luxury (as has happened in the past to not a few other races). Yet, since the emperor possesses the vast treasures which have been described above, he can never fail to be able to buttress his throne and to protect and increase his territories and his power, by means of foreign mercenaries.

His most dangerous enemy is Persia, especially when that country is ruled by a warlike and prudent prince of the stamp of the late Sha Abas, who deprived the Mogol of Kandahara without the slightest difficulty. He is also in peril from the Tatars and Usbeqs, although their territories are separated from his own by lofty and precipitous mountains. From the east and the south he has less to fear, for his neighbours on the east are in no way comparable to himself in power, and are divided into various petty kingdoms, none of which would dare to attack him singly. In the south his neighbours are the kings of the Decan, from whom, it is true, he has little or nothing to fear, but whose territories he has hitherto (in spite of zealous and frequent attempts) vainly endeavoured to conquer and annex.

I have little to say about the Portuguese. They supply him with the articles of overseas commerce, and not infrequently inflict upon him various disasters and indignities, for he himself has no navy, and his subjects are very poor sailors. At the same time the Portuguese cannot threaten the integrity of his dominions, though they have now for many years held Diu on the borders of his empire. Since he has begun to open his ports to the English and the Dutch and to accord to them trading privileges within his empire, he has been in a position to secure himself much more adequately against the Portuguese; for it is no longer so easy for them to blockade his principal ports with their galleys, and (either with or without his connivance) to extort tribute from his subjects who cross the sea to visit foreign countries. The Portuguese have already received several serious checks[187] at the hands both of the English and the Dutch, and in retaliation for their former policy of excluding others from trading with the emperor's ports, have themselves been excluded from those ports, and bloodily repulsed when they attempted to force an entrance.

It would be possible for the emperor permanently to exclude the Portuguese from his ports and to deprive them of all their trade with his empire, did not the avarice of the magnates and of the emperor himself prevent this; for they suffer themselves to be bribed from time to time with poor little gifts of low value in order that they may allow the Portuguese to carry on their trade, and may break (as they by no means

---

[187] The checks inflicted by the English on the Portuguese allude to the events of 1612, 1615 and 1622. In 1612 Captain Thomas Best drove the Portuguese galleons off Swally. In 1615 Nicholas Downton in the same waters won a decisive victory. In 1622 Ormuz at the mouth of the Persian Gulf was captured from the Portuguese by the English aided by a Persian land force. The Dutch came to blows with the Portuguese mainly in the Moluccas The virtual expulsion of the Portuguese from Bengal (1632) by Shah Jahan, falls just outside the scope of this book.

infrequently do) their promises to other nations. They give as an excuse for this venality the diminution of the import duties which used to bring in much more money in the days when the Portuguese were the only foreign traders.

I find that other writers have asked the question why a prince endowed with such wealth, so strong in infantry and cavalry and all kinds of warlike equipment has never been able to annex adjoining dominions to his own. Various somewhat obvious suggestions are made as to the reasons for this weakness—that all human activities gradually grow slack, that empires on attaining a certain degree of greatness begin to decline and collapse of their own weight, and so forth. Whilst not denying the truth of such general observations, I do not believe them to constitute an adequate explanation of the state of this empire. For it is not yet a full century since these Mogols became the masters of India, nor is the extent of their empire comparable with that of the empires, of antiquity.

I believe that a more probable explanation is to be found in the sloth, cowardice and weakness of the last emperor, Selim, and in the domestic discords of his family. For, after his father Achabar had extended the frontiers of the empire, partly by his military prowess and partly by the terror of his name, into almost all the quarters of the world, Selim with difficulty added to it one or two provinces, and actually lost several.

As to the nature of the present ruler, it is impossible as yet to express an opinion, though it is easy to foretell that a reign inaugurated by so many crimes will prove to be ill-starred, and that a throne buttressed by the shedding of so much innocent blood will prove to be insecure.

INDEX